MW00618423

Events That Changed Russia since 1855

Edited by
Frank W. Thackeray

GREENWOOD PRESS
Westport, Connecticut • London

Library of Congress Cataloging-in-Publication Data

Events that changed Russia since 1855 / edited by Frank W. Thackeray.
   p. cm.
 Includes bibliographical references and index.
 ISBN–13: 978–0–313–32815–2 (alk. paper)
 ISBN–10: 0–313–32815–3 (alk. paper)
 1. Russia—History—20th century. 2. Soviet Union—History. 3.
Russia—History—19th century. I. Thackeray, Frank W.
 DK246.E925   2007
 947.08—dc22   2006103476

British Library Cataloguing in Publication Data is available.

Copyright © 2007 by Frank W. Thackeray

All rights reserved. No portion of this book may be
reproduced, by any process or technique, without the
express written consent of the publisher.

Library of Congress Catalog Card Number: 2006103476
ISBN-13: 978–0-313–32815–2
ISBN-10: 0–313–32815–3

First published in 2007

Greenwood Press, 88 Post Road West, Westport, CT 06881
An imprint of Greenwood Publishing Group, Inc.
www.greenwood.com

Printed in the United States of America

The paper used in this book complies with the
Permanent Paper Standard issued by the National
Information Standards Organization (Z39.48–1984).

10 9 8 7 6 5 4 3 2 1

Contents

Illustrations

Preface

Winston Churchill once described Russia as "a riddle, wrapped in a mystery, inside an enigma." Putting aside Churchill's customary hyperbole, the fact remains that for at least a century and a half, Russia's historical development has been erratic if not mystifying. To some, modern Russian history seems analogous to a roller coaster ride with steep ascents, breathtaking plunges, and both centrifugal and centripetal forces of great intensity; to others, Russia has resembled the quintessential soap opera with its strong heroes and weak villains (and vice versa), complex plots and subplots, shocking twists and turns, and enough characters to fill a Tolstoy novel many times over. Through it all, the hundreds of millions of average Russians have persevered, a tribute to the resiliency and endurance of the human spirit and a unique example of dogged determination to survive no matter what the circumstances.

The year 1855 represents something of a turning point in Russian history. The death of the conservative—if not reactionary—Tsar Nicholas I brought his son, Alexander II, to the throne. Although quite conservative himself, Alexander was intelligent enough to know that both domestic and foreign challenges required Russia to modernize. Alexander initiated a series of measures known collectively as the Great Reforms, the most important being the emancipation of the serfs in 1861. Later in the century, the modernization process continued when the Industrial Revolution came to Russia in full force. By the turn of the twentieth century, Russia had become one of the world's greatest producers of coal, iron, and steel.

Nevertheless, for a growing number of Russians, their country's transformation was a case of too little, too late. During Alexander II's reign, intense and sometimes violent opposition to the autocracy (the autocratic form of government that vested all power in the tsar) surfaced among Russia's intellectuals, a miniscule but vocal segment of society. However, by the start of the twentieth century, discontent with the state of affairs in Russia had become almost universal, and the pot boiled over in 1904–1905. Several factors, including an ill-conceived and unpopular war against Japan, the shooting down of peaceful, unarmed demonstrators, and the foolish decisions of a politically myopic emperor, converged to provoke revolution. Amazingly enough, when the relatively bloodless revolution petered out at the end of 1905, Russia had reformed itself politically and, to a lesser extent, socially, and the country appeared poised for a brighter future.

Whether or not Russia would have continued to evolve favorably is a moot point because the outbreak of World War I in 1914 destroyed old Russia. The massive Russian army—poorly trained, poorly led, and poorly supplied—absorbed a frightful beating. The incompetent emperor, Nicholas II, and his meddlesome wife, Alexandra, added to Russia's woes. Staggering under the impossible burden of fighting a modern war, Russia collapsed in early 1917. After several months of mounting chaos, Vladimir I. Lenin and his Bolsheviks, or Communists, gained control over a devastated Russia. Lenin and the Communists worked to implement the ideas and ideals of Karl Marx, first and foremost the collective ownership of the means of production. Along the way, they renamed Russia the Union of Soviet Socialist Republics, or the Soviet Union.

Lenin's death early in 1924 touched off a power struggle within the Communist Party that Joseph V. Stalin eventually won. Stalin, a Georgian and not a Russian, was perhaps the most consequential figure in Russian history since Peter the Great. Under his brutal, unforgiving rule, the Soviet Union experienced the most rapid and far-reaching industrial expansion in history. However, the cost was prohibitive in terms of both human lives and the human spirit. Millions perished, and many of those who survived bore horrible psychological scars. Nevertheless, by 1939, the formerly agrarian Soviet Union had been transformed into an industrial powerhouse.

With the onset of World War II, tragedy once again befell Russia. After a clever maneuver in August 1939 that both kept the Soviet Union out of war and added significant territory on its western border, Stalin saw his country overwhelmed by barbaric Nazi hordes in June 1941. Although the Soviet Union eventually won World War II, it paid an astonishing price— more than 20 million dead and a country in ruins. Moreover, its victory over Germany did not bring true peace to the Soviet Union. On the heels of Germany's defeat, the victorious alliance shattered, and Soviet Russia entered the Cold War, a long, twilight struggle against its erstwhile allies, the United States and Great Britain.

The protracted Cold War sapped the Soviet Union's resources and energy and contributed to a growing sense of malaise and economic stagnation that erratic or uninspiring leaders could not halt. When Mikhail S. Gorbachev assumed power in 1985, he set out to reverse these disturbing trends. But however noble his intentions, Gorbachev's ideas were not practical, and their implementation fared even worse. The result was the disintegration of the Soviet Union in December 1991. The "new" Russia that emerged from the ashes was smaller and physically farther removed from the heart of Europe than any Russian state since the early seventeenth century. Moreover, even though Russia remains an economic and military power, under its current leader, Vladimir V. Putin, it seems to have rejected Western-style democracy in favor of a modified version of the authoritarianism that has characterized Russia in all its permutations since its founding more than 1,000 years ago.

The objective of this book is to provide a short but coherent synopsis of the 10 most important events or developments that have shaped Russian history over roughly the past century and a half. The hope is that this book will enable its readers to place modern Russia in its proper historical context. The volume is presented in a straightforward manner. First, I have provided a factual introduction about each event. Each introduction is then followed by a longer interpretive essay, written by an expert in the field, that explores the ramifications of the event under consideration. Each essay concludes with a selected bibliography of the most important works covering the event.

The 10 chapters are followed by several appendices, including a glossary of names, events, organizations, and terms mentioned in the text but not fully explained; a timeline; a list of Russian or Soviet rulers; and population data.

As with all published works, numerous people behind the scenes deserve much credit for the final product. Mariah Gumpert, Greenwood Publishing Group editor, unfailingly lent her support, insight, and patience. The staff of the Photographic Division of the Library of Congress provided helpful assistance in the selection of the photographs that appear in this book. Megan Renwick served as student research assistant. Her superior editorial skills and her perceptive comments and questions proved invaluable.

Brigette Colligan, who has worked with me on so many projects that she could easily replace me without skipping a beat, deserves a full measure of praise. Various members of the Indiana University Southeast (IUS) staff, but especially the resident computer wizards and the librarians, provided helpful assistance with a smile. Thanks also goes to IUS for the funding that allowed for the student research assistant and that covered other outstanding expenses. Among those who helped in one way or another to bring this project to a successful conclusion are John E. Findling, Stephanie Bower, Yu Shen, A. Glenn Crothers, James M. Beeby, Cliff Staten, Kris Utterbach, and Phil Roberts. Most importantly, I thank the authors of the essays. Without exception, their contributions were insightful, erudite, well-conceived, and thoughtful. It is always a pleasure to work with such conscientious, intelligent, and patient scholars.

Thanks also to Kathy, Sasha, and Max, whose interest in the work—to say nothing of their tolerance of my idiosyncrasies—made it all worthwhile. Finally a rousing "*bolshaia spaceba*" to all my students—past, present, and future. After all these years, they continue to inspire.

Frank W. Thackeray

Note on Dates and Transliteration

Prior to the 1917 Russian Revolution, Russia followed the archaic Julian calendar rather than the Gregorian calendar, the one currently employed almost universally. In the nineteenth century, the Julian calendar was 12 days behind the Gregorian calendar. In the twentieth century, the difference grew to 13 days. The Bolsheviks transferred Russia to the Gregorian calendar in February 1918. All dates given in this book follow the Gregorian calendar, or New Style. However, for events occurring before 1917, the date is also given parenthetically according to the Julian calendar, or Old Style (O.S.). Probably the greatest calendar confusion occurs when dealing with the Communist triumph in 1917. What is known to every Russian as the "Great October Revolution" occurred—according to the Gregorian calendar—on November 7, 1917 (October 25, O.S.).

Russians use the Cyrillic alphabet, based on the Greek alphabet, rather than the Latin alphabet. The task of transliterating from the Cyrillic to the Latin has generated several schemes, none of which is entirely satisfactory. The best—and most widely employed—is that of the Library of Congress. For the most part, this book uses the Library of Congress system, with some modifications. In particular, most first names have been anglicized (e.g., Nicholas rather than Nikolai, Alexander rather than Aleksandr). Moreover, common English spellings are used for names that should already be familiar to the reader (e.g., Moscow rather than Moskva, Yeltsin rather than El'tsin).

1

The Great Reforms, 1861–1874

INTRODUCTION

On March 2, 1855 (February 18, O.S.), Tsar Nicholas I died unexpectedly in the midst of the disastrous Crimean War. For 30 years, Nicholas had ruled Russia with an iron fist, but his death brought to the throne his eldest son, the 36-year-old Alexander II. Alexander was fairly well versed in affairs of state at the time of his accession. He had received a reasonably good if somewhat irregular education and had traveled extensively, being the first member of the royal family to visit Siberia. Alexander was honest and loyal to his subordinates, but he was just as conservative as his father, although he lacked Nicholas' rigidity and bluntness. On that most basic of issues, Alexander never questioned Russia's need for autocratic rule.

Alexander's immediate task upon ascending the throne was to extricate Russia from the Crimean fiasco. Beyond that, however, Alexander was intelligent enough to realize that reforms for Russia could no longer be postponed, despite his own desire to maintain the status quo. In particular, Alexander knew that the ancient institution of serfdom had to go. Reluctantly but with determination, he set out to remake the existing order. Beginning with the abolition of serfdom, he moved on by necessity to reform Russia's judiciary, local government, and military. Collectively, these initiatives are known as the Great Reforms, and in the process of implementing them, Alexander earned for himself the nickname of "Tsar-Liberator."

Recently emancipated Russian serfs pose in their "Sunday finest." The failure to integrate the liberated serfs into mainstream Russian society caused social, political, and economic problems that helped to undermine the Russian Empire. (Reproduced from the Collections of the Library of Congress.)

Traditional Russian serfdom was not far removed from slavery. Control of the land rested with a few institutions, such as the monarchy and the Russian Orthodox Church, and with the hereditary aristocracy. Meanwhile, tens of millions of landless peasants worked the land, totally dependent on their lords. Although statistics from nineteenth-century Russia are notoriously untrustworthy, it is estimated that 80 to 85 percent of the 1858 population of 74 million was enserfed. Slightly more than half of this number belonged to the state and were known as state peasants; the rest, held privately, were serfs. Despite this semantic distinction, there was little of a practical nature to distinguish state peasant from private serf. Each was tied to the land, meaning that in the eyes of the law, he was no different than a barn or a tree and, consequently, would pass with the land when it was transferred from one owner to another. Although illegal, many individual serfs or peasants were sold apart from the land. Neither serf nor state peasant enjoyed any civil liberties or human rights, and inevitably, both found themselves at the mercy of their master, who might prove to be kind and intelligent or brutal and stupid beyond belief. In most instances, the only recompense the serfs or state peasants received for their unrelenting, backbreaking labor was a meager share of the crop they produced.

Although ignorant, illiterate, isolated, and superstitious, serfs greatly resented their condition. Serf revolts regularly disrupted Russia's rural life. In the largest and most serious instance of serf discontent, in 1773–1774, more than a million serfs rallied behind the rebellious Emilian I. Pugachev. It required the full force of the imperial army to defeat Pugachev and the rebels. In the period leading up to the Crimean War, governmental reports indicated a steady increase in the number of yearly serf "disturbances" that required armed intervention to restore order.

In 1856 Alexander initiated public discussion of the serf question when he called upon the Moscow nobility to consider essential reform. At that time, the tsar cautioned the nobles, "you understand yourselves that the existing order of serfdom cannot remain unchanged. It is better to begin to abolish serfdom from above than to wait until it begins to abolish itself spontaneously from below." Alexander subsequently created several governmental committees designed to resolve the question of serfdom. When the inevitable foot-dragging surfaced, Alexander intervened to hasten the process. After several years of deliberation, the emancipation of the Russian serf was proclaimed on March 3, 1861 (February 19, O.S.).

The terms of the emancipation proved to be quite complex because the tsar and his aides tried to protect the interests of the nobility while simultaneously dismantling the system upon which the landowners depended.

Under the emancipation, the Russian serfs received their freedom: no longer did the lord of the land exercise direct authority over the peasants, who could now own property and marry without obtaining their master's permission; no longer were they bought or sold at will; no longer could the master order them to work, send them off to the army to meet a draft quota, or banish them to Siberia for acts of insubordination. Nevertheless, the serfs' newfound freedom was constrained by their duty to pay a head tax and their continued subjection to customary rather than statutory law.

Much to the displeasure of the serfs, they did not receive all the land to which they thought they were entitled. Rather, in order to provide for the nobility who served as the backbone of the regime, the emancipation statute allowed the landholders to retain approximately 50 percent of the land. Moreover, that portion of the land allocated to the nobility tended to be the best portion. Whenever a dispute arose over the division of the land, the nobility usually prevailed. Frequently, they also retained pasture, water, and forest rights at the expense of the newly emancipated serfs.

Not only did the serfs fail to receive all the land, but they also had to pay a heavy price for the portion that they did acquire. In order to compensate the gentry for its loss of land and serf labor, the emancipation statute granted to the nobility interest-bearing notes from the state equal to approximately 75 percent of the value of the land given to the peasants. The statute then required the peasants to pay the remaining 25 percent of the land's value directly to the nobility. Furthermore, the state saddled the peasants with a mortgage for the land they received, compelling the emancipated serfs to submit annual payments to the state over a 49-year period. Although specific arrangements tended to vary from province to province and region to region, the guiding principle was that of protecting the gentry at the expense of the peasantry.

The emancipation statute also reflected the government's fear and mistrust of the serfs. The prospect of hordes of serfs now free to do as they pleased alarmed the state, and it took additional steps to limit peasant freedom. To begin with, title to the land was not given to individual serfs or serf families; rather, title was vested in the *mir*, or village commune, the ancient peasant body presided over by the village elders. The government counted on the hide-bound, deferential, and conservative commune to rein in rambunctious, independent, "uppity" peasants. It was the commune that worked out the division of the estates with the nobility, and it was the commune that assigned landholdings to the former serfs and decided for everyone in the village such basic questions as what to sow and when to plant and harvest. Moreover, the commune periodically reassigned landholdings to its members, a process called repartition that simultaneously strengthened the hold of the commune over its members and inhibited peasant individualism.

Thanks to the emancipation statute, the commune's administrative and judicial role was reinforced. In addition to shouldering responsibility for assessing and collecting the mortgage payments owed to the government, the commune also applied traditional peasant law, issued internal passports (an ex-serf could not move about Russia without an internal passport), and supplied recruits for the army.

The emancipation necessitated several other major reforms. In order to accommodate the newly freed serfs' changed status, Russia reformed its judicial system. Prior to the Great Reforms, the Russian judicial system had earned a well-deserved reputation for sloth, ignorance, corruption, and brutality. However, in 1864 an extensive reform remade Russian jurisprudence into a model for Europe, at least on paper. Russian courts now became a truly independent branch of government; the tsarist administration no longer controlled the court system. Jurists were granted lifetime appointments. Moreover, the reform established the principle of equality under the law, a radical departure from Russia's past. Those accused of a crime gained the right to counsel. New, streamlined, open, and rationalized rules of procedure were inaugurated, and the legal workplace was professionalized. For serious crimes, trial by jury was introduced; for lesser crimes and civil actions, a system of magistrates was established.

Nevertheless, remnants from a benighted past continued to undermine judicial reform. Both ecclesiastical and military courts remained popular. The former dealt with questions involving the clergy, church holdings, and divorce; the latter handled cases from regions under martial law. More important, perhaps, were the courts designated solely for the peasants and for dispensing law on the basis of custom. They were usually ignorant and corrupt.

In the same year as the judicial reform, St. Petersburg initiated a major local government reform based on the principle of limited self-government. The 1864 Statute on Zemstvos provided for district and provincial assemblies elected according to a suffrage weighted in favor of the well-to-do. Its introduction to the Russian countryside, while significant, proved slow; nevertheless, by 1914, 43 of Russia's 50 or so European provinces had *zemstvo* assemblies. Zemstvos were designed to fill the gap between the village communes and the central government's bureaucracy, and as such, they occupied themselves with such tasks as roads, schools, hospitals, and agricultural services. Although they enjoyed the right of taxation, most zemstvos were chronically underfunded. Moreover, tsarist bureaucrats tended to ignore or override them.

In 1870 Russia's municipalities received the urban equivalent of the zemstvo reform. That year's Municipal Reform provided for the establishment of town councils, elected on the basis of the Prussian suffrage (those who paid one-third of the taxes elected one-third of the town councilors; those who paid the next one-third of the taxes had the right to elect one-third of the councilors; the remainder, by far the overwhelming majority of the population, secured the right to elect one-third of the councilors). In turn, the town councils elected a town administrative board that handled such tasks as education, public health and safety, and public works. As with the zemstvos, the town administrative boards suffered from a lack of funds and frequent interference by administrators from the central government.

The final Great Reform modernized Russia's military. Between 1861 and 1881, the Russian military underwent significant change, in no small measure because of its poor showing during the Crimean War. Prior to its reform, the Russian military was quite backward. Its rank and file consisted of disgruntled serfs who had been sent off to the army for a 25-year period of service. As these conscripts left their villages for the army, the local Orthodox priest frequently conducted the mass for the dead in recognition of the fact that few if any of these men were likely to return. Once in uniform, the serf recruits experienced incredible cruelty, suffering brutal discipline and barbaric punishments.

The most important reform measure was the 1874 statute that extended the burden of military service to all Russian males. Drafted by Dmitry A. Miliutin, the minister of war and brother of Nicholas A. Miliutin, who had played a major role in crafting the emancipation legislation, the statute required military service of every able-bodied Russian upon his reaching the age of 18. Moreover, the period of service was reduced to six years, with further reductions contingent upon a recruit's educational level. Mercifully, corporal punishment was eliminated. To upgrade the peasant soldier, provisions were made to provide an elementary education for all recruits. The reform also established a military reserve system and created specialized military schools.

Alexander II introduced additional reforms, but they do not fall under the heading "Great." Among others, they included a general easing of the police state constructed by Nicholas I, a loosening of the ubiquitous censorship regulations, an easing of the prohibition against foreign travel, the extension of greater autonomy and academic freedom to Russia's underdeveloped universities, the opening of a number of elementary and secondary schools, and in 1869 the establishment of two universities for women.

INTERPRETIVE ESSAY
Thomas S. Pearson

The Great Reforms of 1861–1874—beginning with the emancipation of the serfs and encompassing major changes in local administration, justice, and military service and more limited reforms in education, censorship, state finance, and the church—are invariably regarded as the most significant internal development in Russian history between the reign of Peter the Great in the early eighteenth century and the Revolution of 1905. As an act of state-directed social transformation, Tsar Alexander II's reforms had no equal in modern European history prior to the twentieth century. Nevertheless, apart from the abolition of serfdom, the Great Reforms have received relatively little attention from historians. Instead, historians have focused on the connection between the reforms and the revolutions of 1905 and 1917 and, more recently, on the similarity of the Great Reforms era to the process of political change in present-day Russia, including Mikhail S. Gorbachev's *perestroika* in the 1980s and Vladimir V. Putin's current experiment with managed democracy in post-Soviet Russia.

For this reason, the historiographical debate over the origins and outcomes of the Great Reforms is relevant to an understanding of the reforms themselves and their significance. Prerevolutionary Russian liberal historians writing at the time of the 1905 revolution saw the Great Reforms as creating a framework for the rule of law, private property, and public opinion that would open the door for Russia's constitutional development following the 1905 revolution. When Russia's political fortunes took their dramatic and dictatorial turn in 1917, in the form of the Soviet regime, many of these liberal historians emigrated and waxed nostalgic for the tsarist era and the conflict between educated "society" and the autocracy that had lasted up to Russia's brief period of liberal democracy under the Provisional Government in 1917. Soviet historians, by contrast, generally dismissed the Great Reforms as a futile act of tsarism seeking to preserve its rule and the dominant position of the landed nobility in the face of rising capitalistic economic pressures. In their view, the autocracy survived the "revolutionary situation" of 1857–1861 mainly by introducing "bourgeois" reforms to avert mass peasant revolution. Aside from P. A. Zaionchkovsky and his students, Soviet historians paid scant attention to the officials, institutions, and politics at heart of the Great Reforms.

Western historiography initially reiterated the interpretation of prerevolutionary liberal historians who deemed the Great Reforms and the Russian liberals active in 1905–1917 (many of whom were members of the

Kadet Party) as a far preferable alternative to the revolutionary movement with its Bolshevik outcome. Yet, thanks to the influence of Zaionchkovsky, Western and particularly American historians from the 1960s onward focused on the officials and institutions at the center of the Great Reforms. In their view, the imperial government undertook a deliberate but incomplete attempt to modernize the imperial regime and preserve Russia's status as a Great Power. More recently, Russian and Western historians have offered more nuanced views of the Great Reforms, their significance, and their impact on Russia's social classes. In some cases, they have argued that Alexander II's legislation laid the foundation for the development of a civil society with its independent public and professional activity and have claimed that these forces were evident in Russia at the beginning of the twentieth century. Other historians have analyzed the interest-group politics and the international pressures that shaped the reform debates in the 1850s and 1860s, and others, in looking to Russia's "usable past" to discern alternatives to Communist rule, have recently found in Alexander II a strong tsar who introduced bold reforms in a period of internal and international uncertainty.

Given the understudied and much politicized topic of the Great Reforms, it is clear why some of the most basic aspects of the reform era have eluded scholarly consensus. For example, what were the factors that prompted Alexander II and his conservative government to cut the Gordian knot of serfdom and introduce reforms that were startling in their comprehensiveness and complexity? What role did the emperor, his top officials, the landed nobility, and other leaders in educated society play in the reform process? Did the Great Reforms truly provide a wellspring for the development of an independent public voice (obshchestvennoe dvizhenie) that imposed "constitutional" conditions on Tsar Nicholas II following the 1905 revolution? And most importantly, how effective were the Great Reforms in improving conditions for the imperial regime and its subjects, and what, if any, contribution did they make to the downfall of the monarchy?

Although the corrupt and capricious nature of serfdom, rural government, and police justice were well known to top officials prior to 1861—after all, Tsar Nicholas I had organized 11 commissions between 1825 and 1855 to study the peasant question—the autocracy refrained from substantial reform because of its fear of uncontrollable social unrest involving free peasants and because of its belief in the supremacy of its military and political system as a result of Russia's victory over Napoleon in 1812. When technologically superior British and French forces handed Russia an ignominious defeat in the Crimean War (1853–1856), everything changed.

The war and the subsequent Peace of Paris in 1856 cast doubt on Russia's Great Power status by removing its protectorate over the Danubian principalities and the Orthodox Christians in the Ottoman Empire and by denying its warships access to the Black Sea. Even more, the Crimean defeat struck contemporary Russians as irrefutable proof of the bankruptcy of Nicholas I's regime. On his deathbed in early 1855, the tsar admitted as much to his heir, Alexander. Under such circumstances, the accession of a young and well-prepared tsar—who was as conservative as his father on the peasant question—raised new hopes among reform-minded officials and public leaders, who urged Alexander II to petition for peace and introduce fundamental reforms. Unsolicited memoranda in spring 1855 from Nicholas A. Miliutin, Constantine D. Kavelin, Boris N. Chicherin, and Dmitry A. Miliutin, among others, were particularly effective in making that point to the new emperor.

Still, the absence of any definitive statement from Alexander II or a master plan for reform raises the question, What turned Alexander II from a defender of the old order into a ruler committed to sweeping reforms that affected virtually every subject in his realm and had the most far-reaching implications for autocratic rule? Historians over the past century have pinpointed a number of factors, including the role of public opinion at home and in Europe. Given the stigma of the Crimean defeat and the shame of being the only European state (excluding Romania) to retain serfdom after the 1848 revolutions that swept across the Continent, the tsar sanctioned the new "openness" (*glasnost*) that appeared in the press and public discourse. More tellingly, his government established the newspaper *Le Nord* in Belgium in 1855 for the purpose of acquainting Europe with the real situation in Russia and cultivating a favorable European reaction to the state's reform plans. The foreign press and Russian intellectuals in exile such as Alexander I. Herzen, with his underground press in London, were frequently privy to the government's reform plans before they were officially announced in Russia. Nevertheless, the tsar's habit of selectively tuning out public opinion that irritated him suggests that this factor was not the primary consideration in his decision to emancipate the peasants and introduce other widespread reforms.

By contrast, economic and military reasons of state figured prominently in the thinking of Alexander II and the proponents of reform. Besides the loss of over 450,000 men, the Crimean debacle increased the state deficit from 52 million silver rubles in 1853 to 307 million in 1856, triggered a run on Russian banks as the ruble collapsed, and ruined Russia's credit abroad. These conditions, along with the government's costly policy of colonizing the Caucasus (which alone consumed one-sixth of total state income in the late 1850s), brought Russia to the brink of bankruptcy. Judging by the correspondence between the tsar and his brother, the Grand Duke Constantine Nikolaevich, this problem was uppermost in Alexander's mind in 1857–1858. In these conditions, the unproductive nature of serf labor was a significant impediment to Russia's restoration as a Great Power and her development of a modern economy, just as an army based on serf conscripts was no match for the more mechanized forces of Great Britain and France. Deputy War Minister D. A. Miliutin made the case to the emperor during the emancipation debates, as did economists, military engineers, and Michael K. Reitern, the finance minister from 1862 to 1878. Not only did serfs make unwilling and ineffective soldiers with little aptitude for using modern weapons, but serfdom also perpetuated the class divisions that hindered Russia's ability to field a modern professional army. Likewise, as the Crimean War underscored, the absence of railways and a modern transportation system (shunned by Nicholas I because he feared they would accelerate the development of industrialization and a working class, as was the case in western Europe) cost Russia dearly. As the historian Dietrich Geyer has observed, the French government with its railways and ships was able to put its troops into the Crimea at a rate four times faster than Russia, which relied mainly on horseback to move its troops.

Soviet scholars have long emphasized the state's fear of escalating peasant unrest as the principal reason that the state decided to abolish serfdom and introduce the Great Reforms, and there is considerable circumstantial evidence to support that claim. Peasant disturbances during the reign of Nicholas I occurred twice as often as they had in the previous 30 years, and the government and nobles alike worried about the rumors of a black repartition in the 1850s—that is, peasant plans to take land for themselves as compensation for their military service in the Crimea. Alexander II seemingly gave credence to these fears when he told an assembly of land-owning nobles gathered in Moscow on April 11, 1856 (March 30, O.S.), that they should give much thought to the abolition of serfdom, inasmuch as it would be preferable to waiting until peasants took matters into their own hands and abolished the institution from below. However, it is noteworthy that in the same speech, the tsar took pains to quash rumors of his intention to take immediate action on peasant emancipation, and Russian historians such as Larissa Zakharova have recently acknowledged that Soviet scholarship exaggerated the role of the peasant movement in the abolition of serfdom.

Thus, in all likelihood, Alexander II decided in late 1857 and 1858 to embark on peasant emancipation as the way to renovate Russian state and society and make Russia competitive as a great European power without sacrificing his political control or the empire's fiscal stability in the process. What is absolutely clear is that Alexander II was the decisive agent for change in the reform process, just as the controls he introduced to preserve his autocratic authority contributed greatly to the inconsistencies and shortcomings of the reforms themselves. Hence, the traditional view of Alexander II as an indecisive, weak-willed ruler manipulated by his ministers and the nobility is in need of serious revision. Indeed, the tsar's intelligence, common sense, and ability to size up a situation quickly and grasp the big picture served him well in the reform enterprise, as did his administrative experience and talent for judging men. His sense of *realpolitik,* as opposed to any humanitarian inclinations as "Tsar-Liberator" toward the peasants, explained his commitment to intervene at crucial moments in the reform process and make personnel changes and other tactical corrections. As D. A. Miliutin emphasized,

> The tsar showed at this time such unshakable firmness in the great undertaking he had personally conceived that he could ignore the murmurings and grumblings of the clear opponents of innovation. In this sense the soft and humanitarian Emperor Alexander II displayed greater decisiveness and a truer sense of his own power than this father who was noted for his iron will.

In the pivotal period in which the Great Reform legislation was drafted, from 1857 to 1861, Alexander II took three important steps to ensure the enactment of comprehensive reforms. First, when the nobility failed to heed his call for serious proposals on peasant emancipation, and when the secret committee he appointed on January 13, 1857 (January 1, O.S.), proposed that the peasants be freed without land and be required to compensate the squires for their homestead—the so-called Baltic program for emancipation—the emperor took forceful action. In late 1857 he issued rescripts to Vladimir I. Nazimov, Governor General of Vilnius, and Paul N. Ignatiev, Governor General of St. Petersburg, that prescribed that the peasant emancipation would come with land, and he ordered the provincial nobility to meet in committees to come up with suitable proposals for the government. Moreover, the publication of the Nazimov rescript in *Le Nord* and its subsequent dissemination in Russia put the reform on the public agenda as well. The government made it clear that there was no turning back and that the nobility was expected to cooperate. Second, the emperor placed the Main Committee for Peasant Affairs under the leadership of his most trusted confidant, General Jacob I. Rostovtsev. This committee was to prepare draft legislation that satisfied his expectations. Repeatedly from 1858 to 1861, Alexander II supported the minority in the committee who pressed for comprehensive reform. Finally, to do the spadework in preparing the legislation for the emancipation and other associated reforms, the tsar appointed two Editing Commissions under the Main Committee. These commissions of reform-minded nobles, public figures, and especially enlightened bureaucrats *(gosudarstvenniki)* articulated a vision for a new, socially transformed Russia.

Unfortunately, however, by setting the parameters for debate, controlling the political process, and especially preserving at all costs his personal power as tsar, Alexander II undermined the possibilities for successful reforms and for the realization of the vision for social and state development put forth by the enlightened bureaucrats. As U.S. historian Bruce Lincoln has shown, these enlightened bureaucrats, led by N. A. Miliutin, possessed a superior education and a belief in the benefit of rational and systematic state legislation. As a group, they had attained prominent positions in their various ministries (Internal Affairs, Justice, Finance, State Domains) under Nicholas I and enjoyed the support of influential members of the imperial family, most notably Grand Duke Constantine Nikolaevich and Grand Duchess Elena Pavlovna. By the late 1850s, the essence of their vision for a new Russia consisted of the following: the need to emancipate the serfs with land; create a new rural society of small landowners based on property ties rather than traditional social estate affiliation *(sosloviia)*; integrate the small peasant landowners eventually into the ranks of Russian society and, in the transitional period, rely on the peasant commune to replace the serf owner's police powers; engage the public, especially the landed nobility, in the management of local administrative and economic affairs as elected representatives of public (all-estate) self-government; establish the principles of glasnost and respect for the law as the basis for operating all branches of government; and finally, replace the police justice of Nicholas I's era with an independent modern judicial system featuring public jury trials. These principles, especially in the areas of local administration and judicial reform, were derived from a thorough study of French and Prussian practices and revealed a sincere belief that progressive legislation could spare Russia the revolutionary travails that had shaken the Continent in 1830 and 1848. Indeed, N. A. Miliutin made his 1856 memorandum on the emancipation of the serfs at Karlovka (the estate of Grand Duchess Elena Pavlovna in Poltava province) the prototype for the peasant reform of 1861.

At the same time, however, Alexander II's defense of his tsarist prerogative meant that the reformers had to present their vision for a modern activist state in terms acceptable to the tsar and the traditional political culture. This challenge in turn opened up their proposals to attacks from various ministers determined to protect their local authority, nobles eager to achieve favorable land settlements, and peasants and members of society who, for different reasons, balked at the bureaucratic provisions of the peasant reform. To be sure, the reaction to the reform legislation from March 1861 on—as manifested in peasant unrest, noble protests, student demonstrations, mysterious fires in the cities, and the national upheaval in Poland in 1863—dampened Alexander II's ardor for reform and left an imprint on the legislation. Yet, more importantly, the autocrat's unwillingness to create a unified government as part of the reform, combined with his skill in diffusing administrative power and responsibility among his various ministers while maintaining their total dependence on him, ensured that conflicts between the Minister of Internal Affairs and his counterparts in Justice and Finance would be rife for years to come and that the institutions created by the Great Reforms would suffer from a patchwork character. In this vein it is revealing that Alexander II established his Council of Ministers in 1857 not so much to promote collegial and united government as to enhance his control over the reform process. Significantly, the Council of Ministers effectively ceased to operate in 1865. Much to the chagrin of some of his top officials, particularly Minister of Internal Affairs Peter A. Valuev and Grand Duke Constantine Nikolaevich, the tsar entertained but ultimately rejected their proposals to give the local public a consultative role in national policymaking in 1863 and 1866; he considered such projects a step toward constitutional government, for which the Russian people, in his view, were not ready. In short, Alexander II demonstrated the skills of what historian Alfred Rieber has called the "managerial tsar" in functioning as a mediating force between his officials and manipulating them to his advantage, but ultimately at the price of enacting coherent and effective reform.

By the time the peasant reform was implemented in the spring of 1861, the tsar had removed N. A. Miliutin and Sergei S. Lanskoi from their positions as Deputy Minister and Minister of Internal Affairs, respectively, and had appointed Valuev, ostensibly as a concession to the landed nobility. As events soon revealed, the emancipation settlement of March 3, 1861 (February 19, O.S.), consisting of 22 separate statutes totaling 360 pages, disappointed nearly everyone. Although the legislation liberated approximately 23 million male serfs from the personal authority of the landlords and stipulated that they receive some sort of land settlement to be worked out over the next two years, the seigneurial peasants, like their 2 million appanage and 24 million state peasant counterparts (liberated in 1864 and 1866), discovered that they were neither free nor appropriately compensated. On the contrary, they remained tied to the peasant commune according to the principle of collective responsibility (*krugovaia poruka*), thus ensuring that the state would receive its revenues from the village in the event that some peasants separated themselves from it. Even more, the seigneurial peasants were particularly distressed by the land-settlement terms of the legislation, which required that they continue to discharge their servile duties to their former landlords (either as *obrok*, payment in kind or cash, or as *barshchina*, labor service) during the period of "temporary obligations" (1861–1863). In order to help with the process of negotiating land settlements between peasants and landlords, the state appointed nobles who were known to be sympathetic to the emancipation to serve as "peace arbitrators."

Understandably, the millions of peasants who felt that they owned the land because they worked it were bitterly disappointed by the terms of emancipation, and they expressed themselves violently. In the first five months of 1861, there were 1,360 cases of peasant unrest, many of which required military force to subdue. The episode in the village of Bezdna (Kazan province) in the fall of 1861 was especially tragic; 102 peasants were killed as troops sought to restore order. The bloodshed in turn triggered mass student and public demonstrations at Kazan University, which rapidly spread to other cities in the empire. All told, military force was needed to suppress one-third of the peasant uprisings in the first half of the 1860s. And although most peasants managed to get off temporary obligations and onto the system of making redemption payments for their land by 1870, in the end, the peasantry received only about 40 to 45 percent of the land—in other words, 10 to 15 percent less land than they had had before the emancipation. In view of the inflated redemption payments they made for their land allotments up to 1906—when the government, forced with extensive peasant unrest in 1905, decided to abolish them—with good reason many peasants regarded their emancipation as a change in their bondage from statutory to economic.

As for the nobility, most of them spared no criticism of the peasant reforms, especially in 1861–1862. They complained not only about the loss of their police powers over the peasants, which deprived them of an inexpensive labor supply, but also about losing a significant share of their land. Even though they received direct compensation from the state for their losses, many of those funds were used to pay off old debts and mortgages. In fact, 62 percent of all serfs had been mortgaged even before the emancipation. Hence, in many cases, the nobility lacked the resources or aptitude to make the transition to agrarian capitalism, and this had catastrophic consequences for the entire countryside. By the end of the nineteenth century, over 75 percent of the peasants lived on the brink of starvation, and by 1905, the nobility had sold over 40 percent of the land they had possessed at the time of emancipation.

The architects of the Great Reforms, as noted previously, envisioned that the landed nobility would assume the role of elected public servants and provide leadership in local administrative and economic matters, a necessity because the state lacked the personnel and resources to carry out such functions. However, by the time the 1864 Statute on Zemstvos was introduced to provide for public self-government in the countryside, Valuev had taken drastic steps to restrict the authority of the zemstvos in order to prevent them from becoming an independent public sphere within the tsarist administrative order. The legislation of January 13, 1864 (January 1, O.S.), called for the establishment of elected zemstvo assemblies at the district and provincial levels. Chosen from three separate groups (peasants, townspeople, and private landowners) on the basis of meeting property requirements, the elected zemstvo representatives had the responsibility for maintaining and developing rural roads, bridges, hospitals, schools, and food supplies, and for providing essential social services beyond the capabilities of the state. Under the leadership of the nobles, the zemstvos, in the hopes of the reformers, would be the instrument for developing the new social ties and civic consciousness in the provinces that would provide the government with new rural support in the post-reform period. To facilitate their work, the state authorized the zemstvos to levy their own taxes.

Unfortunately, the early experiences of the zemstvos were not encouraging. By the 1870s, they were already finding it difficult to meet their expenses, in part because they had to rely on the local police to collect zemstvo taxes. As state officials, the police attached far greater importance to the collection of state taxes and redemption payments and gave the zemstvos only the surplus funds available as their zemstvo tax revenue (the police collected all of the revenues together). Consequently, by the mid-1870s, some zemstvos were already falling into arrears in meeting their expenses. Additionally, the state prohibited zemstvos in different provinces from meeting and collaborating because it feared such endeavors might spawn a constitutional movement against the autocracy. In fact, in 1862 several provincial assemblies of the nobility, most notably in Tver province, called on the government to "crown the edifice" and convene a national assembly of elected representatives to advise the state on reform and policy. The autocracy rejected such appeals, and in the wake of Dmitry V. Karakozov's unsuccessful attempt on Alexander II's life on April 16, 1866 (April 4, O.S.), as well as several well-publicized conflicts between provincial zemstvos and the local governors in the late 1860s, the state clamped down on zemstvo activities. In these conditions, many of the most enthusiastic original participants in zemstvo work abandoned the cause of public service. These developments, however, did not prevent the government from introducing the Municipal Reform of 1870. Modeled on the Zemstvo Statute of 1864, the Municipal Reform introduced an expanded organization of municipal self-government based on the election of a city Duma or council (according to a three-tiered system of property ownership). Besides creating a common town identity for all urban residents, no matter what their previous social estate, the reform through the city councils provided municipal social services, promoted urban commerce and industry, and contributed significantly to the development of the professions and voluntary civic associations.

More than any of the other Great Reforms, the Judicial Reform of December 2, 1864 (November 20, O.S.), reflected the original vision of the enlightened bureaucrats. Although the emancipated peasants were to remain for the time being subject to their own village and *volost* courts, which operated according to customary law, the judicial reform laid out a modern legal system for a fully integrated society based on the Prussian model of jurisprudence. At the core of the legislation were the establishment of a judiciary separate and independent from the executive branch of government; the appointment of irremovable judges; jury trials open to the public; the equality of all before the law; the establishment of the legal profession and the bar; and the introduction of justices of the peace, elected and paid for by the zemstvos, to decide cases involving disputes between peasants and non-peasants. As with the reforms in education (the University Reform of 1863 and the reform of secondary education in 1866 and 1874), the proposed legislation was submitted for public comment before it was enacted.

By its content, the 1864 Judicial Reform signified a complete repudiation of the arbitrary police justice of the pre-reform era, and it introduced the most progressive judicial system on the Continent. Unfortunately, because of administrative backlash against the public criticism and revolutionary agitation of the 1860s and 1870s, the new institutions, especially the jury system, which allegedly was too lenient, came under government fire. The state became increasingly convinced that the peasants were confused by having to deal with so many legal authorities (namely, the justices of the peace, peasant courts, peace arbitrators, zemstvo officials, and the police), as compared to the simplicity of dealing with one landlord in the pre-reform era. By 1878, crimes involving revolutionary terrorists had reached such high numbers that these cases were transferred to military tribunals. When a jury in the same year acquitted Vera I. Zasulich, a revolutionary charged with shooting the military governor of St. Petersburg, General Fedor F. Trepov, in spite of overwhelming evidence of her guilt and in a verdict that evoked widespread public jubilation, the state determined to curb the autonomy of the courts, and the new judicial institutions were soon subject to counterreforms in the 1880s.

The military reforms of 1866–1869 and 1874 proved to be the most successful of the Great Reforms. In the late 1860s, Minister of War D. A. Miliutin introduced measures to separate the engineering and artillery branches of the army, update the military's armaments, professionalize its schools, and overhaul the officer corps. These measures, and the decision to reorganize the army on geographical lines so that troops were stationed closer to home, all represented improvements to an army badly embarrassed in the Crimean War. Still, the cornerstone of Russia's military reform was the Universal Military Training Act, introduced on January 13, 1874 (January 1, O.S.). Impressed by Prussia's swift victory over France in the 1870–1871 Franco-Prussian War, Miliutin decided to put the Russian army on the same footing as German and French forces. All males 18 years of age were subject to universal military conscription, regardless of their social estate, and were required to perform active duty from six months to six years, depending on their level of education. Even having two years of elementary schooling—not a very common occurrence in the massively illiterate Russian Empire—could reduce a soldier's term of active duty from six to two years.

The military reform paid dividends in three ways. First, the reorganized Russian army scored an impressive victory over the beleaguered Turkish forces in 1877–1878, only to lose the spoils of war through concerted European pressure at the Congress of Berlin (1878). Unfortunately, the tsar's foray into the Balkans brought the state to the verge of bankruptcy and harmed the cause of internal reform. Second, the 1874 military reform abolished the nobility's privilege not to serve the state, a privilege that it had enjoyed since 1762. In this sense, the military reform, more than the other Great Reforms, was consistent with the enlightened bureaucrats' desire to transform the social order from one based on estate affiliation to one based on common experience and economic ties. Third, and most important, the military reform with its stress on education and literacy did much to change the intellectual and social horizons of the peasants. Thanks to military service, schooling, and seasonal work in the industrial cities, peasants found themselves absorbed into a wider world with its new opportunities and risks, but with consequences that the reformers of the 1850s and 1860s did not anticipate.

Any attempt to assess the long-range impact of the Great Reforms must begin by setting a frame of reference. Measured against the conditions of pre-reform Russia, the reforms were truly great in bringing important benefits and opportunities to the Russian Empire. They were fundamental to the development of new professions, especially in law, medicine, teaching, engineering, and even some early social services. The zemstvos brought vital human services to the countryside and through their employees—the so-called Third Element—valuable expertise to zemstvo activities. The judicial reforms provided people of all ranks and backgrounds with legal protection and access to the courts and benefited some of the national minorities of the empire (for instance, the Baltic Germans and the Jews for a brief period). And, of course, the emancipation of the peasants—an act that could not be reversed by any subsequent legislation—profoundly altered the political, social, economic, and cultural landscape of Russia. On the other hand, when assessed against the bold vision and goals that inspired the architects of the Great Reforms, the results were far more inconclusive and even disappointing. Indeed, well before the tragic assassination of Alexander II by revolutionary terrorists on March 13, 1881 (March 1, O.S.), the government had begun to take steps to correct the concrete shortcomings of the Great Reforms that would culminate in Alexander III's counterreforms of the 1880s. Even more important, the reforms and the autocratic state that produced them failed to achieve the aim of a renovated monarchy drawing upon new and wider levels of social support. If anything, the Great Reforms and the counterreforms that followed, particularly as illustrated by the agrarian crisis at the turn of the twentieth century, left the regime more isolated, by its choice, and more vulnerable to revolutionary challenges.

SELECTED BIBLIOGRAPHY

Eklof, Ben, John Bushnell, and Larissa Zakharova, eds. *Russia's Great Reforms, 1855–1881.* Bloomington: Indiana University Press, 1994.
  A collection of essays from Russian and Western scholars that analyzes the state and the politics leading to the Great Reforms and the interaction of state and society in the institutions created by the Great Reforms
Emmons, Terence. *The Russian Landed Gentry and the Peasant Emancipation of 1861.* Cambridge: Cambridge University Press, 1968.
  A pioneering social history of the emancipation that explores the attitudes of the landowning gentry (nobility) on the peasant issue, their participation in the preparation of the peasant reform, their criticism of the terms of the emancipation settlement, and their political challenges to the state's authority.

Field, Daniel. *The End of Serfdom: Nobility and Bureaucracy in Russia, 1855–1861.* Cambridge, MA: Harvard University Press, 1976.

    The most comprehensive account in English of the politics of the peasant emancipation and the progress of the reform legislation, from the government's first commitment to reform through the promulgation of the emancipation legislation in February 1861.

Geyer, Dietrich. *Russian Imperialism: The Interaction of Domestic and Foreign Policy, 1860–1914.* Translated by Bruce Little. New Haven, CT: Yale University Press, 1987.

    An important analysis of the mutual dependence of tsarist domestic and foreign politics that provides important insights into the diplomatic, economic, and ideological issues that shaped Alexander II's policies.

Lincoln, W. Bruce. *The Great Reforms: Autocracy, Bureaucracy, and the Politics of Change in Imperial Russia.* DeKalb: Northern Illinois University Press, 1990.

    The best synthesis of the Great Reform era in English, with particular emphasis on the origins and significance of the reform legislation up to the Revolution of 1905. The work is especially good in analyzing the reformers' contradictory aims of renovating the old regime and creating the framework of a citizen society in place of the rigidly defined social estates order.

———. *In the Vanguard of Reform: Russia's Enlightened Bureaucrats, 1825–1861.* DeKalb: Northern Illinois University Press, 1982.

    A pathbreaking book that argues that the key ideas behind the Great Reforms came from a generation of enlightened bureaucrats who came of age under Nicholas I and had social, economic, and political attitudes very different from those of their predecessors.

Miller, Forrest A. *Dmitrii Miliutin and the Reform Era in Russia.* Nashville, TN: Vanderbilt University Press, 1968.

    A rather cursory but sympathetic overview of Miliutin's life and career and his leadership in introducing military reforms against the opposition of the privileged classes.

Mosse, Werner E. *Alexander II and the Modernization of Russia.* New York: Collier Books, 1958.

    A succinct account of the reign and reforms of the Tsar-Liberator that depicts him as a well-intentioned but weak ruler who succeeded in introducing sweeping reforms that then generated the social and political ferment that led to his assassination.

Orlovsky, Daniel T. *The Limits of Reform: The Ministry of Internal Affairs in Imperial Russia, 1802–1881.* Cambridge, MA: Harvard University Press, 1981.

    A valuable institutional history that analyzes the development of the most powerful ministry in nineteenth-century Russia and focuses on its functions, ethos, and officials. It illuminates the leading role that the Ministry of Internal Affairs had in the emancipation of the serfs and the zemstvo reform and shows why, by the mid-1860s, it had become a force for the retrenchment of the autocracy and the upholder of administrative power.

Pearson, Thomas S. *Russian Officialdom in Crisis: Autocracy and Local Self-Government, 1861–1900.* Cambridge: Cambridge University Press, 1989.

    A revisionist account of the origins of the counterreforms in peasant and zemstvo administration in 1889–1890 that argues that the substantial failures of peasant and zemstvo self-government, as perceived by the state, rather than gentry interests or revolutionary terror, prompted the autocracy to reassert its authority over local self-government.

Radzinsky, Edvard. *Alexander II: The Last Great Tsar.* Translated by Antonina Bouis. New York: The Free Press, 2005.

A massive biography by one of Russia's most popular historical biographers (author of previous works on Stalin and Rasputin), who places Alexander II in the company of Peter the Great as a strong, pragmatic, and visionary ruler who introduced reforms only to come under attack from the right for being too liberal and from the left for not going far enough.

Rieber, Alfred J. "Alexander II: A Revisionist View." *Journal of Modern History* (1971): 42–58.

An influential essay that challenges the conventional view of the tsar as a liberal reformer in the first half of his reign and a conservative autocrat in the second half and that instead depicts Alexander II as a pragmatic ruler who followed military and fiscal reasons of state in abolishing serfdom and introducing reforms in government and society.

———, ed. *The Politics of Autocracy: Letters of Alexander II to Prince A. I. Bariatinskii.* The Hague: Mouton, 1966.

A valuable collection of 42 letters (in French) from Alexander II to Prince Bariatinskii, his intimate friend from childhood, that offer insights into the workings of the tsarist state from 1857 to 1864. The volume contains an extensive and incisive introductory essay by Rieber in which he argues that military reasons of state and the need to create a modern professional army were the main motives for Alexander II's decision to free the serfs.

Robinson, Geroid Tanquary. *Rural Russia under the Old Regime: A History of the Landlord-Peasant World and a Prologue to the Peasant Revolution of 1917.* New York: Macmillan, 1932.

A classic account emphasizing the shortcomings of serfdom that led to its abolition and the impact of the peasant reform on the peasants and nobility and arguing that the state's decisions on the peasant emancipation led directly to the agrarian crisis and revolutions of 1905 and 1917.

Starr, S. Frederick. *Decentralization and Self-Government in Russia 1830–1870.* Princeton, NJ: Princeton University Press, 1972.

Starr attributes the introduction of public self-government in the Zemstvo Reform (1864) and Municipal Reform (1870) not to gentry class politics or the Crimean defeat, but to the state's need to administer its chronically undergoverned provinces.

Taranovski, Theodore, ed. and trans. *Reform in Modern Russian History: Progress or Cycle?* Cambridge: Cambridge University Press, 1995.

A compendium of stimulating scholarly essays that compares and contrasts the politics and patterns of the Great Reforms with later periods of reform in Russian history, specifically the constitutional changes of the years between 1906 and 1917, the 1920s, and the periods of Khrushchev and Gorbachev.

Wcislo, Francis W. *Reforming Rural Russia: State, Local Society, and National Politics, 1855–1914.* Princeton, NJ: Princeton University Press, 1990.

The most comprehensive treatment in chronological terms of the government's reform of rural local government that shows how official reformers anxious to promote civic culture were undermined by the defenders of autocracy and traditional social estates of the realm.

Wortman, Richard S. *The Development of a Russian Legal Consciousness.* Chicago, IL: University of Chicago Press, 1976.

A fundamental reinterpretation of the origins of the Judicial Reform of 1864 that views the legislation as a result of the development of legal specialists in Russian government under Nicholas I and their view of the law as an independent source of authority, and not simply as a sudden reversal of state policy during the brief liberal period of the 1850s and 1860s. Wortman's study also shows how the Judicial Reforms promoted the development of the bar and public appreciation of the law as an independent force, which led to conflicts between the judiciary and the autocracy in the post-reform era.

Zaionchkovskii, P. A. *The Abolition of Serfdom in Russia.* Translated by Susan Wobst. Gulf Breeze, FL: Academic International Press, 1978.

The classic Soviet account, which attributes the abolition of serfdom to the government's fear of growing peasant unrest and its recognition that serfdom (as a form of feudal economy) was no longer economically and politically viable.

Zakharova, L. G. "Autocracy, Bureaucracy, and the Reforms of the 1860s in Russia." *Soviet Studies in History* (1991): 6–33.

A condensed presentation of the argument made in her major work *Samoderzhavie i otmena krepostnogo prava v Rossii 1856–1861* (*The Autocracy and the Abolition of Serfdom in Russia, 1856–1861*) (1984). However, this essay by one of Zaionchkovskii's leading students goes beyond the standard Soviet interpretation and her own earlier work by playing down the importance of popular rebellion as a factor in the state's decision to abolish serfdom; the essay instead emphasizes the influence of public opinion, Russia's image abroad, and the role of enlightened "liberal" bureaucrats in the editing commissions in the reform process.

2

The Rise of the Radical Intelligentsia, 1862–1881

INTRODUCTION

Prior to the nineteenth century, there were two sources of rebellious activity in Russia. The first featured angry peasants reacting violently to the brutal system of serfdom. Spontaneous, unfocused, disorganized, and undisciplined serf uprisings often proved lethal; however, by the nineteenth century, they had become a permanent part of the Russian landscape. The most serious serf revolt, Pugachev's Rebellion in 1773–1774, witnessed more than a million enraged serfs wreaking havoc on the eastern districts of European Russia before being put down with some difficulty. The fear engendered by serf revolts, especially Pugachev's, burned deeply into the minds of Russian officialdom and the landowning class.

The second source of rebellion featured discontented court circles. Unlike the serfs, these aristocratic kingpins did not want to destroy the empire; rather, they struck at specific tsars whose actions or policies alienated and alarmed them, and they feared for the state's welfare and their own security. Court conspirators deposed and then murdered Peter III in 1762 and strangled his son, Paul I, in 1801.

During the early years of the nineteenth century, opposition in Russia assumed a new form. Although serf unrest continued unabated, court conspiracies yielded to new opponents who were frequently lumped together under the awkward name "the radical intelligentsia." The term "radical intelligentsia" is hard to define. Generally, it included all those Russians who were literate and free (a small percentage of the population), who

George V. Plekhanov (1856–1918), universally recognized as Russia's "first Marxist," spent much of his adult life in exile in Switzerland. Initially, Vladimir I. Lenin embraced Plekhanov's interpretation of Marx; however, he subsequently broke with Plekhanov and reworked Marx's ideas to create the ideological foundations of the Soviet state. (Reproduced from the Collections of the Library of Congress.)

had some leisure time, who had an interest in what was happening about them, and who were convinced that Russia was heading down an erroneous path. Initially, the radical intelligentsia was drawn almost exclusively from a discontented nobility; however, throughout the nineteenth century, its ranks expanded to include (and become dominated by) the *raznochintsy*, or those without a defined position in the social order, such as the children of priests and lower-level bureaucrats and students who came from the ranks of the peasantry and the embryonic working class. Egalitarian in nature, the radical intelligentsia eventually included a growing number of educated but angry and disillusioned women. Although the radical intelligentsia provided Russia with its revolutionaries, most of its members sought peaceful change.

Eighteenth-century precursors of the radical intelligentsia included the authors Alexander N. Radishchev and Nicholas I. Novikov. The first significant explosion attributable to the radical intelligentsia occurred in December 1825, when a handful of frustrated Russian noblemen, many of whom were officers in the elite guards units, tried to overthrow the autocracy. Their discontent stemmed from Tsar Alexander I's failure to enact promised reform, a growing realization that Russia was out of step with Europe's mainstream development, and shame over the brutal and backward nature of Russian society.

The revolutionaries, known as the Decembrists, failed for many reasons, including faintness of heart, lack of organization, and absence of real support for their cause among their peers. But perhaps the most important reason for their failure was their unwillingness to tap into popular discontent and enlist the seething serf population. In any event, the revolt failed miserably, and the new tsar, Nicholas I, severely punished the participants. Nevertheless, in executing and exiling the Decembrists, Nicholas inadvertently created martyrs that future Russian revolutionaries looked back to for inspiration and solace.

After the Decembrist revolt, the profoundly conservative Nicholas instituted an even more stifling police regime, but despite Nicholas's best efforts, the radical intelligentsia did not disappear. Instead, Russian radicals now devoted their energies to a seemingly nonrevolutionary discussion of Russia's past and its prospects for the future. During the 1830s and 1840s, Russian intellectuals tended to gravitate into one of two camps, either the Westernizers or the Slavophiles. For the Westernizers, western Europe provided a shining example of what Russia should aspire to be. They acknowledged Russia's backwardness and urged reform along western lines. Because of their implicit criticism of the tsarist state, the Westernizers chose their words carefully. Important Westernizers included Vissarion G. Belinsky, the grandson of a priest and one of the first to employ literary criticism to condemn Russia's status quo and agitate for reform.

Conversely, the Slavophiles attacked Russia for ignoring its traditions and becoming *too* western. They venerated an idyllic Russian past anchored by the Orthodox Church and the village commune. According to the Slavophiles, old Russia was a harmonious, unified, moral paragon that had been corrupted by Peter the Great's importation of Western forms and ideas. Russia's hope for the future rested on discarding these foreign, nefarious influences and returning to its ancient roots.

Although Russia was fairly somnambulant during the 1830s and 1840s, occasional intellectual outbursts roiled the waters. In 1836 the nobleman Peter Y. Chaadaev suggested that Russia was a vacuum, possessing neither a culture nor an ethos and not even a worthwhile history. For his pains, Chaadaev was declared insane and institutionalized. Later, the noblemen Alexander I. Herzen and Michael A. Bakunin made a splash. Herzen, a convinced Westernizer, dismissed the moderate liberalism of the eighteenth century that had appealed to many discontented Russian aristocrats and embraced the revolutionary view that power belonged to the people (in the Russian case, the serfs). Herzen immigrated to western Europe in 1847, and there he founded *Kolokol* (the Bell), a popular periodical that agitated for reform of an increasingly socialist nature. Bakunin also began as a convinced Westernizer who in 1861 escaped from Siberian exile and immigrated to the West. He espoused increasingly radical views, finally earning for himself the sobriquet "the father of anarchism." Bakunin's advocacy of destruction as a prerequisite for subsequent construction found a ready audience among some Russian revolutionaries of the next generation.

The death of Nicholas I in 1855 brought Alexander II to the throne, and the new tsar reluctantly but firmly pushed through a series of measures that became known as the Great Reforms. Alexander's reign signaled not only substantive reform but also a general loosening of the constrictions that his father had placed on society. In this freer atmosphere, the radical intelligentsia flourished. The decade of the 1860s became known as the time of "the word," whereas the 1870s was the time of "the deed."

During the 1860s, an outpouring of radical thought provided much of the philosophical foundation for the turbulence that beset Russia in the following decade. Perhaps the most influential purveyor of "the word" was Nicholas G. Chernyshevsky, the son of a priest and the author of the wildly popular novel *What Is to Be Done?* Chernyshevsky was arrested in the wake of student demonstrations in 1862, and he wrote *What Is to Be Done?* while in jail awaiting the start of his exile to Siberia. Chernyshevsky embraced a rudimentary socialism, and his novel's protagonists, including "liberated" women, successfully establish a series of cooperative workshops. Beyond his endorsement of socialism, Chernyshevsky also painted a picture of the ideal men and women who were to lead Russia into a brave new world. These heroes and heroines were to be determined, relentless, self-sacrificing, critical, and harshly objective. Their duty called them to destroy a moribund Russia that was beyond reform and to lead the long-suffering Russian peasantry into a glorious new future based on a sort of perfect equality. Russia's future revolutionaries, including Vladimir I. Lenin, ranked Chernyshevsky with the Decembrists and consciously modeled their behavior after his prototypes.

Chernyshevsky's contemporary and friend Nicholas A. Dobroliubov, another priest's son and a literary critic in the mold of Belinsky, wrote for *Sovremennik* (The Contemporary), an influential periodical. Dobroliubov rejected the concept of art for art's sake and stressed that all creative activity must have a utilitarian purpose. Dmitry I. Pisarev, the son of a country gentleman, expanded Dobroliubov's injunction when he demanded the destruction of *all* that served no utilitarian purpose. Pisarev wrote, "What can be broken should be broken." For Pisarev, the application of the scientific method to all problems was essential. If in the process, all existing institutions, moral codes, traditions, and values had to be leveled, so much the better. Pisarev envisioned the almost total destruction of the existing Russian state in order to recreate it on the basis of an agrarian socialism rooted in the peasant commune. However, because Russia's newly emancipated serfs were too ignorant and backward to seize the opportunity, a cadre of young, educated, dedicated revolutionaries had to both raise the peasantry's revolutionary consciousness and—for the foreseeable future—provide the leadership necessary to destroy the old Russia and usher in the new.

Pisarev's steely views shocked many Russians, including those hungering for change but unwilling to sanction mass destruction. The character Bazarov in Ivan Turgenev's classic novel *Fathers and Sons* was clearly modeled after Pisarev, and the term "nihilist," or someone who sees destruction as desirable for its own sake, was coined to describe those who subscribed to Pisarev's views.

Later in the decade, the young nobleman Peter N. Tkachev advocated violent revolution. Tkachev saw Russia's future in the rural masses and the quasi-socialistic peasant commune. Nevertheless, Tkachev concluded that the ignorant and superstitious peasantry would take much too long to acquire the necessary level of consciousness through the normal education process. His answer to this dilemma was a tightly knit, fanatical cadre of dedicated, organized revolutionaries who would immediately seize power "in the name of the people" and rule in a dictatorial manner until the proper maturity was achieved. Because their goals were so lofty in nature, the revolutionaries felt they were absolved from abiding by normal conventions of morality.

Peter N. Lavrov, another radical intellectual, accepted Tkachev's emphasis on the peasantry and his reliance on a small, disciplined party to bring change to Russia. However, he rejected Tkachev's calls for the tsar's immediate overthrow. Rather, he concluded that Russia's intellectual elite, who had achieved their status through the sweat of the peasantry, had a moral obligation to create a just and fair social order. In order to achieve this, they needed to go into the countryside and through personal contact over a long period of time win over the peasantry and educate them in the ways of socialist revolution.

Although the 1860s were rich in thought, there was little notable action except for one, a badly botched attempt to assassinate the tsar that only resulted in a police crackdown and, two, the machinations of the psychopathic Sergei G. Nechaev, which revealed the moral bankruptcy of some radicals and provided the story line for Feodor Dostoevsky's famous novel *The Possessed.* However, the 1860s proved to be the incubation period for the revolutionary activity that convulsed the 1870s.

During that decade, the radical intelligentsia adopted the doctrine of *narodnichestvo,* or Populism. As with almost all of the radical intelligentsia's doctrines, Populism is hard to define. However, some of its elements are clear. For one thing, there was an abiding faith in the goodness of the Russian people, or *narod.* Moreover, because the ultimate goal of Populism was some sort of socialism, the traditional peasant commune was celebrated not only as proof of the peasantry's proclivity toward a socialistic society, but also as a model for Russia's future. *Narodnichestvo* also featured a large dose of guilt and redemption: historically, the peasantry's sacrifices had enabled the privileged radicals to enjoy life; now it was time to repay this debt by going to the peasantry in order to enlighten them and help them create a new cooperative society of peace, harmony, brotherhood, and prosperity. However, this utopia could be realized only by destroying the corrupt and cynical existing structures, and that could be achieved only by revolution.

Although the number of committed Populists was small, they came from the "best and brightest" in Russian society, and they were fiercely determined. In 1873–1874, the Populists launched the *v narod,* or "to the people," movement. Sometimes derisively referred to as a "children's crusade," *v narod* saw several thousand young, urban intellectuals, most of whom were university students, descend on the Russian countryside in order to "serve" the peasants and to commence revolutionizing them as well. The peasants, the intended beneficiaries of this act of self-sacrifice, viewed the city folk with a mixture of curiosity, disdain, suspicion, and fright. Sometimes the astonished peasants simply turned the interlopers over to the tsarist police. Subsequently, a series of trials resulted in deportation to Siberia of perhaps 200 *v narod* activists.

The failure of *v narod* shook the radical intelligentsia; however, in 1876 some of its partisans founded a conspiratorial organization called Land and Freedom. When Land and Freedom split in 1879, one faction calling itself Narodnaia Volia, or the People's Will, embarked upon a campaign of terror. Concluding that the peasantry was not yet ripe for the envisioned mass upheaval but that revolution could be achieved by destroying the current regime's leadership, the People's Will set out to murder the tsar. Spurred on by the iron-willed Sophia L. Perovskaia, the daughter of a high government official, and her peasant lover, Andrei I. Zheliabov, the People's Will repeatedly attempted to assassinate Alexander II. For the People's Will, success finally came on March 13, 1881 (March 1, O.S.), when it blew up the royal carriage and Alexander along with it on the streets of St. Petersburg, thereby opening a new phase for Russia's radical intelligentsia.

INTERPRETIVE ESSAY
David C. Fisher

No one wanted to change Russia more between 1861 and 1881 than Populist radicals dedicated to overthrowing tsarism and ushering in socialist egalitarianism. Populists recoiled from the inequality and arbitrariness of Russia's social, economic, and political system and aimed to replace an autocratic tsar and noble landlords with a form of agrarian socialism organized on the model of the *obshchina*, the peasant village commune. They hoped that after a popular revolt, land would be distributed to those who worked it, peasants would govern themselves, and state government would be formed by a freely elected national assembly representing the interests of peasants and workers. The illegal publications in which radicals expressed their views—*The Bell, The Alarm,* and *Forward!*—communicated a sense of urgency and call for action. The names they gave to their organizations—Land and Freedom, The People's Will, Black Repartition (a reference to land redistribution)—described not who they were, but the changes they wanted to bring about. Despite their dedication and discipline, Populists were thwarted by an inexorable tsar and bureaucracy committed to maintaining the political status quo of absolutism.

Populism emerged in the wake of Alexander II's modernizing Great Reforms and the restrictive countermeasures that limited their implementation. The government emancipated the serfs in 1861 but gave them much less land than they had expected, along with the obligation of redemption (mortgage) payments that compelled peasants to pay for the land they had always considered rightfully their own. Alexander II eased censorship during the reform period, and a multitude of newspapers and periodicals became available to literate Russians. Yet the government retained the right to censor writers and publications. Journals were readily shut down and editors jailed when they crossed an arbitrary line imposed by administration authorities. Opportunities for university education and student privileges were expanded and just as quickly retracted when students began to discuss government policy, organize demonstrations, and criticize the arbitrariness of school officials. Government reform created elected provincial bodies, *zemstvos,* to help with the administration of public education and social services. Yet zemstvo representatives were not allowed to bring their professional expertise to bear on the central government's policy making. They were not to discuss politics, advise the tsar, or advocate for any kind of constituent assembly that would represent the interests of the people at the national level. Finally, the reforms introduced trial by jury for the first time in Russia and created a professional body of lawyers. Nevertheless, the government could circumvent the legal reforms in the case of political crimes and could have alleged revolutionaries tried by military courts or committees made up of state senators.

The reforms had been intended to make autocracy and its bureaucracy more efficient and modern. Elites and peasants alike hoped for political change as well, but the counterreforms revealed the inconsistencies and hypocrisies of a system devoted to the preservation of autocracy. Consequently, the failure of the tsar to crown the reforms with a constitution and the unjust settlement with the peasantry engendered a revolutionary reaction.

Russia's revolutionaries came primarily from the *raznochintsy,* people of various ranks who did not easily fit into the ossified categories of Russian estates. Radicals were by and large young intellectuals—the sons and daughters of priests, military officers, emancipated serfs, and impoverished nobles who entered the universities in the late 1850s and 1860s to prepare for professional careers. Students emboldened by progressive and radical ideas challenged the conservative and reactionary policies of university administrators and government authorities. Educated society was generally sympathetic and even financially supportive of their cause. Yet revolutionaries were not coordinated or organized into any kind of centralized or national body or party. Rather, the Populist banner changed hands and was carried by a variety of groups that formed around particularly eloquent writers, magnetic personalities, and dedicated organizers. Groups dissipated and reappeared as the fortunes of revolutionary ideology shifted and, more important, as revolutionaries were arrested and their activities curtailed. Populists gathered in discussion circles where they read the latest revolutionary publications smuggled into the country from Russian exiles. They studied socialist writers and argued over the problems of how to solve the inequalities of Russia's political, economic, and social system. Inspired by literary models for revolutionary behavior and calls for action, Populist organizations formed in the larger cities of the empire—St. Petersburg, Moscow, Kazan, and Odessa.

As discussion turned to calls for action, debate centered on the most effective tactics for revolution. The state's success at parrying the radicals and popular apathy, as well as ideological battles, compelled shifts in the radicals' tactics. Some spread propaganda, others went "to the people" (*v narod*) to agitate for revolt, and still others plotted revolutionary dictatorship and political assassination. The ensuing clash between the state and the Populist revolutionaries drove government authorities into a siege mentality, and the radical movement became increasingly isolated and turned to terrorism as a last resort, a decision that proved to be the movement's undoing.

Populists clearly articulated the shortcomings of the tsarist system and their goal of transforming inequality into egalitarianism. However, the outstanding problem was how to effect change. The idea of going to the people was first put into words in 1862 by Alexander I. Herzen, a member of the radical intelligentsia who came of age in the 1840s. He envisioned an agrarian form of socialism in which peasants would play the leading role in the state's economic and political life. To bring about revolution, Herzen believed the intelligentsia would have to support the peasants, take action to further their interests, and help rule once revolution came. The decree emancipating the serfs in early 1861 disappointed both radicals and peasants. It was confusing in its pronouncements, caveats, and conditions. The freed serfs felt deceived by the government's requirement that they make redemption payments for land they received at overvalued prices. It was during this confusing period of transition in the early 1860s that Herzen's role as an opinion shaper for the radical intelligentsia diminished. He was superceded by a younger generation that was more radical, more demanding of not only enacting reform but also overturning the autocracy, and more willing to organize secret groups to take action. By 1863 Herzen's influence had waned, but not before he had issued marching orders for the nascent Populist movement. If radicals desired to bring about justice and equality for peasants confounded by an odious regime, they would have to "go to the people." However, putting Herzen's words into action proved difficult.

Radicalism spread among university students who picked up the call for revolution. In the atmosphere of impending reform during the late 1850s, universities came alive with debates about the politics, economics, and future of the empire. Government authorities viewed a politically active student body given to self-organization as a threat to stability. Admiral Efim V. Putiatin, the minister of education, restricted student enrollments and the right to organize meetings or mutual aid societies. Nothing could have more effectively politicized students or helped solidify their sense of collective identity and opposition to the regime. In fall 1861, university students held Russia's first public demonstration in St. Petersburg. The authorities responded to this and student demonstrations elsewhere by closing the universities until 1863, a move that failed to prevent radical students from challenging the government.

Peter G. Zaichnevsky stood at the center of a Moscow student circle dedicated to socialism and the revolutionary overthrow of the Romanovs. He struggled with the problem of putting radical ideas into action and proposed a Jacobin solution. Rather than a "go to the people" philosophy, Zaichnevsky envisioned a conspiracy of dedicated radicals who would place themselves at the head of a popular revolt and seize power as a dictatorship in the name of the people. Police arrested Zaichnevsky in the fall of 1861 for his activities organizing socialist radicals. Yet from his prison cell, he authored the most startling and violent call for action to the radical intelligentsia. The leaflet, titled *Young Russia,* and signed simply, "the Central Revolutionary Committee," appeared on the streets of Moscow and St. Petersburg in May 1862. The manifesto declared that a revolution was imminent in which the people would let flow rivers of blood as they massacred the ruling class of the tsar, his family, government officials, and the wealthy. It declared that national and regional assemblies would be elected by the people who would live in, and according to, the traditions of the *obshchina.* The precepts of socialism would govern the state's economic, domestic, and foreign policy. Twenty-year-old Zaichnevsky called on his own generation to form the revolutionary party that would guide the popular uprising and ensure its gains through dictatorship in the people's interest.

The manifesto unnerved the authorities, pushed liberals and radicals further apart, and introduced for the first time a Jacobin thread into the Populist discourse. Patently undemocratic, Jacobinism had little currency among Russian radicals but the idea was not altogether rejected. As Populists continued to seek an effective strategy for action in the 1860s and 1870s, the idea of bringing revolution to fruition and governing by means of a revolutionary party continued to be developed. Nevertheless, at this point, the young people who were becoming radicalized eschewed Jacobinism and more readily adopted the philosophy of scientific positivism and negation of authority that nihilism offered.

Nihilism provided an antiauthoritarian pose for young people but not a plan of action. Nicholas G. Chernyshevsky, the influential critic who guided the popular journal *The Contemporary*, mapped a route out of the nihilist cul-de-sac by providing radicalized youth with models for taking action in the revolutionary movement. Chernyshevsky opposed capitalism and liberalism and, like Herzen, believed that the future of socialism in Russia lay in the collective traditions of the obshchina. Chernyshevsky had an able and enthusiastic protégé in Nicholas A. Dobroliubov, who embodied a political and personal dedication to Populist ideas and communicated them through literary criticism and satire. Dobroliubov's contributions to *The Contemporary* helped shape the radical intelligentsia by arguing that they had a duty to educate the people, represent their interests, and transform Russia. As secret groups began to form and plan a revolutionary movement in 1861–1862, Nicholas Chernyshevsky and *The Contemporary* provided a central point at which radicals and various nascent groups found common ideological ground.

The authorities closed *The Contemporary* in the summer of 1862 and arrested Chernyshevsky shortly thereafter (Dobroliubov had died of consumption in 1861). While imprisoned in the Peter and Paul Fortress, Chernyshevsky wrote *What Is to Be Done? Tales about New People*, a novel whose heroes provided a literary model for radicals who longed to put revolutionary ideas into action. Because of a censor's oversight, *What Is to Be Done?* was published in 1863. Its impact on shaping the determination of young radicals cannot be understated. It was read voraciously by young adults whom Chernyshevsky hoped to transform into the "new men and women" of the book's subtitle. He succeeded. The book's characters are young, scientific-minded intellectuals of a nihilist bent who nonetheless are Populists at heart and dedicated to improving the lives of the people.

The question posed in the book's title found an answer in the character of Rakhmetov, a "new man" who lives and works only to ameliorate the people's condition in an unjust society and to prepare for revolution. Chernyshevsky's readers understood the message: deny oneself worldly pleasures, live and work with like-minded men and women in comradely cooperation, and dedicate oneself single-mindedly to the people's cause. Reward would come in the form of a socialist utopia. Government authorities sentenced Chernyshevsky to hard labor and exile in Siberia. He spent the years of the Populist movement there while newly motivated young radicals continued to organize and develop strategies for action, including terrorism.

Moscow university student Nicholas A. Ishutin, inspired by *What Is to Be Done?*, gathered a group of radicals dedicated to self-sacrifice and the people. A select number formed a society called the Organization to agitate for socialist revolution through education and propaganda. Within the Organization, Ishutin formed a secret cell named Hell whose members planned to incite revolution by terrorizing the authorities and the privileged—and ultimately by assassinating the tsar. Before these plans were put into action, Dmitry V. Karakozov, a disturbed member of the Organization, decided on his own, despite the efforts of Ishutin and others to dissuade him, that the time had arrived to kill Alexander II. On April 16, 1866 (April 4, O.S.), he fired an errant pistol shot at the tsar outside St. Petersburg's Summer Garden. Karakozov's subsequent interrogation led to the arrest of several hundred people, including the entire membership of the Organization. Not only did the assassination attempt destroy the Organization, but it also unleashed a "white terror" of police activity that bore down relentlessly on radicals engaged in anti-tsarist discussions, organizing, and propagandizing. Worse yet for the Populist cause, Karakozov's act elicited an outpouring of loyalty for the tsar from peasants and workers, thus demonstrating all the more that radicals did not understand the people for whom they fought.

The question of putting Populist ideas into action remained unresolved. Jacobinism and terrorism did more damage to the revolutionary movement than to the government, which clearly maintained the upper hand in the battle with radicals. Populists learned a lesson from the Karakozov affair; in the new groups that attempted to form during the white terror, the prevailing belief was that intellectuals had to bridge the gap between themselves and peasants through direct contact, study of peasant conditions, and gradual socialist propagandizing. Nevertheless, the impulse for immediate action, a Jacobin strategy of conspiratorial cells that would merge with and lead a mass uprising, had not been extinguished. It was embodied in the magnetic and mysterious personality of Sergei G. Nechaev.

Nechaev was in St. Petersburg when Karakozov fired at the tsar and was taking university classes in 1868 when the student movement revived. An ambitious young man, Nechaev became involved with radical circles and hoped to lead the student movement. Believing that a peasant uprising against the authorities and against the injustices of the emancipation decree was imminent, he became more involved in clandestine organizing efforts in Moscow and St. Petersburg. In 1869 Nechaev went abroad to establish contacts with Russian exiles. In Geneva he collaborated with the venerable Russian radical, Michael A. Bakunin, and coauthored the *Revolutionary Catechism.* This manual spelled out the characteristics of the ideal revolutionary: dedicated to the organization, loyal to its leader, and ruthless in devotion to the cause for which he would spare neither himself nor others. The young radical's association with, and endorsement by, Bakunin enhanced his reputation. But though influenced by Bakunin's philosophy of anarchism, Nechaev's tactics for revolution focused on the creation of a party of conspiratorial cells whose members would encourage and guide the spontaneous peasant revolt. Nechaev's approach was completely out of step with the majority of Populist radicals who favored democratic policies and believed forming a connection with the people was paramount, yet he gained the most notoriety.

Nechaev returned to Moscow in the fall of 1869 and set about organizing a society he called the People's Vengeance. Despite success at organizing students, the new revolutionary society did not get far. Nechaev plotted the murder of a group member, and the resulting criminal investigation turned up evidence of the People's Vengeance and led to the arrests of the group's members and tangential associates. Eighty-seven defendants were put on trial for their association with the murder and Nechaev's radical political activities. The primary effect of the trial, particularly the revelation of the *Revolutionary Catechism,* was to scandalize the public and reaffirm in radical circles that Jacobinism was anathema to the core ideas of agrarian socialism and doomed to failure.

For most Populists, Nechaev's antics discredited the idea of a revolutionary elite; nevertheless, a Jacobin strategy for bringing about socialism remained alive in a more articulate spokesman, Peter N. Tkachev. Tkachev made a name for himself in the radical movement as a writer and agitator after he was expelled from St. Petersburg University in 1861. In 1869 Nechaev and Tkachev moved in the same radical circles. Tkachev's writing, influenced by Marx and advocating revolution to bring about Communism, led to his arrest in 1869 when Nechaev's plans for revolution were just getting underway. He was tried along with radicals rounded up in the Nechaev affair in 1871, but managed to flee abroad in 1873 and join the exile community in Switzerland. Tkachev was a Populist but he did not idealize "the people" or trust that a popular revolt would produce an egalitarian social and economic structure based on the principle of a collective, communal obshchina. He argued in his newspaper, *The Alarm* (1875–1881), that a popular revolt might destroy the old order, but only an elite, conspiratorial group of disciplined revolutionaries could establish a new order based on class, gender, and economic egalitarianism and self-administration. His lack of faith in the people put him at odds with mainstream Populist ideology even if he shared Populist goals. Reliance on conspiracy and a radical elite were heretical tactics to Populists who placed their hopes in a popular revolt through which the people themselves, with some guidance from intellectuals, would establish a socialist state. Although Tkachev's ideas were out of favor among radicals in the 1870s, they would come back to the fore by 1879 as a response to heightened government repression.

The government's white terror succeeded at breaking up radical circles, but not at preventing them from forming. Radicals continued to question how to proceed in the face of these government successes. They began to focus more intently on Herzen's charge to go to the people. Nechaev's infamy did not deter other radical circles that had, for the time, remained undetected by the police. Chief among them were the Chaikovtsy, a group that rejected Nechaev's Jacobin tactics and emphasized propaganda. The Chaikovtsy eschewed a narrow political program and created a group more open to the various strains of Populist ideology. Consequently, the group flourished and formed the broadest and deepest radical organization yet to challenge the authorities.

The Chaikovtsy did not plot violent overthrow of the government. Their actions were shaped by moral, ethical, and communal sensibilities and a pervasive belief that educated Russians owed a debt for their elevated position to the people who were oppressed by ignorance and an unjust regime. The young men and women—mostly students—of the Chaikovtsy emphasized education through propagandizing socialist ideas. They began by educating fellow students through the creation of lending libraries of socialist literature. They also legally printed materials that analyzed the oppressive conditions of workers and peasants in Russia, and they took pains to distribute pamphlets and books (including Chernyshevsky and Marx) beyond the cities to provincial towns and districts. The Chaikovtsy took propagandizing far beyond the limited reach of their predecessors. Government authorities responded to the Chaikovtsy by tightening censorship restrictions and increasing surveillance. Although the group had fallen apart by 1873, it contributed to the creation of an atmosphere in which Populism reached its high-water mark in the summer of 1874, when several thousand students and activists fanned out into the provincial countryside to live, work, and propagandize among the peasants.

Two additional lines of thought shaped the intellectual atmosphere in which the "to the people" movement occurred. Both Michael Bakunin and Peter N. Lavrov believed radicals had to bridge the gap between the intelligentsia and the people if a social revolution were to take place. Lavrov advocated long-term propagandizing and education of the peasants about the wrongs of tsarism and about the solutions offered by socialism as the best strategy to effect an eventual mass uprising. Alternatively, Bakunin argued that the peasants already understood the inequalities and arbitrariness of the tsarist system. If only given a push by radical agitators, peasants would revolt and destroy the status quo in an anarchic frenzy in which they would seize the land and set up self-government. Bakunin stood for anarchy, Lavrov for patient preparation. Both opposed Tkachev's Jacobin idea of a dictatorial revolutionary party.

Bakunin believed social revolution was imminent in post-emancipation Russia. He argued that peasants were ready to rise up in the same spirit as Pugachev in the eighteenth century. However, a socialist peasant revolt would be more than a jacquerie that terrorized nobles and aspired to place a pretender like Pugachev on the Romanov throne. A socialist peasant revolt would destroy the state, the idea of a mystical bond between peasants and a tsar-protector, and traditional patriarchal authority. The peasant obshchina would supercede the tsarist system as the highest instance of political authority, and Russia would consist of independent obshchinas joined in a free federation.

In opposition to Bakunin, Lavrov theorized that a long period of intellectual self-preparation for radicals and education of peasants about socialism had to take place before revolution could be achieved. Lavrov encouraged youth to abandon the positivistic, self-centered, and destructive nihilist identity in favor of accepting a sense of duty that the intelligentsia bore before the people. Those who had prospered from the unjust Russian economic and social system, Lavrov argued, owed a debt to the peasants to change the system. Lavrov was convinced that patient preparation was necessary so that the people would be ready to transform revolutionary upheaval into a socialist state.

Students responded enthusiastically to Lavrov's social and ethical call to repay a debt and to the injunction to bridge the gap between themselves and Russia's rural masses. In fact, Bakunin and Lavrov overlap here in their emphasis on going directly to the people to effect change.

But students rejected Lavrov's idea of the need for intellectual preparation and gradual propagandizing. They were ready for action and ready to overthrow the system. When students headed into the countryside in the spring of 1874, they were influenced by both Lavrov and Bakunin, but in their sense of urgency and belief that revolution was imminent, they were more Bakuninists than Lavrovists.

There was no central organization directing the "to the people" movement. Neither Lavrov nor Bakunin had ever led an organized group, and the Chaikovtsy were no longer an organized force by the summer of 1874. Taken together, however, the spirit of the Chaikovtsy, the ideas of Lavrov and Bakunin, and the preliminary attempts to spread literature among the peasants by the Dolgushin group in the summer of 1873 had created an atmosphere for a genuine movement. Students were radicalized by propaganda that unleashed their enthusiasm to act. Yet peasants were indifferent or taken aback by the urban strangers who appeared in their midst. Some listened politely to socialist propaganda, others paid the students no mind, and not a few grew suspicious of radicals as troublemakers. No one revolted. Peasants remained loyal to the tsar and showed more interest in owning land and hiring laborers than creating a socialist utopia. The police easily rounded up student agitators, jailed hundreds, and harassed even more. The "to the people" movement failed to instigate an uprising, but it did alter tactics within the radical movement.

A new party, Land and Freedom, revived the organizational strategy of small, conspiratorial cells to operate beyond the reach of the gendarmes and reinvigorated the Populist cause by incorporating a wide variety of radical circles formerly divided by ideological and tactical differences. The party's breadth was its initial strength and ultimate weakness. Lavrovist, Bakuninist, Jacobin, and terrorist strains of the Populist movement intermingled uncomfortably but united in a shared sense of purpose. The goal of agrarian socialism had not changed, but Land and Freedom's founders approached their task more pragmatically than their predecessors had. They attempted to shed their idealization of peasants and the belief that an organic uprising was on the verge of erupting.

Land and Freedom emphasized three primary tactics to achieve change in Russia. First was the organization of radical circles into a cooperative body tied loosely together through the work of a centralized and highly secretive executive committee. Second, the group promoted agitation through word and deed, propagandizing revolution among workers and peasants on the one hand and organizing strikes and uprisings on the other. Finally, Land and Freedom's program directly confronted the problem of fighting back against government repression by declaring the party would engage in "disorganizing activities" aimed at state institutions and officials. In practice, this meant that revolutionaries would use firearms against police to prevent arrest and would plot escapes of jailed comrades, eliminate informers, and take revenge against brutal representatives of the regime such as police chiefs and governors-general through assassination. This final point was embraced by those members of Land and Freedom who had the least patience for agitation and believed no progress could be made without literally doing battle with the state. Their position quickly erased the difference between self-defense and terrorism as a wing of Land and Freedom devoted itself increasingly to political assassination, in lieu of a mass uprising, to topple the tsarist regime.

Differing opinions on resorting to terror split Land and Freedom. One faction argued for continued propaganda and agitation to arouse the people, while advocates of violence argued for concentrating resources on toppling the government through political assassination. Land and Freedom's loose organizational structure could not prevent these two factions from taking separate courses. The question of terror came to a head in the spring of 1879, when Alexander K. Solovev decided to assassinate Alexander II. Solovev's colleagues in Land and Freedom could not agree on whether the organization should assist or forbid his attempt. Indecision produced the half measure of withholding organizational support from the would-be assassin, while not preventing individual members from helping Solovev if they so chose. On April 14, 1879 (April 2, O.S.), Solovev fired five shots at the tsar as he strolled on Palace Square. Solovev missed, and he was tried and executed within eight weeks.

As the opponents of terrorism feared, the assassination attempt provoked heightened vigilance and repression that hobbled the activities of Land and Freedom in the capital. A party conference met in the southern city of Voronezh in June 1879, but only temporarily smoothed over the differences dividing the organization. In August the party dissolved itself and divided its assets between the propagandists and the terrorists. The propagandists' faction, Black Repartition, was led by George V. Plekhanov and Paul B. Axelrod. Their organizational and propaganda efforts produced little because they were quickly hounded out of Russia by the authorities, and they then attempted to lead the Populist struggle from exile in Switzerland.

The terrorist wing took the name People's Will. Born in the atmosphere of increasing oppression by state organs, the Executive Committee of the People's Will guided the organization according to the principles of centralized authority, hierarchy, and discipline. At the center of the Executive Committee, dedicated revolutionaries such as Timofei M. Mikhailov,

Andrei I. Zheliabov, and Sophia L. Perovskaia focused the organization's mission on assassinating the tsar. The orientation of the People's Will toward action and pragmatism attracted committed followers, which made it the leading revolutionary organization in Russia.

The ideology of the People's Will stitched together the goals of Populism and socialism with the tactics of Jacobinism and terrorism. The *Narodovoltsy* (members of the People's Will, or Narodnaia Volia) sought to replace the tsarist system with the "will of the people," as expressed in democratic elections to a national assembly that would represent the interests of workers and peasants. Yet they harbored no hope that a spontaneous popular revolt would occur to topple the tsar and the bureaucracy through which he expressed his will. Rather than rely on the people, the Narodovoltsy believed a dedicated core of revolutionaries could seize power, ensure that liberals and the bourgeoisie did not snatch it away, and deliver it to the people. Within the workings of a newly called national assembly, the Narodovoltsy would not become dictators or impose socialism; rather, they would argue for agrarian socialism in open political debate. Their tactics were similar to those proposed by Tkachev except that the Narodovoltsy shied away from the un-Populist notion of imposing their political agenda by decree. Terrorism would be the key to seizing power. The Narodovoltsy reasoned that tsarist power was a rotten façade that would crumble if sufficient pressure was applied. They believed that assassinating the tsar would create a crisis in government, and then authoritarian rule would collapse, and power would fall into their hands as the population rose in support of revolution.

They were wrong. After six attempts to blow up the tsar with dynamite, including an explosion in the Winter Palace itself, the Narodovoltsy finally succeeded in assassinating Alexander II on March 13, 1881 (March 1, O.S.). The assassination caused shock and fear, but it did not destroy tsarist absolutism. Ironically, at the time of his death, Alexander II was considering a proposal that would permit elected representatives a limited role in his Council of State. But with the tsar's murder at the hands of radicals, any notion of introducing even the mildest reform evaporated. The new tsar, Alexander III, declared that absolute authority resided solely in the hands of the autocrat. The Populist movement came to an end in the repressive crackdown of Alexander III's reign (1881–1894), an era characterized by counterreform and martial law.

Radical revolutionaries changed Russia, but not in the way they had intended. Populists in the 1860s and 1870s had aimed to engender a mass peasant uprising against tsarism and replace autocracy and the rule of landlords with egalitarian agrarian socialism. After 1881, revolutionary

Marxism eclipsed Populism, yet Populism had provided a pathway for radicals to Marxism. Former Populist George Plekhanov gradually rejected agrarian socialism for Marxism and founded the first Russian social democratic party. Young radicals, such as Vladimir I. Ulianov, the future Lenin, studied the Populist writers and then moved on to Marx and the idea that the future of revolution lay with urban workers, not rural peasants.

Populists also contributed to undermining autocracy. Their efforts at agitation and assassination put the state on the defensive and caused government authorities to follow their predisposition toward reaction rather than progress, to become more oppressive and arbitrary, and to ever more staunchly defend the legitimacy of autocratic rule. Public trials of radicals provided a platform from which revolutionaries demonstrated their integrity and eroded the regime's moral authority. The inability of Alexander III and his son Nicholas II, the last two tsars, to exercise any genuine flexibility in their autocratic rule made the system all the more brittle and susceptible to disintegration. Ultimately, the Populists were correct in predicting that Russians would spontaneously revolt and overthrow tsarism. Indeed, the house of Romanov barely contained a nationwide revolt in 1905 and then crumbled in 1917 because of the challenges of fighting World War I and society's utter lack of faith in the tsar to rule competently. In the aftermath of tsardom's collapse, the neo-Populist Socialist Revolutionary Party may have had the most support among the rural masses, but a socialist government was installed by Lenin's Bolsheviks, who seized sole control of the government in October 1917 using Jacobin tactics that Tkachev would have readily recognized.

SELECTED BIBLIOGRAPHY

Baron, Samuel H. *Plekhanov: The Father of Russian Marxism.* Stanford, CA: Stanford University Press, 1963.
> Biography of the former Populist who rejected agrarian socialism for Marxism and founded the first Russian social democratic party.

Bergman, Jay. *Vera Zasulich: A Biography.* Stanford, CA: Stanford University Press, 1983.
> A narrative about Zasulich and her experiences in the revolutionary movement as a Populist including her acquittal for attempted political assassination and subsequent conversion to Marxism.

Berlin, Isaiah. *Russian Thinkers.* Edited by Henry Hardy and Aileen Kelly. New York: Penguin Books, 1994.
> Erudite and accessible collection of essays that comment on key nineteenth-century thinkers including Herzen, Bakunin, and the Populists.

Billington, James H. *Mikhailovsky and Russian Populism.* New York: Oxford University Press, 1958.

Analysis of Nicholas Mikhailovsky's intellectual contributions to Populist ideology.

Figner, Vera. *Memoirs of a Revolutionist*. DeKalb: Northern Illinois University Press, 1991.
     Figner's firsthand account of her conversion to revolutionary Populism and her role in the Executive Committee of the People's Will and assassination of Alexander II.

Gleason, Abbott. *Young Russia: The Genesis of Russian Radicalism in the 1860s*. New York: Viking Press, 1980.
     Analysis of student activism and emergence of Populism from serf emancipation in 1861 to the Nechaev trial in 1873.

Haimson, Leopold H. *The Russian Marxists and the Origins of Bolshevism*. Boston, MA: Beacon Press, 1966.
     Elegant discussion of the transition from Populism to Marxism among radicals and the division of Russian Social Democrats into Bolsheviks and Mensheviks.

Hardy, Deborah. *Land and Freedom: The Origins of Russian Terrorism, 1876–1879*. New York: Greenwood Press, 1987.
     In-depth assessment of the roots of terrorism in the Populist movement.

———. *Petr Tkachev, The Critic as Jacobin*. Seattle: University of Washington Press, 1977.
     Biography of Tkachev's life and intellectual development.

Leatherbarrow, W. J., and D. C. Offord, trans. and eds. *A Documentary History of Russian Thought: From the Enlightenment to Marxism*. Ann Arbor, MI: Ardis, 1987.
     Collection of primary source documents by leading intellectuals and radicals including Chernyshevsky, Dobroliubov, Lavrov, Bakunin, Tkachev, and Plekhanov.

Malia, Martin E. *Alexander Herzen and the Birth of Russian Socialism, 1812–1855*. New York: Grosset and Dunlap, 1971.
     Places the roots of Russian socialism in European influence, as seen in Herzen's thought, whose life and ideas linked the radicals of the 1840s with the new generation of the 1860s.

Mendel, Arthur P. *Michael Bakunin: Roots of Apocalypse*. New York: Praeger, 1981.
     Analysis of Bakunin's background and intellectual development as the father of anarchism.

Pomper, Philip. *Peter Lavrov and the Russian Revolutionary Movement*. Chicago, IL: University of Chicago Press, 1972.
     Intellectual biography of Lavrov.

———. *Sergei Nechaev*. New Brunswick, NJ: Rutgers University Press, 1979.
     Psychological biography of Nechaev.

Venturi, Franco. *Roots of Revolution: A History of the Populist and Socialist Movements in Nineteenth-Century Russia*. Translated by Francis Haskell. London: Phoenix Press, 2001.
     The most comprehensive and definitive analysis of Russian radicalism from the 1820s to the 1880s.

Walicki, Andrzej. *A History of Russian Thought from the Enlightenment to Marxism*. Translated by Hilda Andrews-Rusiecka. Stanford, CA: Stanford University Press, 1979.

Analysis of intellectuals and their ideas from Catherine II's era to Lenin, including Populist thinkers.

———. *The Controversy over Capitalism: Studies in the Social Philosophy of the Russian Populists.* Notre Dame, IN: University of Notre Dame Press, 1989.

Analyzes the role of modernization to illuminate the difference between the Populist and Marxist paths to socialism in Russia.

Woehrlin, William F. *Chernyshevskii: The Man and the Journalist.* Cambridge, MA: Harvard University Press, 1971.

Biography of Chernyshevsky and analysis of his writings and impact on the radical movement.

Wortman, Richard. *The Crisis of Russian Populism.* London: Cambridge University Press, 1971.

Study of how intellectuals' idealized image of peasants was challenged by reality.

Yarmolinsky, Avrahm. *Road to Revolution: A Century of Russian Radicalism.* Princeton, NJ: Princeton University Press, 1986.

A highly accessible survey of radical opposition to tsarism from the late eighteenth century to the late nineteenth.

3

Industrialization, 1881–1913

INTRODUCTION

As was the case for most countries, Russia's Industrial Revolution arrived in fits and starts. For many centuries, Russia had produced "industrial" goods for domestic consumption. In fact, at the end of the eighteenth century, Russia was one of the world's largest producers of iron. However, the technology that yielded these goods was decidedly primitive; the Industrial Revolution that was then unfolding in Great Britain was absent in Russia.

The first unmistakable signs of modern industrial development in Russia appeared only with the Great Reforms. Some experts think that the emancipation of the serfs spurred Russia's industrial development because it freed up labor, a vital commodity for the labor-intensive Industrial Revolution. Although by the early 1870s, Russia had begun to industrialize, it is difficult to generate a clear picture of this process because of the chaotic and unreliable nature of the rather meager statistical data available.

Railroads played a key role in Russia's industrial growth. Beginning in the 1860s, Tsar Alexander II encouraged railroad construction for strategic rather than purely economic reasons. The disastrous Crimean War had revealed Russia's backwardness, and there was fear that if Russia did not modernize, it would fall from the ranks of the Great Powers. Consequently, an extensive rail network was seen as essential. With encouragement from the government, small, newly created firms undertook most of the construction. An economic boom of sorts followed, and the rail

Railroad development, such as this newly constructed cut for a railway line in Ukraine, played a major role in Russia's Industrial Revolution. Between 1857 and 1901, Russia's railroads expanded from 600 miles to 28,000 miles. There were similar increases in coal and steel production. (Reproduced from the Collections of the Library of Congress.)

network expanded from 600 miles in 1857 to more than 11,000 miles in 1876. However, in the early 1870s, the economy turned down, and many of the fledgling railroad companies went bankrupt.

During this initial stage of Russia's Industrial Revolution, the number of industrial enterprises doubled, and by 1880 the value of their output had increased five-fold to one billion rubles, still not a very impressive figure. These companies were organized on a capitalistic basis, with the support and encouragement of an undercapitalized state. With capitalism came a hired labor force, and with industrialization came exploitation of that force. Not surprisingly, labor rebelled at its condition, and in 1878 and 1879, St. Petersburg witnessed its first industrial strikes.

During the 1880s, Russia's industrial pace quickened. Once again, railroads led the way. However, this time, the government moved to bring the rail network under its control and to stimulate the construction of new rail lines. Between 1876 and 1895, the rail system doubled in size to 22,000 miles, most of which the state now owned and operated. Moreover, the nascent petroleum industry located at Baku, south of the Caucasus Mountains, began to expand significantly. The decade was also noteworthy for the development of the Donets Basin, or Donbas, a region in southern Russia rich in both coal and iron.

The Donbas expansion was underwritten by massive foreign investments and loans, and the importation of capital and appeals to foreign investors now became a major feature of Russia's Industrial Revolution. The pursuit of foreign capital featured prominently in the policies of Nicholas K. Bunge, minister of finance from 1881 to 1886. Bunge also eased the tax burden on the peasantry in order to increase their buying power and, thus, stimulate demand for domestic manufactures. In the same vein, he raised tariffs to restrict imports, thereby protecting home-grown industry. His successor, Ivan A. Vyshnegradsky, headed the finance ministry from 1887 until 1892. Like Bunge, Vyshnegradsky insisted upon high import duties and continued to solicit foreign investment. However, Vyshnegradsky emphasized the need for a balanced budget, and to this end he increased taxes on the peasantry and began to export massive amounts of grain even at the risk of depleting reserves.

With the foundation for future growth in place, Russia's industrial expansion took flight during the 1890s. Sergei Y. Witte, Russia's finance minister from 1892 to 1903, superintended this period of rapid industrialization. Witte, like a number of nineteenth-century Russian officials, was of Germanic extraction. He was energetic and hard-working and was something of a self-made man, having come from a comfortable but not noble provincial background. Knowledgeable in the practical aspects of economic matters, Witte had originally made his mark as a railroad official. Throughout his tenure at the finance ministry, he paid careful attention to the expansion of Russia's industrial infrastructure.

During the 1890s, Russia's annual rate of industrial growth averaged about 8 percent, making it the highest in Europe. Once again, railroad construction led the way. Between 1898 and 1901, Russia laid almost 6,000 miles of track. The most impressive rail project was the ambitious Trans-Siberian railroad linking European Russia with its Far-Eastern Pacific shore. Existing railroads were double-tracked, and rail facilities connecting Russia's ports to the interior were significantly upgraded. However, industrial expansion was not confined solely to the rail sector. During the 1890s, the production of pig iron more than tripled and that of coal more than doubled; oil output rose by 250 percent. By 1905 there were more than 40,000 factories in Russia generating an output worth more than 4 billion rubles.

Witte was the driving force behind this spectacular growth. Echoing Bunge and Vyshnegradsky, Witte feared for Russia's future, especially for its Great Power status, because of the empire's backwardness. It took no genius to see that Russia continued to fall further behind the likes of Great Britain and Germany. To reverse this trend, Witte dramatically accelerated the rate of industrialization. Under Witte's direction, the imperial government concentrated on expanding Russia's industrial infrastructure through concessions, subsidies, investments, and tariff policies favoring domestic producers.

During his tenure at the finance ministry, Witte took several major steps to modernize Russia's economy. He invested the state heavily in railroad construction, believing that this would stimulate domestic heavy industry, make Russia's vast resources more accessible for exploitation, and employ surplus labor that in turn would boost the demand for consumer goods. The increase in tax revenues derived from a healthy economy would reimburse the government for its initial capital expenditures.

Following in Bunge's and Vyshnegradsky's footsteps, Witte eagerly courted foreign capital. Russia enjoyed great success in floating loans from the French government and private French banking interests. To facilitate foreign investment, it was necessary to ensure the convertibility of the Russian ruble, thereby creating monetary certainty. To this end, Witte accumulated gold reserves, and in 1897 he moved the ruble to the gold standard.

Witte had other sources of capital for industrial expansion as well. Russia's high import duties generated a tidy sum, as did the government monopoly on vodka. Grain exports were encouraged. Perhaps most consequentially, Witte taxed the lower classes mercilessly. Certainly their increasing penury and desperation hastened the coming of revolution in 1905; however, in terms of industrialization, Witte's policies brought impressive results.

The nature of Russia's Industrial Revolution differed from the European norm. To begin with, the central government played a major entrepreneurial role. Except for the railroads, the state did not own much of the means of production; nevertheless, it placed huge orders with the new factories, extended loans at favorable rates, generously subsidized various enterprises, maintained a tariff policy very favorable to domestic producers, actively promoted Russian industrial exports, and provided modern banking facilities. Unlike other industrializing countries, Russia also encouraged foreign investment on a massive scale. Between 1880 and 1900, foreign investment in Russia grew from 100 million rubles to 900 million rubles; by 1914, foreign capital fully owned almost one-half of Russia's industrial plant.

Russia's late arrival on the industrial scene also shaped its Industrial Revolution because it could take advantage of prior technological improvements in industrial processes to leapfrog over the rudimentary stages and go directly to the latest and most modern forms. Ironically, backward Russia was creating one of Europe's most modern industrial infrastructures. Furthermore, Russia's new factories were massive in size. Perhaps more than one-half of Russia's factories employed more than 500 workers, and many employed more than 1,000. Because Russia did not experience the evolutionary process of building large firms from the merger or acquisition of numerous smaller ones, it was able to proceed directly to an economy of scale. Finally, rather than being spread throughout the country, Russia's industry was concentrated in a few locations. Significant industrial clusters could be found in the Donbas and at St. Petersburg, Moscow, Kiev, Baku, and Warsaw.

Early in the twentieth century, Russia's industrial expansion paused, and a sharp recession occurred against a backdrop of revolution. However, starting in 1906, stability returned, and Russia's Industrial Revolution resumed its impressive advance. Between 1906 and 1914, Russia's industrial economy grew at an annual rate of 6 percent. In 1913, the last full year of peace, Russia produced 4.4 million tons of steel, almost 5 million tons of pig iron, and 38 million tons of coal; it was second only to the United States in total miles of railroad. Nevertheless, foreign capital continued to play a major role in Russia's industry. There was extensive French investment in coal, steel, and iron, and British firms dominated petroleum production. Germany, soon to be Russia's adversary in the murderous World War I, controlled chemical production.

Despite this impressive growth, the quality of Russian finished products remained inferior; consequently, Russia found it difficult to crack the European market. However, its products found ready buyers in the less-developed Middle East and Asia. Another problem—one that defied such an easy solution—was the prevalent poverty of the Russian masses. Without adequate purchasing power, domestic demand stagnated.

Because of the character of Russia's Industrial Revolution, many members of the new entrepreneurial and managerial class were foreigners.

Among native Russians, the rising bourgeoisie emerged from a wide social spectrum ranging from former serfs to the nobility, although quite a few originated from the Old Believer community that had dominated hand production during the preindustrial era.

The number and nature of the nascent Russian proletariat, or working class, remains at issue. Many believe that the number of Russian "workers" at the start of the twentieth century totaled about 2 million, increasing to 3 or 3.5 million by 1914 (the 1897 census calculated Russia's population at 125 million). Almost all of these workers came from the peasantry, and many were only part-time members of the proletariat; that is, a sizeable number of workers regularly shifted back and forth between factory and village. Nevertheless, as the Industrial Revolution became firmly rooted, more and more "peasant-workers" abandoned the village altogether in order to live permanently in the industrial cities.

Although the Industrial Revolution in Russia may have been qualitatively different from the industrial revolutions in Western Europe and the United States, one factor remained constant—the exploitation of the worker. Russian laborers earned low wages, worked long hours, endured wretched working conditions, lacked job security, and lived in crowded, unsanitary, dangerous slums. Sometimes the proletariat resorted to the strike to protest its condition. For example, in 1885 there was a massive strike at Moscow's Morozov textile factory. However, until 1906 both unions and strikes were illegal. Nevertheless, when pushed far enough, desperate people will resort to desperate actions, and wildcat strikes occurred frequently.

During this period of rapid industrial growth, the Russian government periodically tried to ameliorate the workers' conditions. Under Bunge, employers were required to pay wages in money rather than in kind. Furthermore, employers had to pay the contractually agreed-upon wage rate, and restrictions were placed on both child and female labor. However, a system of factory inspectors created at this time proved inadequate. During Witte's ministry, an 1897 law reduced the working day to 11 and 1/2 hours, declared Sunday a holiday, and further limited child labor. In 1903 workmen's compensation was introduced, and three years later, local unions were legalized.

Despite these measures, unsatisfactory conditions and the growing influence of radical agitators sparked further worker rebellion. In 1912 the authorities used force to quell unrest in the Lena goldfields; the resulting "massacre" claimed more than 300 dead and wounded strikers. In 1914, during the months before the outbreak of World War I, more than a million workers were out on strike at one time or another. Obviously, the Industrial Revolution in Russia was not a placid experience.

INTERPRETIVE ESSAY
Randi B. Cox

What is the purpose of an economy? Is an economy merely the means to produce the objects that human beings need to survive and, when we are lucky, to live comfortably? Or is an economy also a way to define social structures by assigning specific tasks and obligations to individuals? What is the role of the economy in determining the power of a state over its neighbors? What happens to a society when its economy begins to change?

The issue of industrialization in Russia gives historians the opportunity to study these complex questions. The Russian monarchs Alexander III and Nicholas II found themselves in a difficult situation in the late 1800s. On the one hand, both were committed to conservative social policies and to the preservation of unlimited autocracy. An economy based on that perspective should be organized in such a way as to preserve the social hierarchy; nobles would dominate peasants, and economic life would center on agriculture. Yet the tsars were also responsible for Russia's international status, which increasingly depended on economic modernization. By midcentury, the Industrial Revolution in Western Europe had put Russia at a disadvantage in international relations, and that situation only worsened as the decades passed. In 1890 Russia's military lacked competitive technology and the capacity to produce sufficient supplies of armaments. In terms of trade, the tsars' advisors worried that Russia was slipping into the role of a colony, exporting raw materials and agricultural products while importing manufactured goods from more industrialized nations. This situation was simply unacceptable, but the solution was equally terrifying. If Russia was going to remain one of the Great Powers of Europe, she had to have modern means of transportation, communication, and industrial production, and that meant embracing economic changes that threatened the social order. It proved to be a challenge that Nicholas's government could not overcome.

In considering the origins of Russian modernization, historians often ask why Russia did not industrialize at the same time as other European nations. Part of the reason lies with geography; situated far from the oceans, Russia did not participate in the overseas exploration and colonization that led to the development of the Atlantic trade network and the ensuing commercial revolution of the seventeenth and eighteenth centuries. As a result, Russia lacked both the capital and the trade institutions that supported industrialization in Western Europe. Just as important, however, is the role of the state, especially in the early nineteenth century. In the United States and Western Europe, governments invested in internal improvements, such as canals and railroads, and passed laws encouraging the formation of banks, corporations, and similar institutions. In Russia, on the other hand, government action was not forthcoming before the 1860s. The ultra-conservative Nicholas I did not approve of industrial development—he feared that it would destabilize society, and he failed to appreciate its military significance.

The turning point was Russia's defeat in the Crimean War in 1855. Largely a result of Russia's inferior weaponry and inadequate rail system (which made it difficult to move troops and supplies quickly enough), the defeat emphasized the growing importance of technology and industry for military preparedness. No longer could Russia rely simply on her manpower and draconian discipline for military strength. To encourage modernization, Alexander II initiated a wide-ranging series of reforms, the most important of which was the abolition of serfdom in 1861. Unfortunately, the terms of the emancipation limited its economic impact by imposing strict conditions on peasants, which made it difficult for them to leave their villages and thus inhibited the creation of a mobile labor force.

Alexander's successors were equally ambivalent toward industrialization. Although Alexander III appointed finance ministers whose policies encouraged modernization, Russian jurisprudence remained oriented toward a system of nobles and peasants, not corporations and entrepreneurs. During the 1880s, Russia's industrial economy grew at a modest but steady pace. In 1892 Alexander III named Sergei Y. Witte to the post of finance minister, and it was under his leadership that Russian industry came into its own. Witte saw the acceleration of Russian modernization as crucial to economic independence and international status. For Witte, the goal of an economy was to ensure the international power of the autocracy.

Drawing on the policies of his predecessor Ivan A. Vyshnegradsky, Witte used the power of the state to promote economic growth through protective tariffs and high domestic taxes, which raised capital to be invested in key projects. He sought out foreign loans and encouraged foreign investment in Russian companies by placing the ruble on the gold standard in 1897; foreign involvement gave Russian factories access to the most advanced industrial technologies of Western Europe. He was a passionate advocate for business. He frequently made statements to the press, sponsored exhibitions and prizes, and even required the employees of the Ministry of Finance to wear business suits rather than traditional civil service uniforms. Under Witte's leadership, the state supplied capital to new industries, guaranteed profits for struggling firms, and acted as a major customer for heavy industry, to whom it often paid above-market prices.

Having previously served as an executive for a private railroad company and as transport minister, Witte placed particular emphasis on accelerating railroad construction. An expanded rail network would increase the volume of domestic and foreign trade by facilitating transportation of goods. On a structural level, railway construction would provide a stimulus to other industries, including iron, coal, oil, and steel production. The production of railroad stock (train cars, engines, and so on) would require factories with sophisticated machine-tooling capacities. Railways had proved a critical economic spur in Western Europe and the United States, and Witte hoped for similar results in Russia.

Witte's attitude toward the railroad also reflected his view of the connection between industrial growth and state power. In addition to its general economic benefits, an expanded rail network would facilitate travel and create links between various regions, which would encourage loyalty to the nation as a whole, rather than to localities. Railroads would make the rich natural resources of Siberia more accessible and encourage settlement there, providing an outlet for the growing land hunger of the Russian peasantry. The Trans-Siberian railroad, built between 1891 and 1905, would open Asian markets to Russian goods, which would give Russia an edge in the European competition for influence in Asia.

Witte thus pursued a traditional goal—international power and prestige—through new methods. Despite his personal conservatism, Nicholas II supported Witte's program for the sake of that goal during the 1890s, when Russia's industry made its most impressive strides. Unfortunately, economic growth slowed down after 1900, and Witte fell from Nicholas's favor. Industrialization had never been popular with the aristocracy, and by 1903 Viacheslav K. von Plehve, the interior minister, had persuaded Nicholas that Witte's policies had impoverished the peasantry and created social unrest in the cities. Plehve believed that an economy should function to preserve social order, and economic change threatened to destabilize the government. Historians consider the conflict between Witte and Plehve an expression of the larger tension between modernization and tradition that haunted the last decades of the Romanov dynasty.

Specialists divide Russian economic performance after the Great Reforms into four periods: slow growth from the 1860s through the 1880s, the rapid growth of the 1890s under Witte's leadership, a depression from 1900 to 1905, and moderate growth from 1906 to 1914. For the period 1861 to 1913, overall factory production increased 1,000 percent, and iron production increased to 14 times its original rate. Under Witte's leadership,

Russian industrial production doubled, and general economic growth averaged a stunning 8 percent a year during the 1890s. Despite these broad gains, there was significant regional variation, and industrial development was concentrated in six regions of the country. St. Petersburg, the Polish provinces, and the Central Industrial Region around Moscow all enjoyed considerable growth in textiles, metalworking, and chemical industries. Ukraine and the Urals had significant coal and iron mines, and in the Caucasus region there were coal mining operations and oil refineries, especially around the city of Baku. By the early 1900s, Russia was also seeing expansion in fields related to industry: banking, retail trade, advertising, and urban entertainment.

Another reason that Russia did not industrialize as early as Western Europe is that Russia failed to develop a cohesive capitalist class. During the infancy of Russian industry in the late eighteenth and early nineteenth centuries, nobles dominated manufacturing and mining, and the traditional merchant class dominated commerce. Given the low prestige of commerce in Russian culture, the merchant class included a large proportion of outsiders, such as religious sectarians, Jews, and descendents of German immigrants. The early nineteenth-century merchant class, because of its marginal position, tended to be cautious, both economically and socially, and discouraged innovation. As a result, the business class of the late nineteenth century was by no means a unified group. Powerful noble families continued to dominate mining and manufacturing, particularly in St. Petersburg, the Urals, and Ukraine. The more guarded sons of traditional merchants continued their conservative cultural practices and generally limited their economic activities to small enterprises. At the same time, Russia saw the rise of a new group of entrepreneurs, especially in Moscow, who boldly embraced modern notions of capitalism and desired the kind of political and social influence enjoyed by Western businessmen.

As might be expected, these groups had little in common and did not interact with one another comfortably. Even many of the new entrepreneurs preferred to organize their enterprises as family businesses and raised capital through the sale of stock only when absolutely necessary. However, after the turn of the century, the largest producers began to see the value of cooperation, and some began to form organizations to coordinate operations. The metallurgy industries created a syndicate in 1902, for example, and coal industries did the same in 1904. Like joint-stock companies, these new syndicates encountered resistance from the conservative government because any kind of autonomous organization held the potential to offer its members a sense of identity and purpose outside the traditional hierarchies of Russian society.

As noted previously, Witte encouraged foreign investment in Russian industry. In 1890, before his appointment as finance minister, foreign investment totaled 200 million rubles; by 1900 it had reached 900 million rubles and accounted for roughly half of capital investment. Most of this foreign capital came from British, French, and German investors, who exerted a significant amount of influence in the factories they invested in. Foreigners also owned companies outright in Russia. The largest department store in Moscow, Muir and Merrielees, was owned by a Scottish company. American firms such as Singer Sewing Machines and Duke Tobacco operated branches in Russia. Although this foreign activity contributed to the economic growth of this period, it also encouraged ordinary Russians to think of capitalism and business as something done by outsiders, something literally foreign to Russian traditions. Many Russians also feared that such investment had made Russia dependent on foreign nations and therefore had resulted in a loss of sovereignty. These fears were misplaced. If anything, economic relations with other nations led to interdependence and mutual obligation, not dominance.

Let us now turn our attention to the workers and the impact of industrialization on their lives. By the turn of the century, approximately 2 million people worked in factories. Russian factories tended to be very large; more than a third employed over 1,000 people. One of the largest, the Putilov Metalworks in St. Petersburg, employed 12,000 workers in plants that produced railroad stock and armaments. An additional 6 to 8 million people worked outside of factories as urban wage laborers, including tram drivers, dockworkers, and shop clerks.

As is often the case in developing countries, workers lived and worked in appalling conditions. Until the 1890s, managers and foremen used corporal punishment to discipline workers, and even after that, they imposed fines for infractions such as tardiness, breaking tools, or excessive waste. Most workers put in at least 12 hours per day, six days a week, and a labor surplus kept wages disturbingly low. Before the Revolution of 1905, it was illegal to form unions or go on strike, although such things happened anyway. Although the state clearly sided with management in the case of disputes, some efforts were made to stem the worst abuses. Legislation in the 1880s limited child labor to 10-hour days and banned night work for women and children under age 17. In response to widespread labor unrest in 1896 and 1897, the state imposed a maximum workday of 11½ hours on weekdays and 10 hours on Saturdays. Factory inspections did take place, but outcomes depended on the diligence and honesty of the inspector. Moreover, entrepreneurs and the state had a common interest in keeping the labor force docile; the finance ministry wanted to keep the

support of entrepreneurs, and the interior ministry did not want workers to think that they could force concessions from the government. As in
Western Europe and the United States, police and soldiers were used to
crush illegal strikes.

Despite these conditions, workers were not always powerless. Although
they could do little to change their overall circumstances, day-to-day practices
on the factory floor allowed skilled workers to negotiate small gains from
foremen, who set the pay rates of each worker. Developing a positive relationship with the foreman was thus crucial. For example, Eduard Dune, a skilled
toolmaker in Moscow, recalled that he pressured a foreman into granting him
an eight-hour day by adjusting his work pace such that he produced the same
number of pieces whether he worked 10 hours or 8 hours. Workers sometimes
took out their frustrations on foremen who abused their power. A small group
of workers would creep up behind the hated foreman, throw a sack over his
head, and shove him into a wheelbarrow. Then they would wheel him about
the factory floor to the hoots and insults of the whole workshop. When the
workers tired of mocking the foreman, they would wheel him outside and
dump him into a garbage heap or latrine. This practice was so well known
that workers sometimes only had to threaten foremen with the "wheelbarrow
treatment" before they gave in to their demands.

Historians have been struck by the diverse experiences of workers in
Russia. Workers rarely saw themselves as a unified group, bound by their
common status as laborers. Instead, they were divided by skill level and
the extent to which they maintained rural ties. Most workers came from
rural backgrounds, and roughly 90 percent were legally considered peasants. Still obligated to peasant communes, such workers either migrated
to villages on a seasonal basis or sent money to their families to help cover
the communes' taxes and other financial responsibilities. These village
ties also provided some security for workers, who could return home
when industrial employment was scarce or in the case of injury or old age.
Ambitious families, urban or rural, might seek apprenticeships for their
sons in factory workshops. These apprenticeships, which began in a boy's
early teens and lasted three to five years, were the most common way for
a young man to become a skilled craftsman who enjoyed higher pay and
more autonomy than unskilled laborers.

The longer workers remained in the cities and the more skills they
developed, the less likely they were to maintain their rural connections.
For example, a 1907 survey of Moscow printers revealed that only 35
percent of skilled typesetters still had village ties, whereas about three-
quarters of unskilled print workers did. Seasonal workers sometimes
had difficulty adapting to the rhythms of factory life, which were very

different from those of farm work. Permanent workers, especially those born into working-class families, often looked down on unskilled seasonal workers. Dune, for instance, complained that the arrival of seasonal workers always disrupted the work in his factory because the new arrivals did not understand the informal arrangements between workers and foremen. In particular, they did not respect the pace set by skilled laborers and instead worked too fast. Workers were paid piece-rates (by the amount of work completed each day), and if workers were too productive, managers would simply lower the piece rate in order to keep total labor cost low. From Dune's perspective, seasonal workers' efforts to earn more as individuals reflected their lack of respect for experienced workers and disregard for established factory practices.

Any discussion of working conditions must take note of the special problems of women workers, who made up roughly a quarter of the workforce. This general proportion is misleading, however, because women were concentrated in certain sectors of the economy. Two-thirds of textile and garment workers were female, and it was common for entire families to work in textile mills; women and girls worked as spinners and performed other unskilled operations, and men and boy apprentices worked as skilled machinists. Female workers received significantly lower wages than their male counterparts, and they were often subject to sexual harassment and even sexual abuse by managers and foremen. Labor activists complained that single workingwomen sometimes had no choice but to turn to prostitution to supplement their meager incomes. Women with families faced additional pressures. Fearful of losing their jobs for absenteeism, pregnant women worked throughout their pregnancies and returned to work almost immediately after giving birth. Wives and mothers had sole responsibility for buying and cooking food, washing clothes, and other such domestic tasks; for childcare, many working mothers relied on "baby farms" run by older women near factories.

As in Western Europe, industrialization led to increased urbanization in Russia. The urban proportion of the population, which had been 10 percent in 1856, had risen to 18 percent by 1913. Moscow and St. Petersburg both saw their populations rise to over 1 million residents, and 11 other cities had populations of at least 200,000 people. Most of the newcomers were peasants seeking jobs in the new factories, and the dramatic increase must have been startling for longtime residents. At the turn of the century, approximately two-thirds of the inhabitants of St. Petersburg had been born elsewhere. In contrast to rural areas, cities were ethnically diverse. Russians, Jews, Armenians, Ukrainians, Poles, Tatars, Latvians, and people from dozens of other ethnic groups flocked to cities to take advantage of new opportunities.

Stunning juxtapositions of wealth and poverty shaped the growing cities of the Russian empire. The slum apartment buildings and outdoor markets of working-class neighborhoods contrasted sharply with luxurious homes and new department stores for the wealthy and middle classes. By 1913, St. Petersburg's Nevsky Prospekt, probably the most glamorous street in the country, boasted two dozen banks, five goldsmiths, the Passazh department store, the Russian headquarters of the Singer Sewing Machine Company, and the Eliseev Food Emporium, all of which were designed in the new "style moderne" by Russia's leading architects. A few blocks away stood the new red and gray granite building that housed the workshop of jeweler Peter Karl Fabergé, best known for his magnificent Easter eggs. In Moscow, architects blended Parisian neo-Gothic styles with traditional Russian motifs for new mansions, department stores, banks, hotels, and corporate headquarters. Both the fine arts and a new urban popular culture flourished, and Russian entrepreneurs became important patrons of the arts. Moscow's famous Tretiakov Art Museum, for example, takes its name from its founder, Paul M. Tretiakov, whose textile fortune allowed him to amass one of the greatest art collections in Europe. Russian entrepreneurs also participated enthusiastically in philanthropic organizations, learned societies, and voluntary associations.

Rapid urbanization created severe housing shortages, which lowered the quality of life in working-class neighborhoods. The population density of St. Petersburg was twice that of any other European capital, and workers there commonly spent half their income on rent and food. Working-class life must have been lonely for many people; 60 percent of all workers lived apart from their families. The housing shortage forced many to rent not an apartment, not a room, but a corner of a room. In 1904 St. Petersburg officials estimated that an average of 16 people lived in each apartment with as many as six people to a room. Fewer than one-third of apartment buildings in working-class neighborhoods had running water or indoor plumbing; workers relied instead on outdoor latrines and courtyard water pumps. Drinking water had to be boiled before it was safe because latrine waste often ended up in the same rivers from which the water supply was drawn. As might be expected, disease haunted the city. Cholera hit once every three years on average, and tuberculosis and typhus were also serious problems. In fact, at the turn of the century, St. Petersburg had the highest mortality rate of any European capital, including Constantinople.

One strategy workers used to cope with the problems of urban life was to form artels, cooperatives of 10 to 20 workers, often migrants from the same region, who pooled their wages to pay for food and housing. Members of the artel elected an elder, who purchased supplies, contracted with a landlord, and hired a cook. For example, 16-year-old Semën Kanatchikov was brought to Moscow in 1895 by his peasant father, who knew an artel elder from their village. This man arranged for Kanatchikov's housing in the artel's apartment and got him an apprenticeship as a patternmaker. No doubt the existence of such artels made it easier—financially and emotionally—for parents to send their sons away to work in the city.

Kanatchikov's membership in the artel spared him the humiliation of living in factory barracks. The housing shortages meant that the poorest workers had no choice but to live in barracks provided either by factories or, in bigger cities, by charities. Photographs of these barracks indicate that as many as 75 workers slept in one large room. The furnishings in the sleeping room at the barracks of Moscow's Prokhorovskaia Trekhgornaia textile mill in the 1890s consisted of six plank beds: long wooden platforms, each divided into more than a dozen sleeping spaces by foot-high partitions. Residents of the workers' dormitory run by the St. Petersburg Temperance Society in 1909 at least had separate beds, which were numbered to prevent confusion in a room housing roughly 70 men. As if the lack of privacy in the barracks was not bad enough, workers also suffered the indignity of knowing that when they were at work, someone else was sleeping in the space they had just vacated; day-shift workers slept in the barracks at night, and night-shift workers occupied those same beds during the day.

Despite these hardships, workers found ways to enjoy the little leisure time they had. They read popular newspapers, visited taverns and bathhouses, played cards, and even attended new amusement parks and movie houses. Spectator sports enjoyed popularity, and soccer games at Moscow's Hippodrome stadium drew crowds of more than 10,000. Religion also played a part in the workers' world; most factory workshops took up collections for candles and oil for icon lamps, and many workers attended church services.

The longer that workers remained in urban areas, the more likely they were to adopt urban culture. Historians understand this process of urbanization as one of the factors that shaped workers' self-image, especially for skilled workers. An act as simple as buying a new suit of clothing or getting one's hair cut in the latest urban style took on great meaning because it allowed skilled workers to distinguish themselves visually from peasants and seasonal workers. Such changes were a way for workers to declare their independence from their peasant pasts.

The acquisition of complex work skills also increased workers' confidence and their desire to be considered reputable members of society. Skilled workers sought self-improvement in a variety of ways outside of the factory. They attended museums and concerts. They formed social organizations ranging from mutual benefit societies to literary circles. Such workers were fastidious in their dress and even gave up alcohol as a way of announcing that they had become respectable men. In short, they understood that a person's economic status in large part determines one's social status, and they demanded recognition for their achievements by adopting the dress and cultural behaviors of their social superiors. However, the respect that skilled workers desired was not forthcoming. The gap between rich and poor was clear to every worker who walked down the streets of St. Petersburg or Moscow, and the combination of growing self-confidence and the frustrations of working-class life drove some skilled workers to political activism. Both Kanatchikov and Dune, like many workers who became revolutionaries, recalled a gradual movement from reading popular literature, such as detective novels and self-help manuals, to reading and discussing political literature.

Finally, industrialization also changed Russia by contributing to the rise of revolutionary movements. Many educated Russians, as they observed the impact of industrialization on Western Europe, wondered if they were looking at Russia's future. Was Russia destined to enjoy the benefits—and face the problems—of economic modernization? Was there anything about Russia that would somehow allow it to avoid the problems of pollution, political conflict, social dislocation, and urban poverty that had followed the development of industry in Western Europe? Intellectuals disagreed on these questions and on the desirability of industrialization. Just as the government's mixed response to industrialization reflected conflicts over the purpose of economic activity, so did the debates of the revolutionary intelligentsia reflect disagreement on how best to structure society through economics.

The Populists of the 1870s and 1880s argued that capitalism was so alien to Russian traditions that peasants would never respond to it. Instead, Russia's future should lie with the peasant commune, which they believed promoted egalitarianism and cooperation, rather than capitalism's competition and individualism—which they saw as mere selfishness. Even if capitalism were to take hold in Russia, the Populists doubted that peasants would be able to afford to buy consumer goods and so would remain outside the capitalist system. Similarly, the Socialist Revolutionaries (SRs) of the early 1900s criticized industrial capitalism and even private property on moral grounds. In their view, factory owners exploited workers, landowners exploited peasants, and both increased suffering and poverty. The only solution, they argued, was a revolution that gave all farmland to the peasant communes and control of factories to workers.

The Social Democrats, on the other hand, embraced industrialization as evidence of Russian progress. As followers of Karl Marx, they believed that the development of industrial capitalism was a necessary step on the path to Communism, which they envisioned as an industrial society without exploitation. Marx, a German philosopher, had theorized that economic activity structures all aspects of a society, everything from politics to culture. Elites control society by controlling the "means of production" and exploiting the labor of the lower classes. Marx also argued that as new technologies emerge and economic systems change, political revolutions become more likely. The advent of industry in Western Europe had swept aside the landed nobility, whose status had derived from control of agriculture, and had empowered the bourgeoisie: factory owners, bankers, and other businessmen. These men dominated governments throughout Western Europe. A Communist revolution would, in turn, bring to power workers who would create an industrial utopia. The Social Democrats believed that Russia would follow this same path, but Marx's theory suggested that it would be a very long time before Communism could emerge in Russia, a country that had only just begun to industrialize. One faction, the Bolsheviks led by Vladimir I. Lenin, emphasized the need to train professional revolutionaries who could perhaps accelerate the revolution. The Menshevik faction, on the other hand, argued that the party should prepare for a future revolution by educating workers about socialist ideas, so that they would better understand the link between their poverty and the political power of elites.

Workers, of course, did not need intellectuals to explain that their lives were difficult. Skilled workers, as noted previously, increasingly resented their low status and the glaring disparities between rich and poor. At the same time, recently arrived peasants, who had come to cities fleeing rural poverty, resented their new conditions, and many were willing to engage in violent protest. Their growing frustration so worried state officials that in 1900 the head of the Moscow police, Sergei V. Zubatov, began to form government-sponsored workers' clubs in the hope that sanctioned outlets for their grievances might lessen the appeal of socialism. Contrary to these expectations, workers in many cities transformed these clubs into de facto unions that called for radical reforms and played significant roles in strikes in 1903 and 1905. After the Revolution of 1905, new legal unions initially focused their efforts on economic demands such as improving salaries and working conditions, and the Mensheviks and SRs gained significant followings. However, by 1910, in response to police harassment and managers' efforts to roll back the concessions of 1905, workers again began to call for political reforms, and their mood shifted toward the Bolsheviks. Tensions worsened in 1912 when the army massacred nearly 300 strikers at the Lena goldfields in Siberia.

Industrialists did not, in fact, enjoy the cozy relationship with the government that Lenin alleged. During the 1890s, most entrepreneurs at least tacitly supported the autocracy because Witte's policies made it easier to do business in Russia. However, Nicholas's reactionary policies alienated business leaders, especially after Witte's dismissal. The government begrudged all autonomous organizations, from labor unions to learned societies, and socially inclined entrepreneurs chafed at restrictions on their civic activities, most of which would have been considered praiseworthy in Western Europe. Like many educated Russians, industrialists resented Nicholas's failures and increasingly came to believe that things could not continue as they were. After the Revolution of 1905, the two main liberal parties, the Kadets and the Octobrists, drew many of their leaders from the ranks of Russia's entrepreneurs.

How, then, had industrialization changed Russia by 1913? It increased living standards, although the progress was unevenly distributed. It led to dramatic improvements in both Russia's military capacity and its railway network, and although this was not sufficient for victory in World War I, it did allow Russia to be far more competitive in that war than would have been possible otherwise. Russia's experience also demonstrates that industrialization is about far more than economics. Industrialization prompted fundamental changes in Russian society, including rapid urbanization that led to the creation of a new working class and a new entrepreneurial class, both of which made unprecedented demands on a conservative regime. The breakdown of traditional social hierarchies, although still incomplete in 1913, and the concentration of frustrated workers in the nation's leading cities destabilized the autocracy. It took only the spark of defeat in World War I to set the entire nation ablaze with revolution.

SELECTED BIBLIOGRAPHY

Bonnell, Victoria E., ed. *The Russian Worker: Life and Labor under the Tsarist Regime.* Berkeley: University of California Press, 1983.
    A fine collection of eyewitness accounts by workers and labor activists. The editor's introduction provides an outstanding overview of working-class life.
Economakis, Evel G. *From Peasant to Petersburger.* New York: St. Martin's Press, 1998.
    A study of St. Petersburg workers with special emphasis on the transition from village life to factory work and urban life.

Gatrell, Peter. *The Tsarist Economy, 1850–1917*. New York: St. Martin's Press, 1986.
A comprehensive statistical analysis of economic performance that stresses rising living standards and dynamic growth.

Glickman, Rose L. *Russian Factory Women: Workplace and Society, 1880–1914*. Berkeley: University of California Press, 1984.
A pathbreaking study of the lives of working-class women, both in the factory and at home.

Grant, Jonathan A. *Big Business in Russia: The Putilov Company in Late Imperial Russia*. Pittsburgh, PA: University of Pittsburgh Press, 1999.
A controversial case study of one of Russia's largest corporations. The author argues that corporations could operate autonomously and effectively in Russia despite the limitations posed by the autocracy.

Gregory, Paul. *Before Command: An Economic History of Russia from Emancipation to the First Five-Year Plan*. Princeton, NJ: Princeton University Press, 1994.
A short but important text that provides an overview of the work of previous scholars and summarizes the author's detailed statistical analyses of Russian economic growth in the late imperial period.

Harcave, Sidney. *Count Sergei Witte and the Twilight of Imperial Russia: A Biography*. Armonk, NY: M. E. Sharpe, 2004.
This biography, by the historian who translated Witte's memoirs, emphasizes the link between economic modernization and Russia's international position.

Hogan, Heather. *Forging Revolution: Metalworkers, Managers, and the State in St. Petersburg, 1890–1914*. Bloomington: Indiana University Press, 1993.
A detailed study that uses an analysis of worker–manager relations to explore the nature of workers' rising political militancy.

Johnson, Robert E. *Peasant and Proletarian: The Working Class of Moscow in the Late Nineteenth Century*. New Brunswick, NJ: Rutgers University Press, 1979.
This important book was one of the first to demonstrate that many Russian workers retained strong ties to the countryside.

Kanatchikov, Semën. *A Radical Worker in Tsarist Russia: The Autobiography of Semën Ivanovich Kanatchikov*. Edited and translated by Reginald E. Zelnik. Stanford, CA: Stanford University Press, 1986.
A fascinating memoir by a peasant who became a worker and revolutionary at the turn of the century.

McCaffray, Susan P. *The Politics of Industrialization in Tsarist Russia: The Association of Southern Coal and Steel Producers, 1874–1914*. DeKalb: Northern Illinois University Press. 1996.
A case study of the coal and steel entrepreneurs in Ukraine and southern Russia that provides an important perspective on industrialization away from Moscow and St. Petersburg.

Melancon, Michael, *The Lena Goldfields Massacre and the Crisis of the Late Tsarist State*. College Station: Texas A&M University Press, 2006.
An outstanding work that uses a case study of a watershed event as a prism to explore the social and political tensions created by industrialization.

Melancon, Michael, and Alice K. Pate, eds. *New Labor History: Worker Identity and Experience in Russia, 1840–1918*. Bloomington, IN: Slavica Press, 2002.

A collection of articles on various aspects of workers' lives, including child labor, religion, political activism, and conceptions of dignity.

Owen, Thomas C. *The Corporation under Russian Law, 1800–1917: A Study in Tsarist Economic Policy.* Cambridge: Cambridge University Press, 1991.
This study of corporate law by the leading historian of Russian capitalism highlights the contradictions inherent in the tsarist government's need to promote industrialization and its efforts to protect autocratic power and prevent the development of autonomous organizations.

———. *Dilemmas of Russian Capitalism: Fedor Chizhov and Corporate Enterprise in the Railroad Age.* Cambridge, MA: Harvard University Press, 2005.
A fascinating biography of a Moscow merchant who sought to blend capitalist entrepreneurship with Russian traditions.

Rieber, Alfred J. *Merchants and Entrepreneurs in Imperial Russia.* Chapel Hill: University of North Carolina Press, 1982.
An excellent study of Russian merchants and industrialists from 1700 to 1917. The author argues that social divisions among traditional merchants, noble industrialists, and modern entrepreneurs prevented the development of a politically unified Russian business class.

Ruckman, Jo Ann. *The Moscow Business Elite: A Social and Cultural Portrait of Two Generations, 1840–1905.* DeKalb: Northern Illinois University Press, 1984.
An important study of the leading Moscow merchant families in the nineteenth century.

Von Laue, Theodore H. *Sergei Witte and the Industrialization of Russia.* New York: Columbia University Press, 1963.
The classic study of Witte's policies. The author emphasizes the necessity of state leadership in fostering economic development in a conservative society.

West, James, and Iurii A. Petrov, eds. *Merchant Moscow: Images of Russia's Vanished Bourgeoisie.* Princeton, NJ: Princeton University Press, 1998.
A fascinating collection of articles by Western and Russian scholars on various aspects of merchant life, ranging from business practices to family life to voluntary associations. All of the articles make extensive use of historical photographs.

Witte, S. Iu. *The Memoirs of Count Witte.* Edited and translated by Sidney Harcave. Armonk, NY: M. E. Sharpe, 1990.
An excellent annotated translation based on Witte's original manuscript.

4

The Revolution of 1905

INTRODUCTION

At the dawn of the twentieth century, imperial Russia faced a myriad of problems, although probably none as serious and intractable as the socioeconomic one. The ignorance, isolation, and alienation of the Russian peasantry was legendary, and despite the emancipation of the serfs almost four decades earlier, little had changed to ameliorate the peasants' condition. Of a total population numbering about 125 million, more than 100 million were peasants scattered throughout the Russian countryside. Most remained firmly tied to the commune—the ancient, hidebound, stifling institution that the state had strengthened at the time of the emancipation in order to maintain authority over the newly freed serfs. The commune controlled the land given to the emancipated serfs, and the commune elders made binding decisions for the peasants that made up the commune. For example, the elders decided what to plant, when to plant, when to harvest, and to whom the harvest should be sold. Individual initiative simply did not exist. Moreover, the commune periodically redistributed the land among commune families. Thus, rather than having an incentive to preserve the land, the peasant household felt compelled to exploit the land ruthlessly for the household's own survival.

Moreover, the state held the commune responsible for taxes, redemption (mortgage) payments, and recruits for the army. These responsibilities made the commune elders even more cautious when it came to innovation or to permitting peasants to leave the commune. To further ensure docility, in 1889 Tsar Alexander III established the office of *zemskii nachalnik*, or land captain, and gave to it extensive jurisdiction over the commune's activities.

Bloody Sunday (January 22, 1905) saw the massacre of peaceful, unarmed workers who had marched on the Winter Palace to petition the tsar for redress of economic grievances. The bloodshed served to push Russia into revolution and permanently sever the bond between the tsar and the common people. (Reproduced from the Collections of the Library of Congress.)

Socially, the peasantry remained a class apart from the mainstream of educated Russian society. Polite society ostracized the peasants, who were easily distinguished by their sunburned skin, crude manners, and rough language. Legal forms and institutions reinforced this societal gulf.

The peasantry was also starving, sometimes literally, as in the horrible famine of 1891–1892, and almost always figuratively. Since the emancipation, Russia's peasant population had almost doubled in size. However, in part because of soaring land values, the amount of acreage held by the peasantry had increased only modestly. Consequently, there were considerably more mouths to feed from virtually the same amount of land. Perhaps this dilemma could have been managed successfully had farming been modernized and had productivity increased, but such was not the case. Russian agricultural methods remained firmly rooted in the Middle Ages.

The end result of all this was a backward, destitute, segregated Russian peasantry sullenly eyeing neighboring gentry estates while trying to stay afloat in a sea of debt and high taxes. Despised by society, feared by the nobility, and exploited by the government, the peasants were a ticking time bomb waiting to explode.

Most of Russia's peasants remained on the land; however, by 1900 a growing number had begun to drift into the cities looking for work in the expanding industrial sector. Russian industrialization also created major problems for the tsarist state. During the industrialization process, the first generation of workers almost always experiences horrible exploitation, and in this instance, Russia was no exception. Driven into the factories by rural poverty, Russian peasants—now on their way to becoming workers—found long hours, backbreaking labor, low wages, abysmal workplace conditions, and no security. Crammed into unspeakable slums, these poor souls struggled to survive. Not surprisingly, their anger was great. For the most part, the rage was directed against the owners of the machines; however, skillful agitators not only attempted to organize this disgruntled labor force, but also tried to channel its discontent against the system as a whole, including the government.

Unhappiness also characterized those who benefited most from Russia's industrialization—the bourgeoisie. Consisting of factory owners and their associates, such as managers, bankers, lawyers, and accountants, this segment of society was growing rich. However, increasingly, the bourgeoisie resented the fact that it lacked political power and social prestige equal to its wealth. When the tsar indicated that he had no intention of addressing these matters, especially the political question, important elements of the bourgeoisie began to consider fundamental reform if not revolution.

For the radical intelligentsia, reform was seen as too little too late; revolution was the only course. Since early in the nineteenth century, some Russian intellectuals—despairing of ever reforming what they had come to regard as unreformable—had advocated a complete restructuring of Russia. Ruthlessly suppressed after their assassination of Alexander II in March 1881, the radical intelligentsia resurfaced by the turn of the twentieth century. Although there were a number of radical groups, two in particular stand out. The Social Revolutionaries (SRs) looked to the Russian peasantry to rise against the regime and sweep it aside in favor of an ill-defined agrarian socialism. The Social Democrats (SDs) took their cue from Karl Marx and placed their hopes in the industrial working class, or proletariat.

Several of the Russian Empire's various nationalities were just as dissatisfied as the peasants, workers, and intelligentsia; however, they marched to the beat of a different drummer. For them, the national ideal was everything. More than 100 different national groups lived within Russia, and though most were docile, several large ones were not. On the empire's western borders, the restless Poles seethed. The Finns, after a long period of lenient treatment, now found themselves subjected to a heavy-handed version of Russification. The tsarist state even denied the existence of a Ukrainian nationality, despite the fact that perhaps 21 million Ukrainians lived in Russia. Other nationalities such as the Estonians, Latvians, and Lithuanians and religious minorities such as the hated and despised Jews expressed their contempt for the status quo.

Unfortunately for Russia's long-term health, responsibility for guiding the empire through these tempestuous times fell to a most uniquely unsuited man, Tsar Nicholas II. Nicholas was born in 1868, the eldest son of the reactionary Alexander III. Overawed by his father, Nicholas proved to be bland, polite, self-effacing, and modest. However, Nicholas manifested shortcomings that proved fatal. He was weak-willed, indecisive, and stubborn. Furthermore, Nicholas was dangerously detached from the world around him, caring more for sailing and romps with his children than affairs of state, which he hated. Nicholas possessed a modest intellect and an unquestioning mind. Constantine P. Pobedonostsev, the influential Russian reactionary who oversaw Nicholas's education, inculcated in his pupil a visceral hatred of liberalism and modernity and a worshipful attachment to absolutism. Shortly after his coronation, Nicholas clearly stated his view on Russia's future when he told a zemstvo delegation that thoughts of reform were "senseless dreams" and that he intended to "maintain the principle of autocracy as firmly and unflinchingly as did [his] father."

Although Nicholas wore the crown, considerable power rested with his wife, Alexandra, a German-born princess and granddaughter of Great Britain's Queen Victoria. Alexandra was a hysterical, nervous, intense, and unhappy woman, but she was also strong-willed and decisive, and she dominated her husband. Despite her extensive exposure to the British system of governance, Alexandra was a committed reactionary. She viewed any suggestion of reform as treason and lived in an imaginary, romantic, semimystical world where the tsar and the Russian masses bonded together in a divinely inspired relationship. She came to rely on incompetent or unscrupulous sycophants such as Gregory E. Rasputin, and she pressed their views on her passive husband.

At the turn of the century, ominous clouds were gathering on the Russian horizon. The volatile mix just described began to congeal into a revolutionary critical mass. Unrest in the countryside spread. In 1902 there were more than 300 peasant "disturbances" requiring armed intervention; in the following year, that figure rose to about 450. The SRs roamed the countryside, spreading their doctrine of rural revolution. In the cities, industrial strikes proliferated. In 1904 there were 2,000 labor actions, chiefly in the south. Late in that year, strikers paralyzed St. Petersburg's giant Putilov steelworks, and by January 1905, there were 140,000 workers on strike in the capital alone. The SDs were as active among the factory workers as the SRs were in the countryside. Even respectable members of the bourgeoisie defied the government. Representatives of the zemstvos met informally to press their demands for reform, and by 1904 they had formed a nascent, albeit illegal, political party called the Union of Liberation. Most spectacularly, the "battle organization" of the SRs carried out a number of high-profile assassinations: in 1901 they murdered Nicholas P. Bogolepov, the minister of education; in 1902 Dmitri S. Sipiagin, minister of the interior; in 1904 Viacheslav K. von Plehve, minister of the interior; and in 1905 Grand Duke Sergei Alexandrovich, the tsar's uncle and governor-general of Moscow.

Amazingly, the tsarist response to this rapidly deteriorating situation was to launch a foreign war. As Plehve argued, "The country is on the verge of revolution. The only way to avert it is to make a small victorious war." Apparently, Plehve and others convinced the tsar that a successful war would generate a surge of patriotism and unite the population behind the government. Then, upon successful completion of the conflict, the subsequently wildly popular emperor could move with impunity against his enemies. Consequently, in February 1904 Russia went to war against Japan over the disposition of Korea and Manchuria. The "small, victorious war" turned into an unmitigated disaster as the racially despised Japanese defeated Russia both on land and at sea. Every setback revealed the empire's backwardness, corruption, and ineptitude, and the tide of revolution—which the war was intended to stem—swelled instead.

In the wake of Plehve's assassination, the new minister of the interior, Prince Peter D. Sviatopolk-Mirsky, relaxed governmental controls and hinted at more extensive reforms. However, these gestures proved to be too little too late. A major turning point occurred on Sunday, January 22, 1905 (January 9, O.S.), when hundreds of thousands of St. Petersburg's workers—many accompanied by their families—marched down Nevsky Prospekt, the capital's main thoroughfare, to the Winter Palace in order to petition the tsar for redress of their economic and social grievances. However, Nicholas had already departed St. Petersburg for his country estate, leaving the local authorities in charge. When the unarmed, peaceable marchers refused to disband, the security forces opened fire. The official death toll was 130 killed, although most authorities place the figure much higher.

The massacre, known as Bloody Sunday, destroyed the tsar's considerable standing with the peasantry and accelerated Russia's descent into revolution. As spring approached, violence in the countryside escalated, as did the number of work stoppages in the cities. Opposition leaders ranging from moderates to radicals became emboldened in their public pronouncements. The borderlands were restless, especially in the west where the Poles once again threatened rebellion. Piecemeal concessions by the tsar only served to increase the demands of the discontented. Moreover, the Japanese continued to pound the hapless Russians in the Far East, exposing the regime's bankruptcy for all to see. Even the military's loyalty came into question in June when sailors on the battleship *Potemkin* mutinied.

In October 1905, a general strike paralyzed Russia. All sorts of Russians, including laborers, transportation workers, bakers, bankers, teachers, and lawyers, banded together to shut down the country. Hardest hit was St. Petersburg, which came to a standstill. In the face of mounting chaos, Nicholas called upon Sergei Y. Witte, his most competent minister but not one of the tsar's favorites. Witte had just completed negotiating the Treaty of Portsmouth, which had extricated Russia from its disastrous war with Japan, and now he proceeded to save the crown by persuading the reluctant tsar to make sweeping changes to the autocratic empire. The resulting document, the October Manifesto, effectively ended the 1905 revolution.

According to the October Manifesto, Russia would no longer be an autocracy; rather, it would move toward becoming a constitutional monarchy. To begin with, Russia would have a written constitution. Moreover, elections would be held for a national Duma, or legislative assembly. Henceforth, the government would have to secure the Duma's approval for all proposed laws, and ministers would be responsible to the Duma and not the tsar. Finally, the October Manifesto extended civil liberties, including freedom of speech, freedom of the press, and the right of association.

Perhaps not unintentionally, the October Manifesto fractured the ranks of the revolutionaries. Moderates accepted it at face value and anticipated working out its details; more radical elements rejected it, demanding instead the dismantlement of the tsarist state and the erection of a democratic successor. By the end of October, the radicals—especially the SDs—controlled the St Petersburg and Moscow Soviets, or Councils, of Workers' Deputies. The soviets, originally created as coordinating organizations and clearinghouses for spontaneous worker demonstrations, now became the SD vehicle for destroying the autocracy. However, Witte grasped the fundamental weakness of the soviets and destroyed them. In December he arrested the leaders of the St. Petersburg Soviet and dissolved it without bloodshed. When the Moscow Soviet refused to go peacefully, Witte violently demolished it.

In May 1906, Witte issued the Fundamental Laws. Promising to flesh out the October Manifesto's barebones structure, the Fundamental Laws instead revealed the insincerity of the manifesto's authors and their true desire to preserve the autocracy. The Fundamental Laws severely limited the Duma's authority over items such as the budget, foreign policy, and the military. They also allowed the monarch to issue decrees in emergency situations or when the Duma was not in session, and they gave to the tsar, who retained his title as Autocrat of All the Russias, an absolute veto over any legislation. Although the Fundamental Laws failed to rekindle the now-spent spirit of revolution, they did have an unexpected result. With their acceptance, Witte became expendable in the eyes of the tsar, and in spring 1906 Nicholas unceremoniously dismissed him.

INTERPRETIVE ESSAY
Taylor Stults

The revolutionary events of 1905 in Russia reveal a tumultuous period in that nation's long history. Nevertheless, they have been overshadowed by the events of the more famous revolution in 1917 that ended the Romanov dynasty and ultimately led to the victory of Lenin and the Bolsheviks. Both revolutions included similar destabilizing conditions: domestic unrest among the population, serious economic problems, an unpopular and costly war, ineffective leadership, emergence of numerous political movements and parties seeking change by either peaceful reform or the overthrow of the government, outbreaks of violence, and an inability or paralysis to identify solutions to respond to these very destabilizing and disruptive conditions. The participants in 1905 could not predict the upheaval to come only a few years later. To them, the dramatic and important events of 1905–1906 represented a major upheaval in their lives. It is an important story of people facing traumatic conditions and an uncertain future.

Besides the disruption and occasional violence, the fundamental challenge in 1905 was to find a workable solution that would maintain the integrity of the nation as a territorial entity and create a credible political system that had sufficient acceptance and support among the population. It was unlikely that everyone would be satisfied with the results, and the story therefore is one of unfinished agendas and unfulfilled aspirations. When the regime reasserted its control by the late spring of 1906, many issues remained to be resolved. This provided the prelude to the next decade, with the final collapse of the regime coming as the result of the double catastrophes of World War I and the revolutionary events of 1917.

This essay focuses on four individuals who played different roles during the 1905 crisis: Tsar Nicholas II, Sergei Y. Witte, Paul N. Miliukov, and Vladimir I. Lenin. They represent diverse backgrounds, ideologies, and objectives: the Russian monarch, a prominent government official, a moderate political reformer, and a dedicated revolutionary. Perhaps the best point of departure for this story is Bloody Sunday, the January 1905 massacre that killed and wounded hundreds of unarmed civilians in St. Petersburg when they peacefully attempted to present a petition to Tsar Nicholas II. Army troops fired on the demonstrators at several locations in the city. This violence triggered the revolutionary events of 1905, unleashing a torrent of anger against the authorities and even the tsar himself, who now appeared to be indifferent to the repression and hardships his government imposed on his subjects.

How did Nicholas react to the tragedy? That evening, the tsar wrote in his private diary of his sadness at hearing the news: "A difficult day! In Petersburg there were serious disturbances . . . as a consequence of the workers' desire to get to the Winter Palace. The troops had to fire, and in various places in the city many were killed and injured. Lord, it is so painful and hard!" In early February, however, he met with a group of workers and admonished them for their audacity in attempting to present the petition. According to Marc Ferro's biography of Nicholas, the tsar demanded that they be more obedient and respectful in the future and told them, "As for coming, in a rebellious mob, to tell me of your needs, that was a criminal act. I have confidence in the honourable sentiments of the workers and in their unshakeable loyalty to me, and for that reason I forgive their offence." The tsar's position as Russia's autocratic monarch did not allow Nicholas to be sympathetic or assume any responsibility for the tragedy that had transpired.

A few weeks later, more violence occurred, but this time directed at the royal family itself. In mid-February a terrorist assassinated Grand Duke Sergei Alexandrovich, the tsar's uncle. His murder understandably shook Nicholas, convincing him that restoring order was the highest priority. Reacting to the widespread public discontent and anger, the government announced several steps designed to lessen the hostile public mood. In March, for example, the tsar announced his intention to establish an assembly at the national level to advise the government on proposed legislation. Nicholas believed this would generate public support for the regime, but by the time details of the group's functions and the selection of its members were published in August, this weak and timid concession proved irrelevant. It only fueled demands for more power and change among the growing number of antigovernment critics.

Nicholas, consistently oblivious to the variety and depth of the serious problems affecting his nation, promised the public that he had the population's well-being as his highest goal. The British academic Bernard Pares, who visited Russia during this period and wrote an important account of these events, recounted a meeting in mid-July when a delegation of elected city and regional officials was permitted to have an audience with the tsar to express their concerns. The monarch quickly assured them of his good intentions: "Throw away your doubts. My will, the Tsar's will, to call together representatives of the people is unchangeable. I every day follow and stand for this work." Those vague words satisfied some, but scarcely resolved all the concerns and issues. Public discontent had not been pacified.

Isolated and sporadic outbreaks of violence occurred throughout Russia during the summer. Even the military had to cope with several mutinies within the armed forces. Nevertheless, by early autumn, the authorities— although still facing widespread criticism—showed few signs of serious weakness. Government institutions and officials continued to perform their assigned functions. On the surface, the monarch apparently had lost little of his power. The peace treaty ending the disastrous Russo-Japanese War in late summer removed one of the major points of public frustration and controversy. Nicholas felt conditions had stabilized sufficiently for him to take a two-week vacation on the Baltic Sea with his family. They left St. Petersburg in mid-September and returned at the beginning of October. To Nicholas, no collapse seemed imminent or even on the horizon.

But October witnessed the outbreak of widespread strikes in major cities that spread quickly throughout Russia. Railroad workers left their jobs, interrupting rail movement across the country and causing massive economic and political disruptions. Workers in numerous occupations also went on strike. The dangers grew daily. Nicholas described these disruptive conditions in his diary in mid-October:

> The strikes on the railways, which began around Moscow, have now reached St. Petersburg. Today the Baltic line stopped working. The persons to whom I was giving audience had difficulty in reaching Peterhof. To keep us in touch with the capital the Dozorny [a boat] provides a shuttle service twice a day. A pretty time.

Nicholas complained about the thousands who left their jobs in peaceful protest against the government, and he also criticized university students for their political agitation. Nicholas particularly detested Jews, blaming them for the vast majority of the problems across the nation. Still, no widespread violence had yet broken out, for the largely peaceful strikers employed passive resistance against employers and public officials. However, the tension steadily built during October. The tsar described this pressure in one of his lengthy letters to his mother, which was later published in the valuable collection of correspondence edited by E. J. Bing:

> So the ominous quiet days began, quiet indeed, because there was complete order in the streets; but at the same time everybody knew that something was going to happen—the troops were waiting for the signal, but the other side would not begin. One had the same feeling as before a thunderstorm in summer! Everybody was on edge and extremely nervous, and of course, that sort of strain could not go on for long.

Finally, hoping to break the impasse, Nicholas authorized General Dmitri F. Trepov, the governor-general of St. Petersburg, to use force if necessary against the strikers. Trepov immediately issued orders to his troops in the capital and even posted throughout the city the threat that his troops would "Fire without warning and [would not] spare the cartridges."

Thus, a potential catastrophe, likely to be even worse than the outcome of Bloody Sunday, appeared imminent. Could a solution be found?

At this juncture, a leading government official tried to resolve, or at least defuse, the crisis. Sergei Witte, a former minister of finance, had led the Russian delegation that had successfully negotiated the end of the Russo-Japanese War during the summer of 1905. A talented and experienced administrator with a sharp mind and a high opinion of his own abilities, Witte understood the great dangers facing the regime. According to Howard Mehlinger's and John Thompson's important assessment of this period, Witte candidly described the domestic situation in July, months before the events of October:

> The world should be surprised that we have any government in Russia, not that we have an imperfect government. With many nationalities, many languages, and a nation largely illiterate, the marvel is that the country can be held together even by autocracy. Remember one thing: if the tsar's government falls, you will see absolute chaos in Russia, and it will be many a year before you see another government able to control the mixture that makes up the Russian nation.

Despite his pessimism, Witte disagreed with the opponents of the regime who demanded sweeping changes. At the same time, he knew of the tsar's orders to Trepov authorizing the use of violence against the population. Witte, therefore, sought a plan that might meet some demands of the opposition while still maintaining the bulk of authority in the hands of the government and the monarch.

In late October, Nicholas met with his closest political advisors to consider possible options and decide on a course of action. In advance of the meeting, Witte prepared a lengthy memorandum for the tsar analyzing the causes of the unrest and giving his recommendations to calm the dangerous atmosphere. As noted in Edvard Radzinsky's recent biography of Nicholas, Witte forcefully identified the fundamental issue: "Russia has outgrown its existing governmental forms. There is still a chance—you must give the people their constitution, otherwise they will wrest one away." Witte argued for making concessions, and the other participants supported his assessment.

Nicholas now made a fateful choice. In yet another lengthy letter to his mother, the tsar described the two alternatives he faced: order the military to break the strikes by force or make concessions to his opponents. He realized the immediate and long-term consequences of the first option:

> There would be time to breathe then but, as likely as not, one would have to use force again in a few months; and that would mean rivers of blood, and in the end we should be where we had started. . . . government authority would be vindicated, but there would be no positive result and no possibility of progress achieved.

Fortunately for his nation and its people, Nicholas chose the second alternative, offering concessions in the famous October Manifesto. This important document promised a constitution for Russia, along with the creation of an elected national legislative body that would place some limits on the tsar's authority. Nicholas had no enthusiasm for this choice because it reduced the autocratic power he had inherited from his ancestors, but fearful of widespread violence, he reluctantly signed the document on October 30, 1905 (October 17, O.S.), describing his feelings two days later in the same letter to his mother: "We discussed it for two days, and in the end, invoking God's help, I signed. . . . My only consolation is that such is the will of God, and this grave decision will lead my dear Russia out of the intolerable chaos she has been in for nearly a year." Harrison Salisbury, a well-known writer of Russian affairs, described the scene as the monarch spoke to an associate after signing the decree. Weeping, with tears streaming down his face, Nicholas sadly concluded, "I feel that in signing this act I have lost the crown. Now all is finished." But the positive consequence was that his unhappy decision avoided the possibility of civil war.

At this critical moment, the tsar also appointed Witte as Russia's new prime minister. Like Nicholas, Witte opposed a constitutional system. Mehlinger and Thompson quote Witte on constitutionalism as follows:

> There is really no love for constitutionalism in my heart or soul. But I urged it as a physician would urge a patient to take a laxative. The remedy was the product of my mind. I realized that this operation, if it may be called so, was absolutely essential. Without it the Russian Government was on the point of . . . crumbling away.

Obviously, the promised reforms lacked the committed support of government leaders and the monarch. The important outcome, nonetheless, was that Russia had survived the immediate crisis. Over the next several months, Witte provided capable leadership, and even Nicholas regained his self-confidence. But problems quickly developed at the highest level. Although the two men initially cooperated, their relationship soon cooled.

Bing's edited volume of Nicholas's correspondence indicates that the tsar almost immediately began to complain in private letters about his prime minister. Writing in early November, he said, "It is strange that such a clever man should be wrong in his forecast of an easy pacification." Shortly after, Nicholas wrote, "I must confess I am disappointed in him in a way." By the end of December, he had lost his patience with Witte, and in January 1906, he wrote, "I have never seen such a chameleon of a man. That, naturally, is the reason why no one believes in him any more."

Likewise, Witte had little respect for the tsar, holding him personally responsible for mishandling the problems of the Russian nation. A sample from Witte's memoirs sufficiently describes his feelings: "His [Nicholas's] character is the source of all our misfortunes. . . . His outstanding failing is his lamentable lack of will power." The final break between the two came in April 1906, shortly before the new Duma was scheduled to meet. Witte resigned under pressure, complaining of the difficulties placed in his way by hostile members of his cabinet and by others, a veiled reference to the tsar's lack of support. Witte's ego and anger at the way he had been treated can be seen in his following observation, as quoted in Ferro's biography of the tsar: "Despite my total disfavor, as soon as the situation becomes critical my name will immediately come up. But they are forgetting one thing: there is a limit to everything." He later complained to Paul N. Miliukov that Nicholas had treated him, in his words, "worse than a household servant."

In the months following the October Manifesto, from November 1905 to the spring of 1906, the government's authority was gradually restored. Nicholas, now increasingly confident that the crisis had passed, saw the promised Duma as his new enemy. According to Ferro, he was determined to prevent it having any significant authority, saying, "I would rather perish than hand over without any resistance all power to those who stretch out their hands for it." Ferro also cites Nicholas's determination to maintain the autocratic system: "I never intended to embark upon that distant and unknown journey which I was so strongly advised to undertake. . . . I have no right to renounce that which was bequeathed to me by my forefathers and which I must hand down unimpaired to my son."

The tsar and his government steadily succeeded in regaining authority. The new Duma met for the first time on May 10, 1906 (April 27, O.S.). Members of the assembly immediately criticized the government, and the deputies discussed topics outside their jurisdiction. In response to these challenges, the authorities dissolved the body in July. This unsatisfactory outcome showed the Duma's failure to establish firmly the parliamentary authority it sought. Its weakness and the government's renewed strength in suppressing the opposition makes it logical to consider the middle of 1906 the termination point of the 1905 revolution. The momentum for reform and change would not return for another decade.

The third person to consider in the events of 1905 and 1906 is a moderate reformer, Paul Miliukov, a distinguished historian and scholar who played a crucial role in this critical period. His historical perspective and personal commitment to political progress ensured that he would be a significant leader of the reform movement in early twentieth-century Russia. Miliukov understood that the major problem facing the antigovernment movements in 1905 was that legal political parties either did not exist in Russia or had only been formed recently. Although many criticized the government and the monarch, it would take time to organize and to have an impact. Miliukov led one reform group that had been created a few years earlier, the Union of Liberation, but it lacked legal status as a formal political party, and its influence was limited.

Miliukov was in the United States on a lecture tour at the time of Bloody Sunday. On his return to Russia, he immediately began to organize the advocates of liberal reform, creating professional and occupational associations to represent their views and pressure the authorities to accede to their broader reform objectives. In May 1905, 14 professions established the Union of Unions to coordinate and promote these efforts, electing Miliukov as the group's chairman.

In early June, Miliukov helped prepare a statement to present to the monarch seeking his support for the democratic goals the liberals sought. Tsar Nicholas gave a positive and soothing response to the delegation, leading Miliukov to observe in his memoirs, "For the first time, we heard from his lips words resembling a promise of reform, and, as it were, an understanding of the necessity of reform." But Miliukov also observed that the tsar's assurances lacked specifics, and he questioned the ruler's sincerity. Therefore, he continued to press for more tangible results.

Miliukov's memoirs recall trying to assess the meaning of the confusing daily events of 1905:

> One's eyes became used to the daily repetition of the same headlines, but it was difficult to perceive the dynamic of the revolution or to feel it from newspaper excerpts. Only later when these same facts were sorted out and classified in books was it possible to grasp the whole forces of the revolutionary wave.

This confirms what history often reveals, especially in unstable or revolutionary conditions. Hindsight and perspective make it possible to organize the flow of events in a logical and interpretive way that the participants at the time were unable to see or comprehend fully.

By late summer 1905, Miliukov's numerous public statements and his leadership in the reform cause had irritated the authorities and led to his imprisonment for a month. To illustrate his prominence in the democratic reform movement, an important national gathering of representatives of regional assemblies and city councils was delayed until his release from jail in order for him to attend the sessions.

Miliukov spent much of the summer and fall months striving to create a moderate political party that could agitate for further reforms. He later recalled in his memoirs, "We were concerned with the creation, not of a revolutionary party, but of a constitutional one, whose task would be to carry on the struggle with parliamentary means." By the end of October, he had successfully formed the Constitutional Democratic Party (KDs, or Kadets). However, he also recognized the challenges of seeking peaceful change in conditions of uncertainty, daily turmoil, confrontation, and occasional violence: "It is difficult . . . to rely on peaceful solutions to the urgent questions of governmental reorganization at a time when a revolution is already taking place around us."

On the evening of October 30 (October 17, O.S.), members of the new Kadet Party cheered the news of the October Manifesto. But Miliukov realized that the manifesto's high-sounding promises provided only vague details of guaranteed civil rights and the idea of a national parliament. According to his biographer, Thomas Riha, Miliukov tempered his colleagues' enthusiasm, telling his listeners that the document "does not represent the last word of possible concessions and does not even represent the minimum of concessions needed today." He warned his stunned listeners, "Nothing has changed: the war continues."

Miliukov also had to decide whether to support public unrest and worker strikes. As might be expected, his reasoning was nuanced. He favored the October strikes, but criticized the advocates of renewed labor action in November and December. According to Riha, Miliukov believed that additional strikes had little chance of success, and he warned the strike organizers of inadvertently triggering a severe backlash by the authorities: "Yes, we are for the revolution insofar as it serves the aims of political liberation and social reform; but we are against those who pronounce the revolution 'continuous' because we consider a continuous revolution only serves the aims of reaction." Of the mounting unrest in Moscow that erupted in violence in late December, he wrote, "I beg of all those on whom the decision depends to reconsider—and to stop—while it is not yet too late." Clearly, Miliukov preferred moderate and peaceful solutions to the challenges facing Russia, but it was difficult to channel and control the unrest in a nonviolent manner.

This energetic reformer worked tirelessly in late 1905 and into 1906 to build the Kadet Party so that it might participate successfully in the upcoming Duma elections. However, he also criticized the Fundamental Laws (May 1906), which defined the new Duma's restricted parliamentary functions and limited authority, calling them a "conspiracy against the people." Despite his concerns, Miliukov drove the Kadets forward. In the elections for the Duma, the Kadets won the largest number of seats in the new body, 179 out of 486, a very impressive showing, for which Miliukov deserves the lion's share of credit.

Unlike Miliukov, the noted revolutionary Vladimir Lenin, the fourth of the famous participants during this tumultuous year, dedicated his life to the overthrow of the monarchy in Russia and to the creation of a socialist system broadly based on Marxism. Russian exiles in western Europe (including Lenin) created the Social Democratic Party in 1903 to achieve these ends. However, the party immediately became embroiled in an internal power struggle, splintering into two factions: the Bolsheviks (led by Lenin) and the Mensheviks (led by Julius O. Martov). These two factions occasionally cooperated but usually saw each other as rivals to be resisted and defeated. This confrontation jeopardized opportunities for common effort against the regime, both in 1905 and in later years.

Living in exile in Geneva in 1905, Lenin heard fragmentary news of Russian conditions. According to his biographer, Robert Payne, on hearing of the Bloody Sunday tragedy, Lenin wrote enthusiastically, "The uprising has begun. Force against force. Street fighting has begun, barricades have been thrown up, rifle fire is crackling, guns are cannonading. Blood flows in rivers, and a civil war for freedom is blazing . . . The slogan of the workers is: Death or Freedom!" His hyperbole, inadequate knowledge of events, and factual errors effectively reveal the dramatic style and excessive opinions so often found in Lenin's political writings. He would not be deterred in pressing his views, no matter what the actual situation.

Despite assessing how the aftermath of Bloody Sunday might be turned to the advantage of his revolutionary goals, during nearly all of 1905, Lenin primarily focused his attention on strengthening his Bolshevik faction against the Mensheviks. He spent copious hours writing vitriolic polemical tracts against his Menshevik opponents. These disputes over questions of ideology and leadership took precedence over making common cause against the regime.

The news coming from Russia during the consequential year discouraged Lenin. He was particularly disturbed that his small Bolshevik movement proved disorganized and ineffective. A very revealing letter in mid-October—quoted in David Shub's biography of Lenin—bitterly complained about the lack of revolutionary activity among his followers:

> It requires furious energy and more energy. I am appalled, truly appalled, to see that more than half a year has been spent in talk about bombs–and not a single bomb has been made. . . . Organize at once and everywhere fighting brigades among students, and particularly among workers. Let them arm themselves immediately with whatever weapons they can obtain—a knife, a revolver, a kerosene-soaked rag for setting fires. . . . Do not demand obligatory entry into the Social Democratic Party. . . . Let the squads begin to train for immediate operations. Some can undertake to assassinate a spy or blow up a police station. Others can attack a bank to expropriate funds for an insurrection. Let every squad learn, if only by beating up police.

His demands expose how out of touch Lenin was with the internal situation in Russia. To beat up a single policeman or initiate isolated street fighting scarcely would suffice to bring about the sweeping political changes he sought. Nonetheless, he favored direct action against the regime, not the passive resistance of worker strikes that in fact had been very effective during October.

Finally, unable to effectively control his followers from so far away, Lenin belatedly left Geneva and returned to Russia. Arriving in early December in the capital, he soon went into hiding to avoid the police. By that time, the October general strike was over and the October Manifesto had been issued. The leaders of the St. Petersburg Soviet also had been arrested, and army troops soon crushed the Moscow Soviet. After these reverses, Lenin decided that his followers would boycott the Duma elections in early 1906. He did not believe that the Duma would be a useful weapon against the regime, and he had no use for the moderate groups and parties like the Kadets, whom he accused of supporting the regime.

Lenin criticized the reformers' aversion to violence and described them as "revolutionaries in white gloves." Payne's biography quotes from a heated pamphlet Lenin wrote in 1906 when he declared war on the Kadets: "The Kadets are the worms in the grave of the revolution. The revolution lies buried. The worms gnaw at it." In later years, he continued his attacks on the moderates and liberals, complaining, "In the decisive moments of the struggle, Kadets . . . have betrayed democracy and have gone to help the tsar and the landlords." His anger against the Kadets and others could not change the fact that his Bolshevik movement throughout 1905 was too small, weak, and poorly organized to act effectively. Finally, in exasperation, he left Russia in disgust in 1907 and returned to his western European exile.

Thus, the year of crisis came to an end, with a tired, defeated, and increasingly divided opposition. By the late spring of 1906, the regime had regained control, sometimes by the ruthless use of military force. The critics of the regime faced the unhappy realization that a few initial gains won in prior months had inadequately fulfilled their objectives. For many who had worked so hard for positive change, 1906 looked more bleak and unsatisfactory than a year earlier, when reform activity had had more momentum and the regime was weaker.

Leon D. Trotsky, the youthful Menshevik radical, provided a perceptive and succinct summary of the transition that had occurred by the end of 1905. The famous scholar Bertram Wolfe quotes Trotsky as follows:

> So a constitution is granted. Freedom of assembly is granted but the assemblies are surrounded by the military. Freedom of speech is granted, but the censorship exists as before. Freedom of knowledge is granted, but the universities are occupied by troops. Inviolability of the person is granted, but the prisons are overflowing with the incarcerated. Witte is given us, but Trepov remains to us. A constitution is given, but the autocracy remains. Everything is given—and nothing is given.

To what extent did these four individuals achieve their goals during this revolutionary period? Each succeeded, but each also failed. Nicholas succeeded in restoring his authority and preventing the Duma from having any meaningful influence. By the summer of 1906, the regime was stronger than during 1905. But Nicholas failed to appreciate the level of discontent among the Russian population and thus remained oblivious to the problems that would reappear during the catastrophe of World War I and that would bring the nation to total collapse. The 1917 March Revolution overthrew the monarchy, with Nicholas and his family among the leading victims of the violence that later ensued.

Sergei Witte, sent into the political wilderness in 1906, played no future leadership role for his nation. He disliked both the monarch and the regime's opponents, but attempted a pragmatic balance of shared authority between the two in 1905 and early 1906. To the extent that he succeeded, he deserves commendation for coping with the extremely serious challenges facing the regime. His primary failing was his inability to secure the needed support of both the monarch and the reformers. Lonely and bitter, he died in 1915 and did not witness the eventual victory of Communism.

Paul Miliukov lived until 1943, seeing his dreams of a liberal and democratic Russia shattered by a Communist dictatorship under Lenin and Joseph V. Stalin. Nevertheless, he played a significant role in 1905 and immediately after, succeeding in creating a moderate political party and devoting his talents to making the Duma a more effective player in Russian politics between 1905 and 1917. His efforts were important early steps in seeking to move Russia toward the type of political system he greatly admired in the constitutional monarchies of western Europe. His primary failure, as a politician and historian, was his inability to understand that peaceful reform would come very slowly in a nation unaccustomed to democratic institutions. His was not a failure of a vision of a better Russia; rather, it was a failure to comprehend fully the depth of the challenges to be overcome.

Lenin, the fourth figure, failed to make any significant impact during 1905. His decision to remain abroad for nearly the entire year was a mistake. Lenin's suspicion of the St. Petersburg and Moscow Soviets because of their Menshevik leadership also shows his limited vision. In addition, he refused to support Bolshevik candidates for the Duma, a decision that hurt the movement's chances for greater exposure and wider public support. A depressed Lenin concluded that a successful revolution in his lifetime was unlikely. But Lenin gradually learned the methods and tactics that would be successful in the continued struggle for power in Russia, and he later described 1905 as a useful "rehearsal" for a future revolution. A decade later, in 1917, Lenin returned once again to his homeland to resume the effort that finally led his party to total victory. This was his ultimate success.

Each of these four individuals played a distinctive role in Russian history. They were part of the first two decades of the twentieth century that saw the decline and fall of the monarchy in Russia and four other major states: Austria-Hungary, China, Germany, and the Ottoman Empire. Modern civilization, with its desire for democratic and representative political systems, increasingly found little relevance in the classic historical models of monarchical and autocratic regimes. But these anachronisms did not disappear easily or without a fight. In several cases, dictatorships replaced monarchies. Nonetheless, the events in Russia in 1905 provide important clues of the coming wave of larger revolutions that would sweep away the old and offer an uncertain opportunity for the future. As of 1905, only time would tell if democratic aspirations could be achieved in Russia and other nations as the new reality of the twentieth century.

SELECTED BIBLIOGRAPHY

Bing, Edward J., ed., *The Letters of Tsar Nicholas and Empress Marie: Being the Confidential Correspondence Between Nicholas II, Last of the Tsars, and His Mother, Dowager Empress Maria Feodorovna*. London: Nicholson and Watson, 1937.

Essential source includes lengthy and candid letters describing events in 1905–1906.

Ferro, Marc. *Nicholas II: The Last of the Tsars.* New York: Oxford University Press, 1994.
Contains personal observations about the 1905 crisis in the tsar's private letters and diary entries.

Fischer, Louis. *The Life of Lenin.* New York: Harper and Row, 1965.
Solid biography by a noted interpreter of Russian affairs.

Harcave, Sidney. *First Blood: The Russian Revolution of 1905.* New York: Macmillan, 1964.
Comprehensive description and analysis of the origins of the crisis, the events of the year, and the outcome.

Maylunas, Andrei, and Sergei Mironenko. *A Lifelong Passion: Nicholas and Alexandra: Their Own Story.* New York: Doubleday, 1997.
Extensive excerpts from correspondence and diaries of Romanov family members in 1905, along with recollections of other contemporary figures.

Mehlinger, Howard, and John M. Thompson. *Count Witte and the Tsarist Government in the 1905 Revolution.* Bloomington: Indiana University Press, 1972.
Important scholarly work assessing Witte's role in the 1905 crisis.

Miliukov, Paul. *Political Memoirs, 1905–1917.* Ann Arbor: University of Michigan Press, 1967.
Essential recollections by a prominent leader of democratic reform in 1905.

Moorehead, Alan. *The Russian Revolution.* New York: Carroll and Graf, 1987.
Comparatively brief account of the first two decades of the twentieth century, with an engaging description of the 1905 revolution.

Pares, Bernard. *The Fall of the Russian Monarchy: A Study of the Evidence.* New York: Vintage Books, 1961.
Pioneering study of the 1905 revolution, World War I, and the Russian Revolution of 1917 by an observer of these events.

Payne, Robert. *The Life and Death of Lenin.* New York: Simon and Schuster, 1964.
Includes Lenin's views and activities in 1905.

Radzinsky, Edvard. *The Last Tsar: The Life and Death of Nicholas II.* New York: Doubleday, 1992.
Provides extensive excerpts from the letters and personal diary of Nicholas II.

Rawson, Don. C. *Russian Rightists and the Revolution of 1905.* New York: Cambridge University Press, 1995.
Traces conservative opposition to the revolution and reform efforts in 1905.

Rice, Christopher. *Russian Workers and the Socialist-Revolutionary Party through the Revolution of 1905–1907.* New York: St. Martin's Press, 1988.
Detailed analysis of the influence of the leftist movement among the lower occupational classes.

Riha, Thomas. *A European Russian: Paul Miliukov in Russian Politics.* Notre Dame, IN: University of Notre Dame Press, 1969.
Essential biography on Miliukov's life and career by a prominent American scholar who mysteriously disappeared in 1969 and was never found.

Sablinsky, Walter. *The Road to Bloody Sunday: Father Gapon and the St. Petersburg Massacre of 1905.* Princeton, NJ: Princeton University Press, 1976.

Very detailed coverage of the origins of Bloody Sunday and Gapon's leadership.

Salisbury, Harrison. *Black Night, White Snow: Russia's Revolution, 1905–1917.* Garden City, NY: Doubleday, 1978.

Fascinating account of the events and challenges facing the Romanov dynasty in its final years.

Trotsky, Leon. *1905.* New York: Random House, 1971.

Memoirs of a revolutionary opposed to the government, focusing on the critical October–December 1905 period.

Ulam, Adam. *The Bolsheviks: The Intellectual and Political History of the Triumph of Communism.* New York: Macmillan, 1965.

Traces both the ideological and practical evolution of the revolutionary movement.

Verner, Andre M. *The Crisis of Russian Autocracy: Nicholas II and the 1905 Revolution.* Princeton, NJ: Princeton University Press, 1990.

Scholarly work assesses the regime's leadership and response.

Witte, Sergei. *The Memoirs of Count Witte.* New York: Fertig, 1967.

Important recollections of the leading government official in 1905.

Wolfe, Bertram. *Three Who Made a Revolution: A Biographical History.* New York: Delta Books, 1964.

Comparative study of the lives of Lenin, Stalin, and Trotsky up to 1914.

5

World War I, 1914–1918

INTRODUCTION

Beginning in August 1914, the catastrophic World War I engulfed Europe's Great Powers, including Russia. Although most historians have determined that Europe accidentally slid into war, few will disagree that Russia played a large and irresponsible role in the coming of the conflict.

In 1871 Germany was unified under the guidance of Otto von Bismarck, who then turned his considerable talents to the task of maintaining Europe's stability. All the major nations, including Russia, enjoyed close relations with a dominant Germany, except for Great Britain, which then practiced Splendid Isolation, and a revengeful France that Bismarck kept isolated. When William II ascended to the German throne in 1888, and Bismarck resigned two years later, Europe's constancy came to an end. Russia was the first to experience the changed circumstances when in 1890 Germany shockingly refused to renew the Russo-German Reinsurance Treaty, thereby setting the tsarist state adrift. However, by 1894 Russia had found a friend. In one of the stranger alliances of recent history, autocratic, reactionary, backward Russia now stood side by side with republican, progressive, modern France. One wonders how many tsars turned in their graves when Alexander III, the Autocrat of All the Russias, stood bareheaded at attention as the band played the "Marseillaise."

Thus, Russia was part of Europe's division into two armed camps. The Franco-Russian alliance added a third friend, if not formal partner, at the start of the twentieth century when Britain abandoned Splendid Isolation and joined what was called the Triple Entente. The Triple Alliance, composed of Germany, Austria-Hungary, and Italy, stood opposed to the Triple Entente.

Russian dead litter the road after yet another World War I defeat. The long and bloody conflict sealed the Russian Empire's fate as its leadership and resources proved inadequate to the task of fighting a modern war. (Reproduced from the Collections of the Library of Congress.)

For several centuries, Russia had evinced a keen interest in the Otto-man Empire and its territorial possessions, including the Balkan Penin-sula. Over the centuries, the Turks and the Russians fought numerous wars, with the latter slowly gaining the upper hand. As Turkey's grip on the Balkans loosened, Russia's interest there intensified. Unfortunately for Europe's peace, the Russians were not alone. Austria-Hungary also took note of the vacuum emerging on its southeastern border, and it also worked to extend its influence in that direction. Austro-Russian rivalry in the Balkans was already a fact at the start of the twentieth cen-tury. However, for the moment, Russia had focused its attention on the Far East, where its competition with Japan over who was to dominate Korea led to the 1904–1905 Russo-Japanese War and a disastrous defeat for the tsarist state, culminating in the outbreak of revolution at home. One important consequence of this setback was that Russia shifted its attention to the Balkans, where it now collided head on with Austria-Hungary.

Having allied itself with the small but restless and ambitious Balkan state of Serbia, Russia faced a crisis in 1908 when Austria-Hungary annexed the lands of Bosnia-Herzegovina much to the displeasure of both Serbia and Russia. War seemed imminent, but a humiliated Russia and Serbia grudgingly backed down when powerful Germany indicated that it would support its Austrian ally in the event of war. Desperate now to retain its position in the Balkans as well as its shaky standing as a Great Power, Russia vowed to never again back down.

A few years later, Russia's determination was tested when Serbian gunmen assassinated Archduke Franz Ferdinand, the heir to the Austro-Hungarian throne, at Sarajevo on June 28, 1914. In short order, a major crisis arose. Austria-Hungary, once again backed by Germany, blamed the Serbian government for the assassination and threatened invasion. Serbia once again turned to its ally Russia, who in turn received assurances from France. Finding itself in a bind, Russia's proverbial backwardness now came into play. Because Russia was so large and dis-organized, it would take much longer than any other Great Power to place its army on a war footing. Thus, in order to have any chance of military success, Russia would have to mobilize well before any other potential belligerent; however, when Russia's opponents saw it start to mobilize, they would take this as a sign of impending conflict and would move as quickly as possible in order to beat Russia to the punch. On July 30, Russia mobilized its army; two days later, Germany declared war on Russia, and Austria-Hungary followed suit four days later. The world war had begun.

Much to everyone's astonishment, during the earliest days of the war, the Russian army launched a major offensive. Initially, the surprise invasion of East Prussia succeeded; however, the Germans regrouped and resupplied, and within a matter of days, the German army dealt Russia a crushing defeat at the twin battles of Tannenberg and the Masurian Lakes. Not only did this debacle cost Russia 300,000 men, but it also revealed profound weaknesses that continued to plague Russia throughout the conflict: incompetent leadership, personal rivalries, lack of equipment, poor training, technological inferiority, logistical failures, and a general sense of doom in the face of a superior enemy. For example, generals Alexander V. Samsonov and Paul K. Rennenkampf, commanders of the invading Russian forces, not only failed to coordinate their movements but also refused to even speak to each other because of a personal feud.

Throughout the course of the war, the Russian rank and file fought bravely and endured extreme hardship. Nevertheless, the numerous military and civilian deficiencies came to undermine this exceptional fighting spirit. Throughout 1915 and 1916, and into 1917, a pattern developed that defined Russia's military campaigns. When facing the even more ramshackle Austro-Hungarian army, Russia enjoyed great success. It soundly defeated the Austrians in their Galician province and more than once threatened to seize the Carpathian passes and flood into the Hungarian plane. The greatest Russian triumph of the war occurred in Galicia in 1916 when General Alexis A. Brusilov's offensive overwhelmed the Austrian defenders, seizing more than 10,000 square miles and taking over 400,000 prisoners.

However, this triumph proved ephemeral because it provoked a German response that can be seen as an integral part of the military pattern. Just as the Russians could beat the Austrians, the Germans could beat the Russians. Whenever the Russian army threatened the Austro-Hungarian forces, the Germans would ride to their ally's rescue, undoing all the Russian gains. Moreover, whenever the Germans conducted their own offensive operations against the Russians, victory was virtually guaranteed. By the end of 1915, the Germans had forced General Michael V. Alekseev to abandon all of Russian Poland, and they were moving into Lithuania and Belorussia. At the start of the war, Russians had spoken glowingly of the "Russian steamroller," but in practice it was the Germans who moved steadily eastward. About the only consistent bright spot for Russian arms was the campaign against Turkey, during which Russia gained Erzerum, Trebizond, and part of eastern Anatolia.

As poorly as the Russian army fared against its German foe, the argument can be made that conditions at home were as bad if not worse.

Apparently, this did not have to be. When the war began, a genuine out-pouring of support for the tsar and his government surfaced. Russians (at least those who were literate and thought about such things) viewed themselves as victims of German aggression and rallied round the flag. In the name of patriotism, the German-sounding city of "Sankt Petersburg" was renamed Petrograd. However, Nicholas II and his advisors not only failed to take advantage of these sentiments, but also behaved in such an aloof, high-handed, and yet incompetent manner that they quickly dissipated this surge of goodwill.

Instead of cooperating with the Duma, which represented the hopes, desires, and opinions of the literate Russian public, the government opted to go it alone, falling back on the traditional bureaucratic, administrative methods that had alienated it from the Russian population on so many past occasions. Given Nicholas's distrust of the Duma and his detestation of anything that threatened autocratic rule, his decisions are understandable; however, the fact remains that such decisions drove a fatal wedge between the government and the people and, in the long run, badly damaged the war effort.

The tsar exacerbated an already perilous situation when he opted for the operational status quo. Seniority and connections rather than ability served as the basis for military appointments. The war minister, Vladimir A. Sukhomlinov, a man of modest abilities at best, was a personal favorite of the tsar. As commander in chief, Nicholas named his uncle, Grand Duke Nicholas Nikolaevich, an imposing man at six feet six inches, who was, however, of small caliber when it came to military matters. When the grand duke's incompetence earned him a demotion and transfer to the Caucasus in August 1915, Nicholas II himself assumed command, despite his painful lack of knowledge about military matters. Nicholas moved from the capital to the front, where he spent his time in the coaches of the royal train poring endlessly over maps and military orders that he did not understand.

Supplying the Russian army proved to be a task beyond the capabilities of the lethargic and corrupt Russian bureaucracy. Already handicapped by a lack of industrial development, Russia now suffered from gross bureau-cratic bungling. The lack of shells for Russia's artillery was scandalous, and by one estimate, 25 percent of Russian soldiers sent into battle lacked rifles (they were told to keep an eye on their comrades who were armed and to grab their weapons when they fell). Nevertheless, during the course of the war, things improved thanks to the Duma, which gradually replaced the bureaucracy as the body organizing the war effort. Linking up with *zemstvo* organizations, municipalities, and industrialists, the

Duma injected a degree of reality into a rapidly deteriorating situation. It instituted relief efforts, increased industrial production, and established a more efficient distribution network.

An inferior transportation system that disintegrated under the strains of war greatly aggravated the supply problem for both the army and the Russian civilians. In particular, Russia's underdeveloped railroad system proved inadequate. Furthermore, Russia's Western allies failed to provide promised support. Because Germany controlled the Baltic Sea, and the Ottoman Empire controlled the straits to the Black Sea, the only way Great Britain and France could supply Russia was through the far northern ports of Archangel and Murmansk (the latter not having a railroad connection to the Russian heartland until 1916) or via the Trans-Siberian railroad from Russia's Far East.

When Nicholas left for the front lines in 1915, responsibility for overseeing the home front fell to his wife, Alexandra, a reasonably intelligent, well-educated, and strong-willed woman who was also hysterical and superstitious and a political reactionary of the first rank. Even though Alexandra was the granddaughter of Queen Victoria and had enjoyed an English upbringing, she was unbending in her hatred of anything that smacked of modernity and liberalism. Furthermore, she selected as her most intimate advisor and confidant Gregory E. Rasputin, an unlettered "holy man" notable for his gargantuan appetites, crude behavior, and boundless corruption. Together, this pair drove the country into the ditch with their unsuitable appointments, bizarre behavior, and ill-conceived decisions.

Meanwhile, somehow the Russian army managed to hold together despite repeated pummeling by the Germans. In fact, it was the home front that finally cracked. Riots first shook Petrograd on March 8, 1917; one week later, the Romanov dynasty that had ruled Russia for more than 300 years was gone. A power struggle for control of the moribund Russian state ensued; meanwhile, the war ground on, and the Germans continued to make headway against a demoralized Russian force. Amazingly, in the midst of the chaos and defeat, the Provisional Government, one of the contenders in the struggle for Russia, ordered the army to mount an offensive. Once again, the Russians attacked the Austrians, and once again, the result was the same— initial success followed by retreat. The only major difference was that this time, the Russian retreat turned into a rout.

A major break came on November 7, 1917, when the Bolsheviks seized power in Russia. Their leader, Vladimir I. Lenin, knew that the Bolshevik chances for remaining in control depended in large measure on successfully extricating Russia from the war. To that end, Lenin reached a cease-fire with the Germans on December 7. Two days later, peace negotiations opened in the fortress town of Brest-Litovsk. Initial discussions proved futile; the Germans asked for the moon, and the Bolsheviks made propaganda. Eventually, Leon D. Trotsky, the leader of the Bolshevik delegation, declared a state of "no peace, no war." The Germans took this as an invitation to resume hostilities.

Unable to defend his regime against the renewed German onslaught, Lenin used all his persuasive powers to convince his fellow Bolsheviks to swallow the bitter pill being offered up by the Germans. His efforts met with success, and on March 3, 1918, the belligerents signed the Treaty of Brest-Litovsk. For Russia, the treaty was draconian. According to eminent Russian historian George Vernadsky, by the terms of the treaty, Russia surrendered 1.27 million square miles, including Ukraine, Poland, Finland, and its Baltic territories (Estonia, Latvia, and Lithuania). It lost 62 million people, 27 percent of its arable land, 26 percent of its railroad system, 33 percent of its industry, and 75 percent of its coal deposits. In other words, the Treaty of Brest-Litovsk pushed Russia back into Asia, surrounded it in the west with German-oriented puppet regimes, and denuded it of the human and material capital required to achieve a recovery. Luckily for Russia, Germany eventually lost World War I, thereby rendering the treaty null and void.

During World War I, Russia drafted more than 15 million men into its army. Of that number, perhaps 1.8 million died, more than 3 million were wounded, and about 2.7 million were either captured or listed as missing. Moreover, untold millions of civilians died as a consequence of the war.

INTERPRETIVE ESSAY
Dana M. Ohren

World War I, or the Great War as it was known to its contemporaries, ushered in a new era of modern European history. For most of the Continent, the war brought with it big government, advanced technologies, and death. Even for those not fighting in the trenches, the home-front experience forced civilians to endure the economic, political, social, and cultural effects of total war in ways unimaginable just a few years before.

The history of the Great War has been a rich field of study for historians, professional and amateur, for nearly a century since the cataclysmic event. This interest stemmed in part from the fact that in western Europe the Great War came to symbolize hope lost. In Great Britain, France, and Germany, the "generation of 1914" was considered a "lost generation."

After the war, Europeans turned their backs on the liberal politics of the nineteenth century, which had emphasized individual rights, in favor of political parties, both socialist and fascist, that stressed the collective. In this regard, the Great War is often considered the watershed event that divided the nineteenth and twentieth centuries. In Russia and the Soviet Union, the Bolshevik Revolution and World War II became the primary events that forged Soviet society and dominated official memory. Nevertheless, the Great War fundamentally altered the course of Russian history and stands among the major events that shaped modern Russia.

On June 28, 1914, a Bosnian Serb assassinated Archduke Franz Ferdinand, heir to the Austro-Hungarian throne. A month later, on July 23, after receiving assurances of support from Germany, Austria-Hungary sent Serbia a series of demands. The Serb government rejected the demand that Austria be allowed to participate in the assassination investigation. To permit Austria's involvement would be a breach of Serbian sovereignty.

The Russian Empire pledged its support to Serbia. In recent decades, both Germany and Austria-Hungary had diplomatically humiliated Russia, and Russia vowed not to see its influence in the Balkans further diminished. Still, Russian military planners disliked the idea of war. Not only did they—along with the rest of Europe—hold the German army in high regard, but they also were in the process of implementing a new armaments program that would not come to fruition until 1917–1918. And yet, if Russia did not appear strong, other countries, such as its ally France, might question its worthiness as a partner. It seemed better to risk war now, while Russia had allies, than to postpone it into the future when its situation might be worse.

As diplomatic efforts waned, military leaders urged mobilization. Because of its large size and lack of organization, Russia would take longer to assemble its forces than other European countries. Tsar Nicholas II was hesitant to call for a general mobilization because such action would be tantamount to declaring war. However, if he did not issue the order, Russia risked being attacked without the necessary troops in place to defend the empire. On July 25, Nicholas ordered a partial mobilization of Russian forces, and Serbia called up its own troops. The next day, Austria mobilized, and on July 29, it invaded Serbia. By the end of the first week of August, each of the Great Powers—Germany and Austria-Hungary on one side and France, Russia, and Great Britain on the other—had entered the fray and the Great War had begun.

At the outset of the war, Russia was at a disadvantage when compared to other belligerent countries. Russian weaponry and military tactics were outdated, and the empire had begun to industrialize only recently. Just as problematic, the empire lacked sufficient transportation infrastructure, including railways, rolling stock, paved roads, and motorized vehicles. These deficiencies not only hampered efforts to transport troops and supplies to the front, but also created difficulties for distribution of materials on the home front. Most problematically, Russia was led by an incompetent ruler who refused to delegate enough authority to more qualified men to overcome these challenges.

Military planners, politicians, and scholars claimed retroactively that Russia lost the war because its people, particularly its peasants, were not fully conscious of belonging to the Russian nation. In total war, armies do not just fight other armies, but rather, entire nations, soldiers and civilians both, mobilize against one another. Although some scholars have recently argued that Russian peasants were not as parochial and ignorant as they often have been portrayed, most still accept the idea that peasants did not understand why they were fighting and were more concerned with local activities than with national or international affairs. Indeed, according to one scholar, the Russian peasant was a "natural pacifist" who was apathetic when it came to fighting a war in which his village was not personally threatened. However, to blame Russia's loss on peasants' lack of national consciousness is misguided. Russian soldiers fought bravely while enduring many hardships. Ultimately, Russia lost the war because both on the battlefront and the home front, soldiers and civilians were poorly led and ill-equipped to wage modern war.

In hindsight, it is easy to point to Russia's shortcomings and pronounce that a revolution of some sort was inevitable given the crushing circumstances of the Great War. Nevertheless, despite apparent military, industrial, and political weaknesses, Russia stayed in the war for three years. To understand this seemingly impossible feat, we must reexamine Russia's World War I.

In August 1914, Germany's Schlieffen Plan inaugurated the war's initial phase. The plan called for German forces to march through neutral Belgium and arc around northern France to take Paris in a matter of weeks. German military strategists believed Russian troops would take the longest to mobilize, and thus, Germany could knock France out of the war before turning its main attention to Russia. In the meantime, Germany had charged Austria-Hungary with holding the Eastern Front. Austro-Hungarian troops were stretched thinly across the immense borders of the Russian Empire, and both Serbia and Russia, which mobilized much faster than expected, gained ground in opening clashes. In response, Germany weakened its forces on the Western Front to send troops east. At the battles of Tannenberg (late August) and the Masurian Lakes (early

September), Germany soundly defeated Russia's first and second armies. Not only did Russian commanders fail to coordinate their efforts, but they also broadcast uncoded messages on open wires because of a lack of secure closed telephone and telegraph lines. Germans just had to listen in and plan accordingly. In the end, Russian losses were staggering. Whereas German casualties were in the tens of thousands, the number of Russian deaths, injuries, and prisoners of war taken was in the hundreds of thousands.

On the Southwestern Front, Russia fared better against Austria-Hungary. After opening battles, Austro-Hungarian forces had lost about 350,000 men. Despite its ability to vanquish the Habsburgs, Russia was unable to defeat the Germans, and it was forced into a massive retreat in mid-1915. The situation was particularly perilous as defensive fallback positions had not been prepared and munitions were running dangerously low. The German offensive continued throughout the summer, and what became known as Russia's "Great Retreat" hastily followed. By autumn 1915, Russia had fallen back some 200 miles east of the line it had held that spring. It was abundantly clear to all involved that predications of a short war with soldiers "home before Christmas" of 1914 were dead wrong.

With no clear path to victory available on the battlefield, the belligerent countries seized upon a new strategy: attrition. Tactics would now involve bleeding the enemy dry, both on the battlefield through the destruction of enemy combat forces and on the home fronts by economic exhaustion. Victory would be determined as much by which home front could outproduce and outlast its opponent as by military strategies. Total war had come to Europe.

To ensure that raw materials were transported to factories, manufactured into war-related goods, and distributed to the front lines took tremendous organization. In Great Britain, France, Germany, and Austria-Hungary, governments, business owners, and workers entered into agreements with one another to ensure that armies received their supplies and civilians were housed and fed. In Russia, the least industrialized of the five Great Powers, this task was overwhelming. Natural resources, such as coal and iron, needed to be mined and distributed across the empire's industrial zone. Here, Russia's lack of sufficient railroad lines and rolling stock impeded efforts. Additionally, like all belligerent countries, Russia struggled with the need to keep enough skilled workers on the job while continuing to meet the enormous demand for soldiers at the front. Women and children entered the industrial workforce in unprecedented numbers, and prisoners of war were put to task doing some of the most difficult work. Although industrial productivity rose from 1913 to 1915, by 1918 figures for all industries were disastrous, with some industrial sectors putting out less than half of their 1913 levels.

One of the main obstacles to industrial mobilization was the need to wrest its control away from the Romanovs. The government stubbornly relied on several big business partners even though the task was greater than their abilities. Businessmen who were not from these favored companies formed war industrial committees (WIC) to pressure the government to give out contracts to smaller suppliers. Nevertheless, the majority of defense orders—some 95 percent—remained with the government's chosen big industrialists.

Like industry, civil administrations reorganized their efforts to meet the challenges of total war. Zemstvos, or self-government boards, had been established in 1864 in rural areas as part of Tsar Alexander II's effort to reform local government after the liberation of the serfs. During the war, the government approved the formation of an All-Russian Union of Zemstvos, as well as its municipal counterpart—the Union of Towns—to care for the wounded and sick. The Union of Zemstvos, led by the capable Prince George E. Lvov, also organized the refugee relief effort. As the front moved further into Russian territory, refugees streamed east, causing even more strains on already overburdened food and housing supplies. By 1915, over three million refugees had been displaced, and by 1917, there were an estimated six million refugees, or approximately 5 percent of the imperial population. Among refugees who fled to the interior, one found not only Slavic peoples, but also Latvians, Lithuanians, and Jews from the western borderlands and Armenians from the Caucasus and Ottoman Empire.

In 1915 the All-Russian Union of Zemstvos and the Union of Towns joined forces as an entity called Zemgor and increased their scope of activities. In addition to relief work, Zemgor also oversaw the manufacturing of clothing, footwear, pharmaceuticals, and war materials. Although Zemgor's activities were necessary to maintain the war effort, Nicholas and his ministers still could only see a political threat to the tsar's authority.

When the war had first begun, many members of the Duma, Russia's parliamentary body, had pledged their full support to the tsar. Only a small number of extreme leftist members had refused. Nicholas, who had always been wary of sharing power with the Duma, had then taken advantage of the politicians' submission and dismissed the Duma. In January 1915, the Duma was recalled for three days in response to the seemingly desperate shell shortage and was then sent away again. When the Duma was reconvened in summer of 1915, a significant proportion of it formed a Progressive Bloc. Members of the Bloc called for a competent government not only to wage a successful war, but also to stave off the growing threat of a social revolution. Nicholas was convinced by the conservative Chairman of the Council of Ministers, Ivan L. Goremykin, to dissolve the Duma again in September 1915.

In doing so, Nicholas made a crucial error. In other European countries, governments allowed specialists, working in conjunction with the government, to manage the war effort. Although governments curbed certain liberties such as the right to privacy and freedom to change jobs voluntarily, the governments of Great Britain, France, and Germany nonetheless conceded some power to societal forces and fostered a sense of shared responsibility for the waging of war. Nicholas, steadfast in his belief that God had appointed him autocrat of Russia, held on tightly to the reins of power. Consequently, it was Nicholas who bore the blame for ensuing shortages and defeats, and he appeared to be a callous and unfeeling tsar who did not properly care for his people.

Exacerbating matters, Nicholas personally assumed command of Russian military forces in September 1915. Although to some this move was a brave attempt to inspire the troops, it was ruinous both militarily and politically. Nicholas, unlike many of his Romanov kin, was not a military man, nor did he possess the personal charisma that could inspire troops to persevere despite hardships. General Michael V. Alekseev, who was in charge of Russia's army in 1915, was able to circumvent Nicholas when it came to most military matters, but he could not prevent the tsar from appointing inept military personnel simply because Nicholas liked them.

Even when success did come, Russia was ill-prepared to capitalize on it. For example, in the summer of 1916, Russia launched an offensive in coordination with Allied plans on the Western Front. General Alexis A. Brusilov, who had recently been appointed the commander of Russian forces on the Russian Southwestern Front, improved coordination between artillery and infantry units and changed tactics so that Russian troops attacked at multiple points instead of a single spot. He chose this strategy because Russia lacked the necessary railways to concentrate troops sufficiently in one place while not allowing the enemy enough time to detect the movement and respond accordingly. The Russian army also benefited from an increase in weaponry and improvements to the supply system. To Brusilov's dismay, however, simultaneous attacks by other Russian generals did not proceed as planned. Instead of having to respond to multiple assaults at once, the Central Powers concentrated their efforts against Brusilov's advance, and by the end of July, Brusilov had been stopped. Although Brusilov's troops had taken almost 400,000 prisoners of war before they were halted, Russian casualties for the campaign were nearly 1 million.

When faced with Germany's superior military and industrial might, Russia fell back upon its primary asset, its people. However, Russia failed to make the most of this advantage. Generous exemptions for only sons or sole male breadwinners in a family, certain minority groups, and some vocations (such as policemen) meant that only 5 percent of Russia's male population actually served. In contrast, Germany mobilized 12 percent and France 16 percent. To make matters worse, Russia's reserve system did not adequately train soldiers. General Brusilov complained that reservists made poor soldiers because all they had been taught to do was march. Newer recruits received even less training. The Romanov men were notorious for liking military parades, but their fondness for precision marching did not help armies win an industrialized war.

As the conflict continued, governments struggled to find innovative ways to inspire soldiers and civilians to continue the fight. In the days before television and the public use of the radio, each government primarily relied upon print journalism and posters to reach its citizens. In Russia, postcards and posters included satirical portrayals of Russia's enemies, battle scenes, and allegorical calls to patriotism. One of the most well-known scenes depicted a single, injured soldier leaning against a wall with his rifle held against his side. Next to the figure were four simple words: "Aid to War Victims." Such imagery was both emotional and realistic and therefore conveyed a powerful message to Russians to give more to the war effort. Other posters and postcards advertised "patriotic concerts" or urged Russians to buy war bonds.

The Russian government needed ever-increasing amounts of money to continue its efforts. It implored Russians to purchase treasury bills and war bonds. Short-term treasury bill debt already had reached 800 million rubles by January 1915. On the eve of the Bolshevik Revolution, this debt stood at 18,747 million rubles. Long-term domestic loans totaled 11,400 million rubles by 1917, and foreign loans, primarily from Britain and the United States, reached 11,194 million rubles. Russia's need to borrow so heavily resulted from the enormous cost of industrialized war. Whereas expenditures for the Russo-Japanese War of 1904–1905 totaled 2,295 million rubles, the Great War's cost reached 38,650 million. The government also introduced a tax on excess corporate profits, initiated a personal income tax, and raised duties on items such as tobacco and sugar, although these efforts achieved little.

Despite the great strides made by Russian industry in 1915 and 1916, the war was still not going well. Soldiers grew increasingly weary, and letters from home brought news of worsening social and political conditions.

As defeats on the battlefield mounted, poorly trained replacements were called up, and Russia's infamous "steamroller" of men seemed to be running out of steam. When in 1916 the government tried to conscript Central Asian Muslims—who had previously been exempt from the draft—to work in noncombat positions in the rear, a massive uprising erupted. Troops were called in to quell the disturbances, and Russia's manpower pool was further drained. Similar to its effects on social and political tensions, the Great War exposed serious ethnic rifts that had long been simmering.

As Russia's position deteriorated, Nicholas received the blame. Even middle- and upper-class Russians came to view the tsar as an obstacle to victory. In November 1916, a leading liberal in the Duma, Paul N. Miliukov, gave a stirring speech in which he asked if the tsar and his ministers were guilty of "stupidity or treason" because they managed the war effort so poorly. Although Miliukov intended his rhetorical flourish to point to the answer of incompetence, rumors swelled that the tsarina, German by birth, was purposefully betraying Russia. Although there is no evidence that the tsar, tsarina, or Russian ministers were treasonous, they were ultimately responsible for their own downfall. Had they allowed Zemgor activists greater latitude in their efforts or had they appointed capable men to run the military instead of relying on court favorites, Russia might have fared better. Members of society, both high and low, would not have been able to blame the tsar so universally for all failures. In this respect, Russia lost the war and the Romanovs lost their throne not because of the backwardness of Russian industry and peasantry, but because Russia entered the war with an inflexible political system headed by a man who did not have the foresight to know his own limitations and allow more competent individuals to do their jobs.

The tsar's most loyal supporters targeted the royal family's spiritual advisor, the monk Gregory E. Rasputin. They accused him of holding enormous influence over the tsar and especially the tsarina, who had been left to run the government in Petrograd (as St. Petersburg had been renamed shortly after the war began) when Nicholas departed for the front. Under Rasputin's influence, Tsarina Alexandra had appointed and dismissed ministers at a rate that earned the label "ministerial leapfrog." For example, between September 1915 and February 1917, Russia had four prime ministers, three ministers of war, and five ministers of internal affairs. In December 1916, several Russian noblemen murdered Rasputin in order to release the royal family from his hold. Despite their success, Russia's fortunes did not improve. Every level of Russian society had lost confidence in Nicholas's ability to lead the empire.

It was the winter of 1916–1917 that led to the downfall of the Romanovs. Other countries faced severe crisis as well, yet neither Germany's so-called "turnip winter" of 1916–1917 nor the mutiny of French troops in 1917 led to an all-out revolt against their respective governments. In Russia, mismanagement of food supplies did. The problem began as agricultural output declined over the course of the war because of the decrease in rural manpower, draft animals, and agricultural machinery. The government took to fixing prices for foodstuffs, causing grain merchants and some peasants to withhold their products in the hopes of higher prices. Others switched to a self-sufficiency model and therefore did not produce as much food for sale as they did in peacetime. Because the production of consumer items also fell during the war, peasants had slight incentive to sell their goods, having little to purchase with the money they would have earned. Local concerns took precedence over what was good for the country at large, and food supplies to the industrial cities were in peril. As winter 1917 began, food shipments to Moscow were down by 60 percent, and Petrograd had but a few days of grain reserves to sustain it. Dwindling food supplies and soaring prices led to an increase in labor strikes. On March 8 (February 23, O.S.), a massive strike eventually led to the end of Romanov rule.

The Romanov dynasty that had ruled Russia for 300 years crumbled quickly. As inhabitants of Petrograd gathered to protest worsening conditions, Nicholas ordered that the riots be stopped by whatever means necessary. However, troops refused to fire on protestors, and a full-scale mutiny swept the capital. Tsarist authority had been called into question earlier, but never before had it been so completely devoid of support among every segment of society. In this respect, the war had exacerbated already existing social, economic, and political tensions that plagued the empire. Perhaps with several decades of peace, the Romanovs could have survived, either through brute force or through slow reformation. But regardless of such possibilities, it was clear in the winter of 1917 that the tsar's authority was no longer accepted.

As urged by his advisors, Nicholas soon abdicated in favor of his brother, Grand Duke Michael Alexandrovich, who declined the throne. In the meantime, two alternative power bases developed. Members of the Duma set up a committee to act as a Provisional Government, under the leadership of Zemgor's Prince Lvov, until elections could be held to decide who would rule Russia. Considering itself to be truly provisional, the Provisional Government thought of itself as a caretaker, not a policymaker. The other main seat of power was the Petrograd Council, or Soviet, of Workers' and Soldiers' Deputies. Although the Soviet had the support of many of the capital's laborers, its representatives feared that riots would spin out of control. They looked to the Duma's Provisional Government to restore order, and the Duma liberals relied on the Soviet for credence on the street.

In spite of the tremendous political revolution that had taken place, Russia was still at war with the Central Powers. Members of the Provisional Government believed in upholding Russia's agreements previously made to allies. The concept of "revolutionary defensism" was employed to keep soldiers and civilians fighting. However, the fragile alliance between the Provisional Government and the Petrograd Soviet (and other soviets that had sprung up at the front lines and in various localities around the former empire) did not endure the strain of war. Indeed, a series of mishandled opportunities related to the war discredited the Provisional Government.

At the front, soldiers were restive. Taking advantage of this, in March the Petrograd Soviet issued Order Number One, which subordinated military decisions to the Petrograd Soviet and called for the formation of soldiers' committees at the front. Order Number One also abolished the death penalty and called for elected soldiers to be in charge of disciplinary actions. These measures destroyed military discipline.

The first true test of the Provisional Government's authority came in April 1917. The new Minister of Foreign Affairs, Paul N. Miliukov, refused to renounce Russia's previous war goals, including acquisition of the Bosphorus and Dardenelles Straits from the Ottoman Empire. Control over the Black Sea region had long been a goal of the Russian Empire. To the people, such ambitions were not part of "revolutionary defensism." In April, a note written by Miliukov circulated in which the minister upheld Russia's right to the annexations. Demonstrations against the Provisional Government and subsequent counter-demonstrations in favor of it ensued. Both Miliukov and Minister of War Alexander I. Guchkov resigned over the issue. As a result, some moderate socialists were brought into or promoted within the Provisional Government, including Alexander F. Kerensky, who went from Minister of Justice to Prime Minister of Russia.

Under such chaotic conditions, Russia launched an offensive against the Central Powers in June. Troops were not well led, and some, after voting on the matter in committees, refused to fight at all. The offensive was a disaster, and news of it helped fuel disturbances in Petrograd in July. In the meantime, Germany initiated a successful counteroffensive that pushed Russian forces further into retreat. Recognizing that order needed to be restored within the ranks, the Provisional Government reinstated disciplinary measures, including the death penalty, for soldiers.

Following the failed June Offensive, Kerensky appointed General Lavr G. Kornilov as the new commander of the Russian army. Many saw in

Kornilov a strong man who could reestablish order in the country. On the other hand, soldiers thought Kornilov a counterrevolutionary who was not to be trusted. In August 1917, Kornilov's forces attempted to march on Petrograd and seize power. They were thwarted by railway workers who stopped the trains and by troops mobilized by the Soviet. After both the June Offensive and Kornilov's attempted coup, many soldiers and workers became more distrusting of the Provisional Government, and the appeal of Bolshevik slogans, such as "Peace, Land, Bread," grew.

By November 1917, the situation had not improved, and the Provisional Government continued to limp along. Meanwhile, the Petrograd Soviet fell increasingly under the control of the Bolsheviks. The Bolshevik-dominated Soviet created the Petrograd Military Revolutionary Committee (MRC) under the command of Leon D. Trotsky, a hero of the 1905 revolution who had recently joined with the Bolsheviks. Trotsky stationed Bolsheviks in military units throughout the capital. When on November 5 (October 23, O.S.), Kerensky attempted to regain authority by arresting some Bolsheviks and closing down several of their presses, Bolsheviks rallied the MRC to take over various parts of the city to defend the Soviet. There was relatively little bloodshed, and within days, Vladimir I. Lenin declared the formation of a new Soviet Government.

As head of the new government, Lenin called for Russia's immediate withdrawal from the war. Of course, calling an end to war and actually negotiating a peace settlement with one's enemies were two different matters. At first, both Lenin and Trotsky, the new People's Commissar for Foreign Affairs, hoped for a general peace. The Allies, however, did not respond to the Bolsheviks' call to come to the negotiations. Instead, Russia alone faced Germany, Austria-Hungary, Turkey, and Bulgaria, and peace talks opened at Brest-Litovsk, in Russian Poland, in December 1917. The Russian delegation, which included representatives from Russia's workers, soldiers and sailors, women, and peasants, was led by Adolf A. Ioffe, an emerging Bolshevik diplomat. On December 7, the two sides agreed to a month-long armistice while negotiations for a permanent peace continued. The Austro-Hungarians desperately needed a peace settlement because their home front was collapsing under the threat of famine, and Germany wanted peace with the Russians so that it could concentrate its forces on the Western Front. General Max von Hoffmann, the German representative at the talks, proposed that areas currently occupied by Germany, such as Poland and parts of the Baltic region, could join with the German Empire if the local populations so desired. The Bolsheviks detested parting with such territory because the proposal went against their slogan "peace without annexations." However, without a viable army in the field, the

Bolsheviks' opposition could not be backed up by force. Ioffe called for a recess to discuss the terms with his superiors.

When talks resumed in January, Lenin sent Trotsky to Brest-Litovsk with orders to stretch out the negotiations in the hopes that either peace or revolution would occur in Europe. Trotsky, a master orator and skilled debater, kept the talks going for weeks. When the talks broke up again so that he could discuss with Lenin proposed German territorial gains, Trotsky faced a divided Bolshevik Party. Lenin argued for the acceptance of German terms because he believed that Russia had little other choice and that the party's primary concern should be protecting the revolution within Russia. The other extreme and the largest single bloc within the party, led by Nicholas I. Bukharin, called for a revolutionary war against Germany. In the middle was Trotsky with the slogan "No War, No Peace." Trotsky wanted to declare peace with Germany without accepting the victor's terms, a proposal unheard of in European diplomacy. In the face of Bukharin's majority, Lenin agreed to support Trotsky's "No War, No Peace" formula with the understanding that if it failed, Trotsky would support Lenin's decision to sign the peace agreement.

Upon resumption of negotiations, an incredulous Germany rejected Trotsky's proposal and declared that it would resume fighting. As German forces rapidly advanced into Russian territory, they took more ground in a few days than they had in the preceding three years. Recognizing Russia's weak position, Germany demanded more rapacious terms. Russia was to surrender the Baltics and Russian Poland as well as withdraw troops from Finland and Ukraine. It was also to recognize Ukrainian independence from Russia. These demands far exceeded Hoffman's original proposal, but Lenin saw no other choice but to accept them. If not, German forces would overrun Russia and the Bolsheviks would be blamed for the final humiliation. At this point, Lenin's chief concern was to save Russia's own revolution and his leadership of it. His position won out by the narrowest of margins within the party. On March 3, 1918, the Brest-Litovsk Treaty was finally signed. According to its terms, Russia lost 1.27 million square miles of territory, approximately 62 million people, 9 thousand factories and mills, around 75 percent of its iron mines and coal fields, and its best agricultural lands. According to one scholar, the agreement put modern Russia on a par with seventeenth-century Muscovy.

During its involvement in the Great War, Russia had called up approximately 15 million men, more than half of whom were dead, wounded, or taken prisoner by the end of the war. Despite the catastrophic nature of the event, the postwar generation in Russia did not obsess about it as West Europeans did. In Russia and then the Soviet Union, monuments were not erected to the war, and scholarly and popular books were not dedicated to the subject. Instead, the Bolshevik Revolution of 1917 and, later, World War II captured this attention. The "lost generation," so poignant and painful a subject in western Europe, simply did not exist in Russian public memory. According to Communist ideology, the revolutions that brought down the tsar and established Bolshevik leadership were the result of long-standing political, economic, and social developments, not the war. Accordingly, the Bolsheviks dismissed the war as an imperialist, capitalist conflict and discouraged its public commemoration. In this regard, although Russia does not have a "lost generation," it does have a "lost war."

SELECTED BIBLIOGRAPHY

Acton, Edward, et al., eds. *Critical Companion to the Russian Revolution, 1914–1921.* Bloomington: Indiana University Press, 1997. Includes short articles on World War I, the February (March) and October (November) Revolutions, and the civil war by specialists in each field.

Engel, Barbara Alpern. "Not by Bread Alone: Subsistence Riots in Russia during World War I." *The Journal of Modern History,* 69 (1997): 696–721. Description and analysis of the types of riots stemming from food and consumer-good shortages during the war.

Figes, Orlando. *A People's Tragedy: The Russian Revolution, 1891–1924.* New York: Penguin Books, 1996. A thorough and highly readable account of Russia's Great War, revolutions, and civil war.

Gatrell, Peter. "Russia's First World War: Remembering, Forgetting, Remembering." In *Extending the Borders of Russian History: Essays in Honor of Alfred J. Rieber,* ed. Marsha Siefert, pp. 285–298. New York: Central European University Press, 2003. Exploration of how and why World War I is and is not remembered in the former Soviet Union and Russia.

———. *Russia's First World War: A Social and Economic History.* Edinburg Gate: Pearson Education Limited, 2005. Full of statistics regarding Russia's industrial and economic situation during the war.

———. *A Whole Empire Walking: Refugees in Russia during World War I.* Bloomington: Indiana University Press, 1999. Detailed account of the empire's millions of war refugees and efforts made to manage the crisis.

Jahn, Hubertus F. *Patriotic Culture in Russia during World War I.* Ithaca, NY: Cornell University Press, 1995. Interesting descriptions of wartime propaganda and entertainment.

Joll, James. *The Origins of the First World War.* London: Longman, 1991. A multifaceted account of the causes of the war from a pan-European perspective.

Lieven, Dominic. *Russia and the Origins of the First World War.* London: MacMillan, 1983.
> Russian involvement in international politics and diplomacy leading up to the war.

Lincoln, W. Bruce. *Passage through Armageddon: The Russians in War and Revolution, 1914–1918.* New York: Simon and Schuster, 1986.
> Classic account of the social, political, economic, and military history of Russia's war and revolutions.

Sanborn, Joshua A. *Drafting the Russian Nation: Military Conscription, Total War, and Mass Politics, 1905–1925.* DeKalb: Northern Illinois University Press, 2003.
> Political and social history of late imperial and early Soviet military conscription.

———. "The Mobilization of 1914 and the Question of the Russian Nation: A Reexamination." *Slavic Review* 59 (2000): 268–89.
> Part of a discussion involving Russian peasants and questions of citizenship during the war.

Seregny, Scott J. "Zemstvos, Peasants, and Citizenship: The Russian Adult Education Movement and World War I." *Slavic Review* 59 (2000): 290–315.
> Part of a discussion involving Russian peasants and questions of citizenship during the war.

Stone, Norman. *The Eastern Front: 1914–1918.* London: Hodder and Stoughton, 1975.
> Classic military account of the eastern front.

Wildman, A. K. *The End of the Russian Imperial Army.* 2 vols. Princeton, NJ: Princeton University Press, 1980, 1987.
> A social history of the Russian army at war.

Winter, Jay. *Sites of Memory, Sites of Mourning: The Great War in European Cultural History.* Cambridge: The Press Syndicate of the University of Cambridge, 1995.
> An interesting exploration of the cultural effects of the war on western Europe.

6

The Russian Revolution and Civil War, 1917–1921

INTRODUCTION

"Preposterous!"

Most assuredly that would have been the astonished response of most observers of the Russian scene at the start of the twentieth century had they been told that within two decades the Bolsheviks would rule Russia. In 1900 those who would deceptively come to call themselves Bolsheviks ("men of the majority") were part of the Russian Social Democratic Labor Party (SD), an illegal revolutionary movement that barely registered on the consciousness of politically aware Russians.

The origins of Russian social democracy can be traced back to George V. Plekhanov, a radical intellectual of noble birth who in the early 1880s drifted away from the Socialist Revolutionary (SR) movement, or Populism, because he disagreed with its use of terror as a weapon. Furthermore, he rejected the fundamental SR belief that the Russian peasantry was an unstoppable juggernaut of revolution. Casting about for a new theory of revolution, Plekhanov hit upon Marxism. From his exile in Switzerland, in 1883 Plekhanov founded Liberation of Labor, the first Russian Marxist movement.

The voluminous writings of Karl Marx—although often confusing and contradictory—consistently and clearly identify the working class, or proletariat, as the most vital revolutionary force. According to Marx, the bourgeoisie, or the owners of the industrial means of production, will invariably exploit the proletariat for financial gain. The distressed proletariat will rise

On November 7, 1917, Bolshevik forces successfully stormed the Winter Palace and seized control of Russia. The Bolshevik triumph, achieved against daunting odds, inaugurated 74 years of sometimes tumultuous communist rule in Russia. (Reproduced from the Collections of the Library of Congress.)

up against the bourgeoisie, and although it may suffer many setbacks, it will eventually triumph, and in victory it will usher in a revolutionary socioeconomic system based on the principal of socialism, or the collective ownership of the means of production. Marx's ideas had been coursing through Europe since the middle of the nineteenth century, penetrating Russia in the 1870s, but for Russia it was Plekhanov who organized the Marxist movement.

Marxism envisions a working class that is both large and class-conscious, and for a long time Russia's working class was neither. However, Russia's industrial development during the last decades of the nineteenth century signaled a change. Although Russia remained overwhelmingly agrarian, pockets of industrial concentration began to appear, especially around St. Petersburg, Moscow, Kiev, and Warsaw. With industrialization came a mercilessly exploited working class and, consequently, fertile soil for Marx's ideas.

The paucity of Russian workers was not the only obstacle to social democracy's success. The tsarist police frowned upon any organized activity not under governmental control, regardless of its ultimate objective. Russian Marxists were harassed, arrested, and exiled with monotonous regularity. Finally, like all Russian radical organizations at the start of the twentieth century, the SDs spent considerable time and energy combating other radical organizations and arguing incessantly within their own ranks.

For the SDs, this internecine warfare reached a climax in 1903 at a gathering billed as the Second Congress of the Russian Social Democratic Labor Party, held, tellingly, in London. There, the SDs formally organized themselves and then split into two competing factions over the issues of party membership and the road to socialism. The Bolsheviks, led by the dynamic intellectual Vladimir I. Lenin, insisted upon a small, tightly knit party composed of dedicated revolutionaries; the Mensheviks ("men of the minority") opted for a more inclusive approach.

Despite their obvious problems, the SDs in general and the Bolsheviks in particular possessed some important assets. To begin with, the SD leadership cadre was excellent. Figures such as Plekhanov, Julius O. Martov, Leon D. Trotsky, and especially Lenin possessed real intelligence as well as organizational and propagandistic skills. Moreover, the SDs were a dedicated bunch. Struggling against long odds and an ubiquitous tsarist police force, the SD cadres consistently exhibited determination, conviction, and fierce loyalty to the cause. And that cause—a Marxist vision of the future in which a dictatorship of the proletariat would ensure the collective ownership of the means of production—provided a clear and compelling purpose for these revolutionaries. Finally, the SDs, especially the Bolsheviks, were very well organized. For the Bolsheviks, this was both a practical and an ideological necessity, but it paid huge dividends when Russia dissolved into chaos during World War I.

During 1905, all of Russia's radical groups participated in that year's revolution. As might be expected, the SDs concentrated on organizing the urban labor force. As the revolution moved toward a climax, soviets, or councils, of workers' deputies formed in Russia's major cities. The most important soviet appeared in St. Petersburg, where Trotsky played a leading role in its activities. The government's October Manifesto contained a number of concessions, thereby splitting the revolutionaries. Most accepted the manifesto; others, such as the soviets and SDs, demanded imperial Russia's destruction, a call that fell on increasingly deaf ears. In December the authorities destroyed the Moscow Soviet at the cost of perhaps one thousand dead. Trotsky and other SD leaders either fled into exile or were arrested and deported to Siberia.

With the end of the 1905 Revolution, radical fortunes in Russia declined. A reinvigorated tsarist government led by Peter A. Stolypin cracked down on dissidents of all shades, and the forces of revolution seemed confused, divided, and demoralized. The SD leadership functioned from abroad: Lenin on the run for quite a while before coming to roost in Switzerland; Trotsky in Vienna and briefly in New York, where he had a bit role in an early American film; and Plekhanov in Switzerland. Smaller SD fry continued to agitate with slight success among the Russian workers, whereas others, such as Joseph V. Stalin, carried out robberies to generate money for the cause, thus earning for themselves a stay in Siberia. Trotsky estimated that by 1910 there were barely 10,000 active Bolsheviks, and a number of those were police informants. More time was now spent wrangling over the intricacies of Marxist theory than challenging the tsarist regime.

The onset of World War I split the international socialist movement. Although most socialists placed patriotism before class-consciousness, others such as Lenin saw the war as an opportunity for the working class to rise up and destroy capitalism. Nevertheless, as the war dragged on and the proletariat remained quiescent, even the most dedicated Marxists began to despair. For example, early in 1917 the 46-year-old Lenin wrote that it was unlikely that his generation of revolutionaries would "live to see the decisive battles of the approaching revolution." Needless to say, the collapse of the tsarist state in March 1917 caught Lenin by surprise.

With the assistance of Germany, who wanted to undermine Russia's war effort, Lenin returned to Russia. Upon his arrival at Petrograd's Finland Station on April 16, 1917, he found a skeleton Bolshevik organization led by young and inexperienced revolutionaries including Viacheslav M. Molotov, who would later be Joseph Stalin's foreign minister. Lenin immediately set a radical course. In his "April Theses" he denounced those who would cooperate with more moderate, albeit revolutionary, Russians, condemned the war as a capitalist adventure, proclaimed the advent of socialism in Russia, and declared that the events in Russia had inaugurated a "worldwide socialist revolution." Subsequently, he co-opted the slogan "peace, bread, and land" and demanded "all power to the soviets."

The fall of the tsarist government had led to the rebirth of the soviets. Serving as an umbrella organization for Russia's radical intellectuals, the Soviets of Workers' and Soldiers' Deputies also included—as the name indicated—disgruntled workers and peasants and politically active soldiers. The soviets competed for power with the Provisional Government, the putative successor government to the toppled autocracy that was made up chiefly of moderates, many of whom had served in the last Duma, or legislature. Initially, the Bolsheviks did not dominate the soviets, but they did make their presence known with their extreme agenda.

Throughout the spring and early summer, the soviets and the Provisional Government struggled for control of a Russia that was fast becoming a corpse thanks to the ongoing war and the growing chaos within the country. As the Provisional Government steadily moved toward the political left, the soviets moved even further leftward at an accelerating pace. The Bolsheviks, who encouraged the leftward movement of the soviets, saw their ranks expand a bit as they now began to play a more prominent role in the soviet decision-making process. Still, the Bolsheviks were far from commanding the soviets.

In July 1917 Petrograd erupted in two days of violence. The capital city's more extreme elements took to the streets, whipped into a frenzy in part by Bolshevik propaganda. This rioting, known as the "July Days," quickly petered out, but the Bolsheviks, who did not quite know how to respond to this spontaneous outburst, now found themselves targeted by the Provisional Government. Their newspaper, *Pravda,* was shut down and their offices seized. Leaders such as Trotsky were arrested, and others, including Lenin, fled. Lenin later described the July Days as "something more than a demonstration and less than a revolution."

Fortunately for the Bolsheviks, the Provisional Government proved to be weak and inept. Two months after the July Days, fear of a coup from the right panicked the Provisional Government into releasing Bolsheviks from prison and arming their militia, the Red Guard, in order to "protect the revolution." Meanwhile, thanks to their radical positions, the Bolsheviks increased their standing with the people of Petrograd, and by early September, they had gained control of that city's soviet.

Lenin now worked feverishly to bring down the Provisional Government and claim Russia for the Bolsheviks. Against the advice of many of his closest collaborators, Lenin insisted that the time was ripe for the long-awaited Marxist revolution. His views carried the day, and his optimism was rewarded when the Bolsheviks toppled the friendless Provisional Government on November 7, 1917.

The Bolsheviks were now in charge of Russia, but the revolution was far from over. Almost immediately, Russia's new masters initiated a series of fundamental reforms. Under Lenin's guidance, the victorious Bolsheviks quickly nationalized the banking industry and transportation; turned the factories over to the workers; issued the Decree on Land permitting the peasants to seize estates belonging to the nobility, church, and royal family; made foreign trade a state monopoly; provided for the election of army officers; recast the judicial system; abolished titles and ranks; confiscated property belonging to the well-to-do; outlawed all other political parties; declared the separation of church and state and seized church property; and converted the calendar to the more modern Gregorian version.

After concluding that the Bolsheviks had no chance of retaining power unless they devoted all their time and energy to the task, Lenin insisted that negotiations between Bolshevik Russia and Germany open in December. When it became apparent that a victorious Germany intended to claim its spoils of war, Trotsky, the frustrated Bolshevik representative, declared a policy of "no war, no peace." Angered by this response, Germany resumed its drive to the east. At this juncture, Lenin demanded that Russia accept Germany's terms. Drawing upon all of his prestige and authority, Lenin barely managed to convince the Bolshevik leadership to support him. The result was the March 1918 Treaty of Brest-Litovsk, an utter disaster for Russia that—luckily for the Russians—was nullified by the Western allies' subsequent defeat of Germany.

Lenin's argument for accepting Brest-Litovsk rested on his belief that the Bolsheviks needed a "breathing space" in order to cement their grip on power. However, a few weeks after signing the treaty, Russia plunged into civil war. The "Whites," or those opposed to the Bolsheviks, gradually morphed into a reactionary, nationalistic force that held the periphery of the old empire. Their retrograde vision of Russia's future, their contempt for Russia's minorities, and their lack of unity destroyed their chances for success despite the fact that several Western countries, including Great Britain, France, Japan, and the United States, entered the civil war on their side. Not only did this half-hearted intervention fail to bring a White victory, but it also inadvertently provided a rallying point for the Bolsheviks, who condemned the foreigners and portrayed the Whites as traitors to Mother Russia.

Initially, Bolshevik chances for success appeared slim. However, Leon Trotsky employed his exceptional organizational abilities to create a Bolshevik force, the Red Army, which proved to be formidable.

As the civil war raged, Lenin imposed War Communism, a Bolshevik initiative that combined elements of both total war and a rapid transformation to the Marxist ideal of collective ownership of the means of production. War Communism called for the nationalization of Russia's productive forces, requisitioning, rationing, conscription, and compulsory labor. A sprawling, inefficient, and obtuse bureaucracy arose to guide the economy. In the countryside, the Bolsheviks turned the peasants against each other, enlisting the poorest peasants in "committees of the poor" and pitting them against the *kulaks,* or better-off and thus "bourgeois" peasants.

To enforce iron discipline, the Bolsheviks created the Cheka under the leadership of the brutal Polish Communist Felix E. Dzerzhinsky.

By early spring 1921, the civil war was almost over and the triumphant Bolsheviks ruled Russia. One can only guess at the number of civil war dead, but no one doubts that the final figure reached into the millions. Nevertheless, this was a price the Bolsheviks were willing to pay for the triumph of their revolution.

INTERPRETIVE ESSAY
Barbara C. Allen

In 1917 Russia witnessed an uprising of the dispossessed and disenfranchised against the representatives of privilege. Long-standing peasant grievances, imperial overextension, the social stress of modernization, and a war-induced economic crisis culminated in political and social revolutions. The March Revolution brought down the tsarist regime, ending over 300 years of Romanov dynastic rule and ushering in a short-lived liberal leadership. The November Revolution brought to power the first self-proclaimed Communist government in world history. The Russian revolution inspired uprisings in developing countries, spurred reform in traditional liberal democracies, and influenced the rise of fascism in less stable democracies. The revolution's history has been the subject of much debate: Why did revolution occur in Russia in 1917? Did liberal democracy have a chance? How did the Bolsheviks come to power? What diverted the Bolsheviks from their course to create a fairer society based on the equitable distribution of goods? Did the Russian Revolution constitute a bold new social experiment, or was it merely a continuation of wartime violence and social breakdown? The revolutionary project in its liberal and socialist forms was undermined and shaped by two chief developments: war-induced economic crisis and a shortage of personnel capable of administering a modern state and economy.

On the eve of revolution, Russia was a world leader in culture, but its economic, social, and political development lagged behind. Russia had emancipated its serfs only in 1861; following emancipation, a host of other reforms had laid a weak foundation for the growth of professions and civil institutions in Russia. Reforms were frustrated by a conservative social system and reactionary rulers (Alexander III and Nicholas II) who barely managed to keep a lid on simmering social and political tensions. Large-scale industrialization beginning in the 1890s produced industrialists and managers, including foreigners as well as Russians, but it also generated sharp tensions between owners and workers. Although Russian industrial workers were a small percentage of the population (10 percent in 1917), they were concentrated in large factories in major cities and often came from the same hometowns or regions; thus, revolutionary propaganda circulated all the more easily among them. Little common ground could be found among members of liberal "society," urban laborers who sought better working conditions and higher pay, and the still overwhelmingly large numbers of rural people, who resented the small size of their landholdings, their high taxes, and bureaucratic interference in their lives.

World War I aggravated social and political tensions in Russia but gave Russians a common goal—to end tsarist rule. The war overstrained Russia's transportation, fuel, and food-distribution systems. Russia's disastrous defeats at the hands of Germany devastated Russian soldiers' morale. Perhaps two million Russian soldiers died during the war, and there were 7.5 million casualties, thereby feeding the universal impression that the government placed little value on combatants' lives. Demoralized soldiers played a crucial role in the revolution. Radical socialists decried the war as an imperialist slaughter and illegally met, organized, and agitated among garrison soldiers as well as among industrial workers and peasants. Russian liberals strove to set up organizations to cope with Russia's wartime crises, but faced enormous obstacles in doing so from the tsarist government's aging and conservative ministers. This provoked a Duma leader, Paul N. Miliukov, to ask in November 1916 whether the government was guilty of "treason or stupidity." Thus, liberals threw their support behind the same short-term goal as Russian socialists: the end of the autocracy, not merely its modification. Even conservatives had tired of the tsar's incompetence in military matters. By early 1917, the tsar had lost the support of the forces of order in the army, police, and bureaucracy.

In March 1917, the crisis broke in Petrograd, the capital, a northern city with dire supply problems because of its distance from Russia's agricultural regions and the drastic wartime reduction in sea shipping. No party or group planned or organized the March revolution. Rather, the catalyst was women workers' protests over food shortages. Beginning on March 8, women, who bore the double burden of working outside the home and providing for their families, called on male factory workers, who had just reluctantly returned to work after a failed strike to join them in taking to the streets to demand greater access to food. Protests then spread to students, to middle-class professionals, and finally to the Petrograd garrison. Even members of the military high command and top liberal members of the government began to see this as an opportunity to achieve change in the management of the war. Russians mobilized to demand the tsar's abdication because this step seemed to be the single solution to a multitude of problems.

Tsar Nicholas II had no choice but to abdicate for himself and his son (the family was eventually executed in July 1918). It appeared that the Russians finally had their chance for popular democratic rule. Nevertheless, ominous signs of future conflict appeared as nascent representative institutions formed along class lines. In Petrograd, "dual power" emerged. The Duma extended power to rule to the Provisional Government. The Provisional Government assumed authority over government ministries, direction of the war, foreign trade, and the Petrograd city bureaucracy and municipal government. At first, liberal Constitutional Democrats (Kadets) prevailed in the Provisional Government. The Kadets were talented leaders, but they had little support outside the rather tiny group of wealthy Russian industrialists and educated professionals. They sought to continue the war to victory and were reluctant to define the nature of Russia's primitive political system or promulgate social reforms (a shorter working day, higher wages, unemployment insurance) until a Constituent Assembly could be held to write a constitution defining Russia's form of government. Despite the importance the Provisional Government placed on the Constituent Assembly, it kept postponing elections. The Kadets more than any other party shaped the Provisional Government's policy and acted as if they constituted a legitimate government, rebuffing the popular soviets' attempts to co-govern.

The Petrograd Soviet representing workers and soldiers intruded into the Provisional Government's affairs, assuming oversight of city functions, transportation, food distribution, and housing and commanding the crucial allegiance of garrison soldiers. The Soviet was dominated by moderate socialists such as the Socialist Revolutionaries and the Menshevik faction of the Russian Social Democratic Labor Party (SD). The greatest support belonged to the Socialist Revolutionaries (SRs), who expanded the definition of an exploited class to include peasants as well as workers and the definition of exploiters to include landowners along with capitalists. Their program advocated a democratic republic and socialization and equal distribution of the land to those who tilled it. Their tactics ranged from organization and propaganda to terrorism; they had no central organization. One of their leaders, Alexander F. Kerensky, became head of the Provisional Government in spring 1917. SR leaders joined liberals in seeking to continue the war to victory and were opposed to the quick introduction of social reforms. In fall elections to the Constituent Assembly, the SRs would win the largest number of votes. Mensheviks in early 1917 were influential in the country's numerous soviets and trade unions; they largely favored working with the Provisional Government and agreed with Kadets on allowing a Constituent Assembly to decide Russia's future form of government. Nevertheless, they pressed for social reforms. The soviets did not challenge the Provisional Government for power because moderate socialists thought a socialist revolution was premature.

Outside Petrograd, government varied. In many areas of European Russia, public committees representing political parties, legal workers' organizations, professionals, and the middle class took charge. Kadets usually controlled the public committees. Simultaneously, soviets of workers and sometimes soldiers' deputies were formed. Street demonstrations typically followed the formation of these new institutions. In rural areas, tsarist-era police and courts disappeared, and peasant adult males (and sometimes females) elected village committees to make decisions for their communities. Minority nationalist governments took charge in outlying regions and clashed with ethnically Russian workers' soviets.

Despite these harbingers of future conflict, a great deal of optimism existed in Russia in the early months of revolution. For the first time in their history, Russians had freedom of speech, organization, and press. Newspapers sprouted like mushrooms, championing a wide range of views. Formerly banned political parties began operating openly; socialist leaders who had fled or been exiled returned; trade unions that had been shut down now reorganized. Membership in parties, unions, and other civic organizations soared. Urban women created groups to press for women's political rights and social progress. Moreover, new organizations called factory committees formed, championing the workers' right to supervise factory directors and managers to ensure that workers were not arbitrarily laid off or deprived of pay.

But continued economic crises played an immense role in the fluctuating fortunes of political parties. Bottlenecks remained in transportation, fuel supply, and food distribution. Inflation rose. Factory directors laid off workers and refused to grant wage increases. Inflation discouraged peasants from marketing their produce. Peasants took advantage of the rural power vacuum to seize and redistribute land. The peasant revolution had military repercussions as peasant soldiers eagerly returned home to take their portions of land. This was not simply a matter of laying down arms and voting with their feet. Soldiers left the front in bands, taking their weapons with them and wreaking havoc on the way. Some never returned to farming, remaining instead in large bandit groups that contributed to the general disorder during the revolutions and civil war. Soldiers who helped set up new revolutionary governments often had participated in crime-like violence; demarcating a line between thuggery and revolution was difficult, especially in the traditionally anarchic Russian borderlands.

Economic crisis increased support for radical leftists such as the Bolshevik faction of the SDs and leftists among SRs and Mensheviks, especially in important political and industrial centers and in large garrisons. Radicals thought revolution was the only way to bring true social, economic, and political change to Russia, but they disagreed over when and how to take power. Before returning to Russia, the Bolshevik leader Vladimir I. Lenin had called for an immediate seizure of power; however, after his April arrival in Petrograd, he called instead for a transfer of power to the soviets. The triumph of the radicals over the more moderate revolutionaries would be a critical development among the Bolsheviks, as would the decision of radicals from other socialist parties to cast their lot with the Bolsheviks. Both the Bolsheviks and the leftist SRs appropriated the basic demands of the rural and urban dispossessed by calling for bread, workers' supervision of the factories, land for the peasants, an end to the war, and all power to the soviets. The trick was in defining exactly what "power to the soviets" meant.

Despite their differences, revolutionary socialists continued to cooperate and even maintain common organizations outside Moscow and Petrograd. Support increased for the socialists in all their guises. In order to give the Provisional Government more popular legitimacy, in spring 1917 its leaders invited moderate socialists to share power. In the long run, this step did little to reinforce the government's authority; instead, it only associated moderate socialists with unpopular policies. Foremost among these was the government's determination to continue the war. Radical leftists in the SR and Menshevik parties began to desert their moderate leaders. By summer 1917, leftist SRs had already become an independent force. Meanwhile, the Bolsheviks stayed outside government and avoided being associated with the decision to remain in the war.

Kerensky's Provisional Government precipitated a revolutionary crisis in July 1917 when it ordered a major military offensive. This caused alarm in Petrograd, with soldiers of the garrison fearing dispatch to the front; their fear increased all the more when news spread that Kerensky had reinstated the death penalty at the front. Radical Bolshevik activists incited both soldiers and workers; however, Lenin worried that the Bolsheviks had no support among peasants. Nevertheless, party leaders were forced to take nominal charge of the July Days uprising even though they had little control over it. The uprising's failure was sealed when the Provisional Government effectively slandered the Bolsheviks as German agents. In the wake of the July Days, Bolsheviks were jailed, other radical leftists were persecuted, Lenin fled the capital, and Bolshevik party operations were temporarily disorganized. But the crisis continued, and even some Kadets began to advocate military dictatorship.

Military dictatorship appeared likely to come from General Lavr G. Kornilov, whom Kerensky had named supreme commander in an attempt to prevent the military from falling apart. However, Kerensky relieved Kornilov of his duty when he suspected the general of seeking to overthrow the government. When Kornilov began marching Cossack divisions toward Petrograd in September, soldiers and workers rallied under radical socialist leadership to thwart Kornilov's plans. They encountered his troops along railway lines and persuaded them to halt. The attempted coup discredited the Provisional Government and its moderate socialist leadership and enhanced the radical socialists; in fall elections to the soviets, the radicals—Left SRs and Bolsheviks—gained delegates.

In Petrograd and Moscow, moderates and reactionaries began to fear a leftist coup, and Lenin urged his fellow Bolsheviks to seize power, even though many of them feared another disaster like the July uprising. This time, however, radical Bolsheviks in trade unions had become disillusioned with the lack of progress in talks with factory owners on wage agreements. Therefore, they swung their support behind Lenin's proposal to seize power, but only in the name of the Second All-Russian Congress of Soviets. In opposition to most Bolshevik leaders, Lenin insisted on taking power before the Congress would meet in order to send a signal abroad and encourage uprisings in other combatant countries.

As the crisis deepened, Lenin gained support; however, some moderates within the Petrograd Soviet cooperated with Kerensky in preparing to suppress the Bolsheviks. They feared that radicals would take control of the Soviet, and they wanted Kerensky to close the Bolsheviks' printing press and dissolve the radical Military Revolutionary Committee (MRC) of the Soviet, which seemed likely to do the Bolsheviks' bidding. Leon D. Trotsky, a former Menshevik who joined the Bolsheviks in 1917, was a key figure within the MRC, which included leftist SRs and anarchists as well as Bolsheviks. After Kerensky ordered the closure of the Bolshevik printing press and prepared to move against the MRC, Lenin gave free rein to his supporters in the MRC to rise. The insurrection began as a defensive move, but quickly escalated. The MRC enlisted loyal troops to seize key transport and communications points and only then took action against the government.

Thus, in November 1917, the Bolsheviks and their radical leftist allies seized executive power on the eve of the Congress of Soviets. Outraged moderate socialists (Mensheviks and mainstream SRs) abandoned the Soviet in protest as Trotsky called after them to "go . . . into the dustbin of history." The SRs expelled their leftists for siding with the Bolsheviks, and the leftists became a separate party. Thus, the moderates surrendered control of the upcoming congress to the Bolsheviks and Left SRs. Did this represent a lost possibility for democracy in Russia? It is questionable: moderates sometimes used undemocratic methods, but did so far less consistently than did radicals who scorned compromise and tolerance.

The first government formed by the Soviet, the Council of People's Commissars (Sovnarkom), was composed exclusively of Bolsheviks. Lenin resisted coalition government, but other Bolsheviks thought that workers and soldiers would not support a solely Bolshevik dictatorship. When the Union of Railway Workers, dominated by Left SRs, threatened a devastating strike unless a coalition government of all parties in the Soviet was formed, negotiations began over Lenin's objections. However, these talks broke down when moderates insisted that Lenin and Trotsky not sit in the new government. Nevertheless, after failure of these talks, Left SRs agreed to join the Bolsheviks in governing. This was enough to convince many Bolsheviks that coalition had been achieved.

The Second Congress of Soviets quickly issued a series of decrees that indicated its support for key popular demands: peace, socialization of land, the eight-hour day, abolition of capital punishment, and workers' supervision of industry. The Congress reiterated the Soviet's support for convening a Constituent Assembly. The Decree on Land came directly from the SRs' program; as Marxists, the Bolsheviks opposed private property ownership and so favored nationalization of land. However, the Bolsheviks did not have the power to enforce nationalization of land; moreover, to many of them, it was not clear what form common owner-ship of land should take. Socialization of land, on the contrary, allowed peasant communes to take possession of land and dispose of it as they wished. Thus, the Bolshevik stance was both a concession to the Left SRs and a legitimization of what peasants were already doing. It guaranteed peasants that the new government would not take the land away from them, thus defusing much potential peasant resistance.

As with the Decree on Land, the Decree on Workers' Supervision confirmed a process that was already underway. In the industrial econ-omy, the balance of power had swung in favor of trade unions and factory committees. As factory owners and engineers (especially foreigners) fled the revolution's chaos, these workers' organizations took over factory operations and sought government support to keep factories running. Despite changes in ownership and management, workers, managers, and revolutionaries faced the same obstacles in maintaining production that had plagued former owners.

Bolsheviks debated how much to rely on administrative and technical personnel who had served the tsarist and interim governments or worked for private industry. Some factory directors and engineers remained in their jobs and cooperated with workers' representatives; some joined new government commissariats and worked with radicals, who had mixed feelings about their presence. The Bolsheviks, or Reds, found former managers' expertise useful, but suspected their loyalty because they were former agents of "capital." Skilled administrators and managers were urgently needed, and the new government faced a bureaucrats' strike as soon as it claimed power. The new commissars used various methods in dealing with this strike; responses ranged from coercion or intimidation to persuasion, negotiation, and finding alternative sources of personnel (trade unions were one source). Commissars disagreed on how to eliminate resistance to the new government. A hard line, of which Trotsky was a key proponent, carried the day.

A similarly hard line was followed in politics. Three events signified the hard-liners' strength and set the stage for future repression: creation of the Cheka, suppression of the Kadet Party, and dispersal of the Constituent Assembly. The Cheka, created in December 1917 to combat counterrevolution and sabotage, quickly became a political and economic police force. Cheka terror intensified after an attempt to assassinate Lenin in August 1918. The banning of the Kadet Party set the stage for the proscription of political parties other than the Bolsheviks. The Bolsheviks, who distrusted parliamentary government as less "democratic" than the soviets, initially soft-pedaled their stance toward the Constituent Assembly. However, the Left SRs insisted that the assembly proceed, and the Bolsheviks feared how the country might react to a failure to convene it. Nevertheless, by the time the Constituent Assembly met in January 1918, the general public had become largely apathetic toward it, underlining the weakness of Russia's civil society. Peasants cared chiefly about the new government's legitimization of their seizure of land. Thus, Bolsheviks and some Left SRs easily shut down the Assembly. Only subsequently would it become clear that the Assembly's dispersal marked a key step on the Bolsheviks' road to dictatorship. Those Bolsheviks who supported a broad coalition government in November had lost their resolve and succumbed to the desire to hold on to power.

There was not a straight line between early political repression and the consolidation of Bolshevik dictatorship. Rather, persecution of non-Bolshevik political parties and suppression of individual freedoms fluctuated. For example, Left SRs were banned and legalized several times during the civil war that followed the Bolshevik seizure of power. Nevertheless, by 1922 only the Bolshevik Party, or Communist Party of the Soviet Union (CPSU), was permitted. As other socialist parties were banned, some of their members joined the Bolsheviks, who in March 1918 renamed themselves the Communists. Others remained politically active as independent and unaffiliated socialists. The Bolsheviks suppressed "bourgeois" newspapers but did not maintain a consistent policy toward non-Bolshevik socialist publications. Press restrictions were relaxed several times during the civil war.

The Communists (Bolsheviks) worked to assert party control over rival centers of power. In particular, trade unions and factory committees posed a challenge. In 1917, Mensheviks, whose policies were relatively moderate, led many trade unions. Before the November Revolution, even the large metalworkers' union, the most Bolshevized of unions, concentrated mainly on negotiating a wage agreement with factory owners in order to organize workers. The Communists accomplished their takeover of the trade unions in various ways, including elections, as was the case with the metalworkers' union, and, in other instances, simply by appointing leaders. However, in some unions, such as the railway workers', independent attitudes remained strong, and the Communists had to resort to forcible reorganization.

Despite the Decree on Peace, Germany continued to press Russia; its advance toward Petrograd threatened the new government's survival. Consequently, the Communists moved the capital to Moscow and evacuated government institutions and much industry from Petrograd to other industrialized areas of Russia. Although Petrograd remained an important political and industrial center, it was now second to Moscow. With their move to Moscow, the Communists commanded the hub of Russia's railway transportation, a factor that would contribute to their civil war victory. Moreover, advanced working-class cadres of the revolution in Petrograd were dispersed across Russia and so had less influence on Communist leaders and policy. Those who were transferred to administrative positions in Moscow soon confronted the traditionally intransigent attitudes of Moscow's lower-level bureaucracy.

Facing continued German invasion and occupation, on March 3, 1918, Communist leaders signed the Treaty of Brest-Litovsk, which stripped Russia of its Baltic territories and much of Belorussia and Ukraine. Having taken power during an unpopular war against a more powerful enemy, the Communists had to ensure the survival of their revolution. Despite his calls before the revolution to turn the imperialist war into a civil war between the proletariat and bourgeoisie in all combatant countries, Lenin pragmatically advocated a treaty with the Germans to end the war and allow the Communists time to consolidate their political control. Other more idealistic Communists opposed peace and wanted to call on the German proletariat to rise up against its rulers. The Left SRs agreed with those Communists who opposed the Brest-Litovsk peace. Although dissatisfied Communists eventually came into line, the Left SRs protested by leaving the government. Their departure left only the Communists in power, but the government still included many who had been Mensheviks, Left SRs, and unaffiliated socialists in 1917 and before. After departing the government, the Left SRs undertook a campaign of violence aimed at forcing changes in Communist policies. As was the case in their struggle against the tsarist government, they resorted to terror. This campaign included the July 1918 assassination of Count Wilhelm Mirbach, the German ambassador, and a nearly successful attempt on Lenin himself. Subsequently, the Left SRs were banned.

Although they had extricated Russia from the war, the Communists still faced the challenge of a deteriorating economy. Economic problems that had contributed to the tsarist government's fall and the Communists' rise were exacerbated by the outbreak of civil war. Hostilities started in May 1918 when Czech prisoners of war, whom the tsarist government had organized into the Czech Legion, began an uprising on the Trans-Siberian railroad. During the summer, former tsarist generals began to form White armies. Right SRs created governments in Siberia, and Allied states (Great Britain, the United States, France, and Japan) sent forces to Russia in order to protect Allied military stores there. However, some Allied agents attempted to overthrow the Communist government.

The Communists responded by organizing a Red Army in May 1918 after Trotsky decided a conventional army would be more effective than the existing decentralized conglomeration of Red Guards and other radical militias. When insufficient numbers of volunteers enlisted, Trotsky introduced conscription. Harsh discipline included execution, and tsarist officers were used in command positions, with their families held hostage to ensure their loyalty. Thus, the Red Army hardly resembled the army that revolutionaries had envisioned in 1917, the army that was supposed to feature abolition of ranks, election of officers, and the end of corporal and capital punishment.

In fighting the civil war, the Communists had far more advantages than did their enemies. They controlled the center of the country and thus the hub of transportation and communications. Although they constantly complained of problems in these sectors, they were more successful in ferrying troops and supplies from the center to outlying regions than were the Whites in doing so across regions. The Red Army was larger than the counterrevolutionary forces—five million soldiers versus the Whites' two million. The Reds' centralized military organizations were an advantage. White generals were geographically isolated and often riven by personal rivalries; the Communists' opponents were also politically divided. Most White generals were nationalists and favored either military dictatorship or monarchy; they would not concede to minority nationalities' dreams of independence. Other opponents of the Communists included liberals and moderate socialists who could find little ground in common with White generals. Communists were by no means monolithic, but they were more united than were their enemies.

Peasants played an important but not decisive role in the civil war. On one hand, they feared the loss of the land they had seized if traditional forces proved victorious; on the other hand, Communist actions had alienated them, especially an emergency measure providing for the seizure of peasant grain in order to feed the urban population. This measure provoked violent resistance from peasants as early as 1918, and peasant uprisings intensified greatly toward the end of the civil war. However, this challenge to the Communists did not tip the scales in favor of the Whites. A third force in the civil war was the Greens, peasant bands largely active in Cossack regions of southern Russia and Ukraine. Some of these professed to be anarchists, but in practice, they robbed, looted, and fought with both Reds and Whites.

Despite military success, the Communists continued to face economic problems. For example, the transportation and supply bottlenecks that had helped to bring down the tsarist and provisional governments also posed tremendous challenges to the Communists. During the civil war, Communist economic policy blended utopian urges with everyday rationalism. There was an urgent need to bring order to an economy disrupted by war and by the flight of capital and skilled managers and engineers. Nationalization of industry in the summer of 1918 put industrial employees on the government payroll. Sinking enterprises came under government protection, thereby draining state resources. With rising inflation, the currency rapidly lost value, and the economy became based on rationing, barter, and the black market. Under the pressures of civil war, the Communists resorted to a command mode rather than enlisting initiatives from below in order to stabilize the chaotic economy. Command became the prevailing tendency not only in the military, but also in politics and the economy.

In distributing scarce resources, military personnel and party and state administrators received highest priority. Industrial workers were supposed to receive priority over other workers, but in reality, personnel in supply offices and in transportation and distribution centers often siphoned off supplies before they reached the workers. Thus, discontent among workers grew during the civil war over shortages of basic necessities and over corruption among party elites. During 1920–1921, the number of strikes grew. Although strike demands usually were not anti-Communist, they had the potential to become so. In Petrograd and Moscow, party leaders usually defused worker discontent by scrambling to obtain necessary items, but in other areas, party leaders and Red Army commanders blamed worker discontent on counterrevolutionaries, foreign agents, and "backward" elements and suppressed workers' uprisings with great force.

Growing tensions between Communist leaders and workers gave rise to debates within the party over the best way to ensure the revolution remained on track and did not fall into the hands of "bureaucracy." Lenin firmly believed that the party had to control all other institutions, but that workers' organizations—under party control—should review the work of government institutions and expose corruption and red tape. Some trade union leaders advocated strengthening trade unions' role in directing and managing the economy, given that trade unions by definition were composed of and controlled by workers. The party rejected this view and, instead, further subordinated trade unions to party authority. Party leaders portrayed workers in a new way; they claimed the working class had degenerated during the civil war and was no longer capable of being the beacon of revolution. Henceforth, workers needed to be "educated" before resuming this role.

Finding workers increasingly unreliable, Communist leaders turned more frequently to the Red Army, Russia's largest institution, which had successfully brought Ukraine, the Transcaucasus, Central Asia, and Siberia under Communist rule. Communists began to accept military intervention as a legitimate means of spreading their ideas. The Bolsheviks had taken power under the assumption that revolution in Russia would spark revolutions in the more advanced industrial powers such as Germany and England. But these hopes did not materialize; uprisings in central and eastern Europe were abortive, and labor unrest in western Europe did not coalesce into a movement capable of toppling the state. In 1919 the Red Army marched into Poland under the belief that oppressed Polish workers and poor peasants would rise against their native landowners. Instead, a nationalist resistance repelled the Red Army. Thus, at the end of the civil war, the Communists faced the prospect of long-term rule in a socialist country surrounded by hostile powers. This likelihood necessarily shaped their mentality. Service in the Red Army proved an important formative experience for those who would go on to staff the party, government, trade unions, and other essential institutions of Soviet power.

Coercion was proving to be a dangerous policy in the countryside, as peasant violence in response to grain requisitions increased in frequency and intensity. When resistance spread to the Kronstadt naval base just outside Petrograd, Communist leaders were alarmed. Kronstadt sailors had been at the forefront of revolutionary action in 1917, but because Left SRs dominated the Kronstadt Soviet, the Communists were wary. Although they suppressed the Kronstadt uprising, party leaders decided to mollify the peasantry by replacing grain requisitions with a tax-in-kind. From this initial step emerged the New Economic Policy (NEP), which until 1929 allowed limited private trade and small private enterprises.

Amid the social chaos of Russia's revolution and civil war, groups and individuals determined to remake Russian society on a more just basis emerged. Revolutionaries not only engaged in violence and expressed hatred of privilege but also demonstrated optimism, popular initiative, and the desire for autonomous organization. The revolutions of 1917 derived from the optimistic belief that popular forces could overcome the stagnation created by the conservative tsarist government's opposition to change. Both the highly educated and those schooled only in common sense displayed initiative in attempting to create a better life for themselves and their fellow Russians. Nevertheless, just as war's ruinous economic consequences served as the catalyst for revolutionary upheavals, war's violence and barbarism infiltrated the revolutionary project. Coercion appeared indispensable as the Communists faced difficulties implementing new policies because of the shortage of qualified personnel devoted to revolutionary change. Thus, the end result was dictatorship and the nullification of the revolutionary dreams of 1917.

SELECTED BIBLIOGRAPHY

Carr, E. H. *The Bolshevik Revolution, 1917–1923.* 3 vols. New York: Macmillan, 1951–1953.
    A classic study of domestic politics, the economy, and foreign policy in early Soviet Russia.
Fitzpatrick, Sheila. *The Russian Revolution.* New York: Oxford University Press, 1982.
    A concise study that takes a broad approach to the Russian Revolution, covering 1917, the civil war, NEP, and the radical break of 1929 (forced

collectivization and intensive industrialization). The author argues that the revolution ended when Stalin created a new elite in the 1930s.

Holquist, Peter. *Making War, Forging Revolution: Russia's Continuum of Crisis, 1914–1921*. Cambridge, MA: Harvard University Press, 2002.
A study of the Don Cossack region; approaches war, revolution, and civil war as a "continuum of violence."

Lih, Lars T. *Bread and Authority in Russia, 1914–1921*. Berkeley: University of California Press, 1990.
Groundbreaking study of the food-supply policies of the tsarist government, the Provisional Government, and the Bolsheviks. Lih is the first scholar to make a case for viewing the period from 1914 to 1921 as one of continuity. He sees the problem of food supply as a formative influence on the Communist regime.

Lincoln, W. Bruce. *Red Victory: A History of the Russian Civil War*. New York: Simon and Schuster, 1989.
A highly compelling narrative of the Russian Civil War designed for a popular audience.

Pipes, Richard. *The Russian Revolution*. New York: Knopf, 1990.
An engaging narrative offering a conservative view of the Russian Revolution. Pipes argues that the Bolsheviks seized power in a coup and proceeded to tear apart Russian society in order to establish a dictatorship.

Rabinowitch, Alexander. *The Bolsheviks Come to Power: The Revolution of 1917 in Petrograd*. New York: Norton, 1976, reprinted by Pluto Press, 2004.
Well-researched, detailed, and fast-paced account of how the Bolsheviks seized power in Petrograd in 1917. Rabinowitch demonstrates that the Bolsheviks in 1917 were flexible and responsive to the desires of the urban population.

Raleigh, Donald J. *Experiencing Russia's Civil War: Politics, Society and Revolutionary Culture in Saratov, 1917–1922*. Princeton, NJ: Princeton University Press, 2003.
A study of the civil war in a provincial city; Raleigh concludes that the civil war was formative for the Soviet system and that it created conditions that blinded Bolsheviks to nonauthoritarian alternatives and contained the seeds of Stalinism.

Rosenberg, William. *Liberals in the Russian Revolution: The Constitutional Democratic Party, 1917–1921*. Princeton, NJ: Princeton University Press, 1974.
The author traces the Kadets' decisions and actions during the revolution and explains their failure in terms of their small constituency, the nature of modernization in Russia, and their insistence on maintaining positions on land distribution and war that in 1917 were at variance with the desires of the majority of the population.

Sanborn, Joshua. *Drafting the Russian Nation: Military Conscription, Total War, and Mass Politics, 1905–1925*. DeKalb: Northern Illinois University Press, 2003.
Argues for a close connection between mass politics and mass killing as both the tsarist government and the Bolsheviks strove to create a citizens' army and define the nation.

Smith, S. A. *The Russian Revolution: A Very Short Introduction*. New York: Oxford University Press, 2002.

Employing a Marxist approach, the author sees revolution as an experiment in modernization that failed to liberate human beings from oppression.

Steinberg, Mark D. *Voices of Revolution, 1917.* New Haven, CT: Yale University Press, 2001.

This collection of documents reveals how ordinary Russians experienced and perceived the revolution.

Stites, Richard. *Revolutionary Dreams: Utopian Vision and Experimental Life in the Russian Revolution.* New York: Oxford University Press, 1989.

Explores revolutionary experimentation in culture and shows how Bolshevik authoritarianism prevailed over popular libertarian trends.

Sukhanov, Nikolai. *The Russian Revolution, 1917, a Personal Record.* Edited, abridged, and translated by Joel Carmichael. New York: Oxford University Press, 1955.

The Menshevik leader of the Petrograd Soviet provides a compelling eyewitness account of the revolution.

Wade, Rex. *The Russian Revolution, 1917.* Cambridge: Cambridge University Press, 2000.

The most recent, thorough, and clearly written synthesis of new research findings on the political and social history of 1917 Russia.

Wood, Elizabeth A. *The Baba and the Comrade: Gender and Politics in Revolutionary Russia.* Bloomington: Indiana University Press, 1997.

Wood studies the women's section in the Russian Communist Party, focusing on the interaction between Bolshevik state-building and Bolshevik policies toward and perceptions of women.

7

The Stalin Era, 1928–1953

INTRODUCTION

Perhaps the most consequential figure in twentieth-century Russian history was not even a Russian. Joseph V. Stalin, the Soviet-era dictator who ruled with an iron fist, was born Josip Dzhugashvili in 1879 in Gori, a small village not far from Tbilisi, the capital of Georgia, then part of the Russian Empire. He was the son of a violent, alcoholic shoemaker and a pious mother. Only after becoming an active revolutionary did he adopt the pseudonym Stalin, meaning man of steel, and throughout his life, he spoke Russian with a thick, almost unintelligible Georgian accent. Sent by his mother to an Orthodox seminary in preparation for a career as a priest, he was expelled in 1899 and soon gravitated into the ranks of the Bolsheviks. For a number of years, he labored for the Marxist cause, even going so far as to rob banks in order to fill the party's coffers. For his pains, he was repeatedly arrested and exiled to Siberia, from where he would escape to resume his activities. Although Stalin occasionally traveled abroad, he was one of the few future Bolshevik leaders who did not spend significant time in European exile.

When the Russian Empire collapsed in 1917, Stalin, who was in exile in Siberia, hurried back to Petrograd, where he attached himself to Vladimir I. Lenin. Characterized by humility, constancy, and retiring behavior in the midst of a unique collection of egomaniacs, Stalin was also exceptionally industrious, efficient, and thorough. Not surprisingly,

Joseph V. Stalin (foreground) viewed his colleague, Sergei M. Kirov, head of the Leningrad Communist Party, with growing suspicion. Kirov's mysterious murder in December 1934 gave Stalin an excuse to launch a purge of the Communist Party that ultimately became a national campaign of terror that claimed the lives of millions. (Reproduced from the Collections of the Library of Congress.)

the Bolsheviks dumped considerable amounts of paperwork in his lap. One revolutionary of the time described Stalin as "a gray blur sometimes emitting a dim and inconsequential light."

During the early years of Bolshevik power, Stalin held several important but not very visible posts, most of which required seemingly dull and boring administrative duties. To many, Stalin seemed to be a born "paper pusher." However, in his various capacities, the ambitious but pragmatic Georgian managed to pack both the bureaucracy and the party with men and women who owed everything to Stalin. This proved invaluable when, after Lenin's death early in 1924, Stalin maneuvered skillfully to defeat his chief rival, Leon D. Trotsky, and by 1928 to gain control over both the Communist Party and the Soviet Union itself.

As ruler of the Soviet Union—the name given to Russia in 1922 by its new communist rulers—Stalin pursued a number of ambitious goals, including the modernization and further industrialization of the Soviet economy. At the time of his triumph, the Soviet Union remained primarily an agrarian country featuring millions of peasants working small farms in an inefficient, labor-intensive, traditional manner. Even though Russia had begun to industrialize toward the end of the nineteenth century, Russian industry had not yet reached a fully mature state when World War I and the subsequent upheavals associated with the Russian Revolution retarded additional growth. During the 1920s, Russia's industrial expansion resumed under the Communists; however, agriculture continued to dominate economic life. Stalin knew this, but he concluded that both practical and ideological concerns demanded that the Soviet Union concentrate its resources on a massive, rapid expansion of its industrial infrastructure. The vehicle he created to achieve this was the Five-Year Plan, first announced in 1928 and covering the period 1928 to 1933.

The first Five-Year Plan provided for a "command economy." State planning agencies (in this instance, Gosplan, the State Planning Commission) working at the behest of the Soviet Union's leadership (in this case, Stalin) mapped out a detailed program for the country's economic development. It allocated all resources, including labor, capital, and materials, to whichever projects it deemed necessary to achieve the plan's aims. There was no feedback from the grass roots and no market mechanism to allow consumers a choice. Such planning was integral to Marxist-Leninist philosophy, but Stalin raised it to an art.

Reflecting Stalin's insistence on rapid industrial expansion, the first Five-Year Plan called for a 200 percent increase in coal and petroleum production, a 300 percent increase in steel production, and a 400 percent increase in electrical output—staggering figures under any circumstance. Overall industrial production was to jump by 250 percent, and heavy industry alone was to increase by an astonishing 330 percent. The plan called for entire new industries to be constructed virtually from scratch, including the automotive, aviation, chemical, and electrical fields. New sections of the country were designated for industrial expansion, particularly the Ural Mountains region and western Siberia.

Among other things, capital—both human and financial—had to be secured in order to make Stalin's soaring vision come to life. With this in mind, Stalin turned on Russia's peasants with a vengeance, squeezing them mercilessly. Under his policy of collectivization, Stalin sought several goals: free up labor for the massive industrial projects; generate money to finance these projects; break the back of an independent peasantry; and conform more fully to the ideological dictate of "collective ownership of the means of production."

Collectivization required Russian peasants to "voluntarily" combine their small plots of land into a much larger unit or *kolkhoz* (collective farm) that operated on a communal basis. This resulted in an agrarian economy of size that freed up millions of peasants for industrial labor. It also ended private ownership of the rural means of production, and by herding peasants into something vaguely resembling the prerevolutionary Russian commune, the government could exercise control over their lives. Moreover, because the state enjoyed a monopoly on the purchase of the peasants'—now collective farmers'—crops, the state bought these crops at an extremely low price and then either sold them abroad to generate capital for the industrial expansion or used them to feed the industrial workers at very little expense.

Many Russian peasants fiercely opposed collectivization. Stalin, as was his wont, responded with massive violence to get his way. Peasants who challenged collectivization were branded *kulaks,* literally "fists," and stigmatized as "enemies of the people." Eventually, Stalin ordered that the kulaks be "liquidated as a class"; in other words, he ordered their destruction. Nevertheless, throughout the Soviet Union, peasants resisted. Estimates are that between 20 and 30 million were either killed or deported to Siberia or Russia's far north. Although this figure may be excessive (no one was diligently keeping score), there is general agreement that 5 to 6 million peasants were deported during the first stages of collectivization. When local Communist thugs could not bring the peasants into line, the Red Army was called upon to do the job. Reacting to this opposition, in early 1930 Stalin signaled a relaxation of the pressure to collectivize; however, this was only a temporary respite. Special mention should be made of the artificial, or man-made, famine of 1932–1933 in Ukraine. There, Stalin's agents purposely condemned millions of peasants to death by taking their crops and then preventing the importation into the area of food for subsistence.

In response to the collectivization drive, disgruntled peasants frequently broke their farm implements, burned outbuildings, and slaughtered their herds rather than allow them to fall into the hands of their tormentors. But despite Stalin's brutality and peasant resistance, the collectivization drive succeeded. In 1928 individuals had controlled about 96 percent of the land, whereas by 1938 the state controlled more than 94 percent.

At the same time that collectivization rolled through the Soviet Union like a tidal wave, the rapid industrial expansion that Stalin ordered took flight. The goals of the first Five-Year Plan were declared fulfilled in four years, and a second Five-Year Plan featuring even more ambitious targets was announced. Surplus labor from the collective farms flocked to the cities, where it was put to use building industrial plants from scratch. This labor was mercilessly exploited, and the standard of living—already abominable—declined further. Any signs of discontent were quickly squelched.

The emphasis remained on heavy industry—coal, steel, iron, petroleum, electricity, chemicals; light industry or the production of consumer goods was largely ignored. The level of inefficiency, chaos, and confusion was staggering. Projects were never started, were abandoned in midstream, or proved to be duplicative or unworkable. Because of a total absence of quality control, many finished products were worthless; the "back yards" of Soviet factories were littered with the unusable. Shortcomings were frequently blamed on allegedly subversive managers, engineers, and workers. Branded "wreckers," these unfortunates faced firing squads or internment in Siberian concentration camps. In order to avoid this fate, those who oversaw individual factories, mills, or mines often fudged statistics to make it appear that all was well.

Despite these obvious and painful shortcomings, by 1940 Stalin had transformed the Soviet Union into one of the world's great industrial powers. Even though Soviet statistics are notoriously unreliable, it was manifestly apparent that when the outbreak of World War II cut short the third Five-Year Plan, the Soviet Union stood among the world's greatest producers of the building blocks for an industrial society. In comparison with 1928 production figures, the output for 1940 (the last year of peace for the Soviet Union) showed a nine-fold increase in electric power, an eight-fold increase in chemical output, and an almost five-fold increase in machine production. During this period, the Soviet economy expanded at an annual average rate of 12 to 14 percent. Significantly, however, the same data show that agricultural production remained flat, while real wages, urban housing, and per capita consumption declined.

Stalin's commitment to the Soviet Union's economic development and his ruthless determination to achieve it were equaled by his desire to rule absolutely and his willingness to go to great extremes to realize this. When approaching a task, Stalin usually exhibited a fair amount of flexibility; however, at bottom he was always willing, perhaps eager, to use force to get his way. Stalin once told French leader Charles de Gaulle that the way to motivate people was to strike fear into their hearts, and clearly, the Soviet dictator believed this. During the 1930s, Stalin made himself the unchallenged leader of the Soviet Union by destroying his real and potential rivals within the Communist Party. This process, known as the Great Purge, was first directed against the Old Bolsheviks, or the longest serving party members, many of whom had played prominent roles in the revolution itself. In a series of show trials, the party's senior figures confessed to all sorts of traitorous behavior. Most were convicted and shot; many lesser figures were also shot or sent to labor camps to perish. Within the party, Stalin reigned supreme.

Once Stalin had disposed of his erstwhile comrades, he perfected a mode of ruling that continued until his death. He would elevate to high positions opportunistic individuals who owed everything to him; then, after several years during which these individuals grew comfortable and, perhaps, began to build their own power base, Stalin would cut them down with the help of a new generation of loyal opportunists, and the process would begin anew.

Successfully using fear to strike terror into the hearts of Communists, Stalin applied the same tactics on a much larger scale against the entire population. In order to achieve complete obedience, Stalin unleashed the NKVD, the dreaded Soviet secret police. In the course of just a few years, about eight million people (according to Nikita S. Khrushchev) were arrested and either executed or sent to slave labor camps.

Stalinism also meant deification of the leader, who was variously described as omnipotent, as a genius, or as infallible. Especially during his last years, Stalin's huge propaganda machine turned out tribute after tribute to the crusty old dictator, leading to later accusations that Stalin had created a "cult of personality" for himself. Another feature of Stalinism was the attempt to forge a national—as opposed to class—consciousness with the creation of the "Soviet nation" that placed the concept of being "Soviet" on a higher plane than being a member of a traditional nationality. Stalin short-circuited this exercise in nation building when, after World War II, he glorified the Russian nation, or people, at the expense of the many other nationalities that made up the Soviet Union.

Despite Marx's vision of a classless society, Stalin encouraged social differentiation. Consequently, there arose a growing distinction between a Soviet elite, the *nomenklatura*—consisting of party members, successful managers, and cultural stars—and the common folk of the Soviet Union, a situation not unlike George Orwell's famous line from his novel *Animal Farm*, "All animals are created equal, but some are more equal than others."

Certainly one of the more striking features of Stalinism was bureaucratic proliferation. Perhaps unavoidable given the nature of Marxism-Leninism, Stalin took bureaucratization to a new level. He greatly accelerated the growth of the *apparat,* the ubiquitous, inefficient, corrupt Soviet bureaucracy that intruded in every way imaginable into the life of the Soviet Union and its citizens.

World War II forced the Soviet Union to cooperate with Western, liberal democracies, and Stalin needed the support of his people. This circumstance brought about a loosening of the many constraints that Stalin had imposed on the Soviet masses; however, with the war's end, mature Stalinism was reimposed, and it remained in place until Stalin's death in March 1953.

INTERPRETIVE ESSAY
Kevin C. O'Connor

Now and again during the Cold War, a debate would resurface regarding the political and economic system created by Joseph V. Stalin, the "unquiet ghost" who has haunted Russians and other peoples of the former Soviet Union for more than half a century. What, intellectuals asked, was the historical significance of Stalinism? Was Stalinism comparable to German Nazism? Where did Stalinism fit in the context of Russia's thousand-year history? Perhaps most significantly for a world divided into two heavily armed and mutually hostile camps—one liberal-democratic and capitalist, the other Communist and egalitarian—what was Stalinism's relationship to socialism and to the November Revolution? (Note that, according to the Gregorian calendar, the November Revolution occurred on November 7, 1917. According to the Julian calendar, which was used in Russia at that time, the revolution occurred on October 25, 1917. Both terms—November Revolution and October Revolution—refer to the Bolshevik/communist seizure of power in Russia.) Did Stalinism represent, as some scholars believed, a horrific betrayal of the revolution's principles, or was the Stalinist state one that simply fulfilled its Leninist potential? By the 1970s and 1980s, many scholars who studied the Stalinist era identified themselves with one of two groups. The first group emphasized the "totalitarian" nature of the Soviet state and stressed the role of ideology in the creation of the Soviet Union's "revolution from above." The second group, called "revisionists," rejected the traditional assumptions about the monolithic and all-powerful nature of the Soviet state. While de-emphasizing the role of ideology, many revisionists focused instead on the "interests" of the various groups that made up Soviet society.

And so the field remained until the end of the Cold War in the late 1980s and the implosion of the Soviet Union that quickly followed. Soviet studies in the West grew less polarized, and the wall that had separated Western and Russian researchers crumbled, with conditions for scholars changing dramatically for the better. Many researchers, typically younger and having had little stake in the ideological battles of the Cold War, shifted their focus from social history to cultural studies and began to mine the archives and other hitherto untapped sources of information. The result has been an explosion of books and articles that allow students and scholars to reimagine Stalinism in a way that was unthinkable not very long ago.

Among the most impressive scholarly works of the post–Cold War era was Stephen Kotkin's *Magnetic Mountain: Stalinism as a Civilization* (1995). Stalinism, according to Kotkin, was not simply a matter of power, ideology, or even forced modernization; Stalinism was "a set of values, a social identity, a way of life." Moreover, the Stalin revolution was enduring, for it created the political, economic, cultural, and social structures that remained in place for half a century. Archival research, supplemented with unpublished memoirs and interviews with people who knew Stalin personally, enabled another young writer to reconstruct the court life of the "Red Tsar." Simon Sebag Montefiore's Stalin is portrayed as an ordinary person of extraordinary intelligence, ambition, and ruthlessness; "a man of many faces," he was a "thin-skinned, neurotic egotist," incapable of giving his family or anyone else happiness.

Despite incessant but false claims that portrayed the Soviet leader as the deified Lenin's closest partner and intended heir, Joseph Stalin—Koba to his friends, Soso to his family, and Josip Dzhugashvili to the tsarist authorities who arrested and exiled him no fewer than four times—was not always the Great Stalin, the visionary "man of steel." Nicholas N. Sukhanov, one of the Russian Revolution's early chroniclers, remarked that the young Stalin gave the impression of "a gray blur sometimes emitting a dim and inconsequential light." Likewise, Leon D. Trotsky, second only to

Lenin in making the revolution, found Stalin in the political shadows at the end of Russia's civil war; Trotsky's Stalin was little more than a pathologically willful cog in a bureaucratic machine. Although it is true that Stalin did not play a leading role in 1917 and was not Lenin's designated successor (indeed, Lenin deemed none of his colleagues worthy of succeeding him, including the "rude" Stalin, with whom Lenin had strained relations at the end), Stalin proved his worth to Lenin during the civil war as the Bolsheviks' principal troubleshooter in the border regions.

From the beginning, Stalin's interests were organizational rather than ideological: remaining silent during the party's early controversies, by 1921 Stalin was the only leading Bolshevik to sit in both the Politburo, which was concerned with making policy, and the Orgburo, which saw to its implementation. Appointed general secretary of the party in 1922, Stalin spent the next decade transforming administrative power—which allowed him to place his own people at every level of the party structure—into a sort of personal power equaled only by the likes of Hitler, Mao, and Kim Il-Sung. Stalin's early genius was that, unlike the arrogant Trotsky, he gave the impression of moderation, saying nothing at party meetings until everyone had had their say and then ultimately giving voice to the conclusion toward which the majority had been heading. Once Lenin died in January 1924, Stalin fashioned himself as the interpreter of Leninism, quoting directly from Lenin during party debates, having his embalmed corpse put on display in a mausoleum, and deliberately identifying himself with the departed leader as he confronted Lenin's other heirs.

Stalin was derided by critics such as Trotsky for having a second-rate intellect, but the reality was otherwise; not only was Stalin a brilliant political intriguer, but he was also a voracious reader with an astounding memory. It is unlikely that he possessed from the beginning a master plan to eliminate all challengers, but Stalin understood better than anyone the rules of the game, and he manipulated them to his advantage. First he united in a triumvirate with Gregory E. Zinoviev and Leo B. Kamenev to undermine the ambitions of the despised Trotsky, Lenin's most obvious successor. In the process, they coined the phrase "Trotskyism," which would be used to murderous effect in the 1930s. In the next phase, Stalin united with Nicholas I. Bukharin against Zinoviev, Kamenev, and Trotsky, who by 1926 had recognized their common interest in opposing Stalin. Accusing his enemies of "defeatism" for their criticism of the peasant-friendly New Economic Policy (1921–1928), Stalin crushed the United Opposition (Trotsky was exiled in 1928, and Zinoviev and Kamenev were expelled from the party) before turning on his ally Bukharin, whose opposition to forced collectivization constituted, in Stalin's words, "a betrayal of the working class, a betrayal of the revolution." With Bukharin's expulsion from the Politburo at the end of 1929, it was clear that Stalin had won the battle for succession. However, he was not quite yet the Great Stalin, and his enemies were allowed to live and work; in fact, most were readmitted into the party before being annihilated during the Great Terror, or Great Purge.

Knowledge of the improvised maneuverings of the 1920s—from the moderate center, Stalin destroyed his rivals on the left, and then, having adopted the left's program, he demolished his challengers on the right—is essential for understanding the nature of Stalinism. Stalinism was power politics. Its essence was the destruction of enemies, both real and imagined, in a quest to attain unchallenged personal power. From this unassailable position Stalin would be able to realize the transformation of Russia from a backward peasant country to a mighty industrial power capable of exercising influence in world affairs. Even if the international revolution anticipated by the Bolsheviks failed to materialize abroad, under Stalin there would still be "socialism in one country."

The Stalin era began in 1928 with the introduction of "emergency measures" to forcibly take grain from the peasants, who objected to the low prices being offered by the state. Resolving to abolish the compromises of the New Economic Policy (NEP), which allowed a degree of capitalism to flourish in the countryside, Stalin, whose psychological need to match Lenin's revolution with one of his own outweighed all practical and human considerations, launched a new socialist offensive intended to transform all Soviet citizens into servants of the state. In turn, this would harness the country's limitless resources. The very existence of a prosperous peasant "class"—the members of which were labeled *kulaks*—able to withhold its grain from the market served as a constant reminder to party activists that the socialist revolution had stalled; thus, many Communists viewed the campaign against the peasantry as a necessary step in eliminating the barriers that blocked Russia's path to industrialization and, hence, to modernity.

Robert Conquest's *Harvest of Sorrow* (1986), a classic treatment of Soviet collectivization, shows how the policies of collectivization and "dekulakization"—the fomenting of class warfare in the countryside that involved the killing or deportation of millions of relatively prosperous peasants—were combined with an all-out attack on the Ukrainian nation. Indeed, no group in the Soviet Union—with the exception of the population of Kazakhstan, one-quarter of which perished during the resulting famine—suffered more in the early 1930s than the Ukrainian peasantry, who were fated to suffer further during World War II and still further in the postwar famine.

In order to cope with their re-enserfment, desperate peasants adopted various strategies, including both violent and passive resistance, accommodation, and manipulation (denouncing others for one's own benefit). One form of peasant resistance was flight to the towns. In 1932 the regime responded by introducing internal passports that were denied to the peasants, who were now placed in a legally inferior position vis-à-vis the country's urban inhabitants.

Despite a temporary retreat in 1930, the collectivization campaign soon resumed and was completed in most places by the mid-1930s. The results were disastrous; private farming was all but eliminated, and agricultural production, especially animal husbandry, plummeted as untold numbers of peasants slaughtered their animals rather than surrender them to the state. While six million peasants died of hunger during the resulting famine (a further two million were deported to the Soviet interior, where many succumbed to cold and hunger), the Soviet Union exported massive amounts of grain to finance its leap into industrial modernity. Collectivization was one of Stalinism's most enduring legacies; the seeming intractability of the agricultural problem stymied Soviet leaders from Khrushchev to Brezhnev to Gorbachev.

According to an article published in *Pravda* on the twelfth anniversary of the October 1917 revolution, 1929 was the "Year of the Great Breakthrough": it was the year of Stalin's fiftieth birthday (even though he was actually born in 1878), which was celebrated as a national event; it was the year that the resistant peasants were dealt a smashing blow; and it was the year that the first Five-Year Plan—backdated to the previous October—was put into effect. Under the slogan "There are no fortresses the Bolsheviks cannot storm," Stalin set impossible targets in all areas of industry—and then raised them still higher. The original plan called for coal production, for example, to double from 35 million tons in 1927–1928 to 75 million in 1932; soon Stalin demanded 105 million tons. "Shock-workers," who gathered at the end of 1929, took their cue from Stalin and called for the plan's fulfillment not in five years, but in four! Although the targets themselves were not always achieved, output—with the use of machinery imported largely from Germany and the United States—rose dramatically across the board.

Although the production statistics of the first Five-Year Plan are impressive by almost any measure, perhaps the Stalin revolution's most significant achievements were its successes in rejuvenating the faith of the party and in mobilizing the population around ambitious goals. Millions of peasants, transforming themselves into industrial laborers and hence builders of socialism, swamped the towns. The practical problem of providing this labor force with adequate housing was met with the construction of tent cities, makeshift barracks, and dormitories, which in turn bred crime and hooliganism. Yet amid the chaos of muddle, disorder, waste, inefficiencies, and shortages, there was also enthusiasm and production. Shock-workers initially set the pace for the new undisciplined workforce; by 1935 the standard was being set by superhuman "Stakhanovites," a name given to those who followed the example of the extraordinary miner Alexis G. Stakhanov, who in a single shift hewed 102 tons of coal instead of the usual seven. Even for those who could not hope to match the achievements of the Stakhanovites (who were rewarded with more food, better pay, and other material incentives), a new social identity was being created. Many Soviet citizens, despite their ambivalence, confusion, doubts, and misgivings, sincerely believed that they were "building socialism."

The large industrial city of Magnitogorsk, built from scratch in the southern Ural Mountains, was but one example of Stalin's penchant for "gigantomania," which also manifested itself in monster projects such as the Belomor Canal and Dnieprostroi. These projects were intended not only to meet the real needs of Soviet industry and security, but also to demonstrate to the Soviet people and to the world the successes of central planning and socialist civilization. Indeed, at a time when Soviet peasants were suffering from a horrific and almost entirely man-made catastrophe, the world's attention was focused not on the tragedy of collectivization, but on the Soviet Union's monumental industrial achievements. Western visitors such as Sidney and Beatrice Webb, George Bernard Shaw, and H. G. Wells trumpeted the achievements of Soviet planning as the capitalist West sank ever deeper into the Great Depression. Meanwhile, thousands of foreigners, disenchanted with capitalism and seeing in the Soviet experiment the creation of a better, more egalitarian civilization, willingly offered their services. From the vantage point of its dynamic cities and industrial centers, the Soviet Union was all movement and enthusiasm. The achievements of female workers, now emancipated from domesticity and "women's work," were also widely acclaimed, as they were mobilized to work in all areas of industry—most notably the building of the Moscow subway (this being one of Stalinism's few positive legacies).

But when things went wrong, as they surely did, there was always someone to blame. The scapegoats for the Soviet economy's shortcomings were not haste, poor planning, and impossible expectations, but legions of saboteurs, wreckers, and spies who had infiltrated the new enterprises and who had to be unmasked. The first show trials of wreckers took place in 1928, when 50 engineers—"bourgeois specialists"—were denounced for conspiring with foreign powers to sabotage the Shakhty mines. Although class warfare against "bourgeois specialists," whose expertise was crucial until a generation of suitably red specialists could be trained, was relaxed during the second Five-Year Plan (1932–1936), Stalin intended this trial to set a precedent that would further his consolidation of power.

The hunt for spies and saboteurs reached fever pitch at the height of the Great Terror in 1937–1938, which represented the final stage in Stalin's drive to eliminate all challengers to his one-man rule. The first general party purge *(chistka)* took place in Lenin's day in 1921, and a second swept the party in 1929, removing thousands of members who had either voted against Stalin or supported an opposition platform. But these purges were not deadly. Although the Old Bolsheviks, whose mentalities were shaped by their experiences as underground revolutionaries, were certainly well accustomed to destroying their enemies, it was only in the 1930s, when Stalin gave the NKVD (secret police) extraordinary powers to root out "enemies of the people," that the revolution began to devour its own children. Internal opposition to Stalin had been mounting since Michael N. Riutin circulated a document in 1932 that criticized Stalin's policies and called for his removal from office. A month later, Riutin and others involved with his "platform" were arrested, and another general purge removed 800,000 (out of 3.5 million) party members, followed by another 340,000 in 1934.

The Seventeenth Party Congress, held in January–February 1934 and dubbed the "Congress of Victors," was intended to celebrate the achievements of collectivization and the Five-Year Plan; even old enemies such as Zinoviev and Kamenev were allowed to speak to praise Stalin. However, it was Stalin's friend Sergei M. Kirov, the charismatic boss of the Leningrad region, who proved most popular in the election to the Central Committee; only three votes were cast against Kirov, whereas 270 delegates—nearly one-quarter of those voting—rejected Stalin. Of the 1,966 delegates who attended the "Congress of Victors," 1,108 would later be arrested on charges of revolutionary crimes; of the 139 members and candidate members elected to the Central Committee, 98 would be arrested and shot. Stalin was responsible for these arrests and executions. As the Bolshevik party was destroyed, in its place a new Stalin party was created.

The signal for the bloodletting was the murder of the popular Kirov on December 1, 1934. Stalin reacted by immediately issuing an emergency decree that created a climate of suspicion, paranoia, and fear in the party. Paradoxically, it was just after Stalin unveiled a new constitution in 1936, one designed to impress Western opinion, that his reign of terror began. A conspiratorial atmosphere enveloped the country; any sign of opposition in the present or past was regarded as treason—a crime punishable by death or a sentence in the Gulag, the vast network of labor camps that stretched from the Arctic Circle to the furthest reaches of Siberia. For allegedly having fallen behind in the hunt for enemies of the people, Genrikh G. Yagoda, the head of the NKVD, was removed and replaced by Nicholas I. Yezhov, whose name became nearly synonymous with the Great Terror of 1937–1938. A "Trotskyite-Zinovievite Center" was held responsible not only for Kirov's murder, but also for plotting a terrorist campaign to wipe out the top Soviet leadership, including Stalin. A series of show trials between 1935 and 1938 eliminated old comrades such as Zinoviev, Kamenev, and Bukharin. Stalin no longer even needed to consult the Central Committee to order the arrest of his colleagues—his power was now almost absolute.

The only remaining areas of potential opposition to Stalin's dictatorship were the NKVD and the army. Yezhov did his part to cleanse the "organs," executing thousands of his predecessor's officers in 1937 before becoming a victim of the terror's logic at the end of 1938, when he, too, was arrested and executed. However, the terror did its greatest damage to the Red Army, whose commanders stood accused in June 1937 of conspiring with the German General Staff. Between 1937 and 1941, approximately 43,000 officers were dismissed, sent to the labor camps, or shot. The destruction of the Red Army's leadership—mainly those who had shown the greatest capacity for independent thought—would prove devastating in the opening months of World War II, or what the Russians call the Great Patriotic War, or Great Fatherland War.

By the time the war broke out in Europe in September 1939, the cult of Stalin was firmly in place. Stalin was the "father of the peoples," the "Lenin of our time," the "friend of the children." It was Stalin whom Soviet children thanked for their happy childhood; it was to Stalin that urban workers owed their flats and their bread; later, Stalin would be praised for the firm and decisive leadership he displayed during the Great Patriotic War. Perhaps filling the voids created by the harsh suppression of religion and the elimination of the tsar, the celebration of the Stalin cult acquired a quasi-religious iconography in a land of peasants and former peasants accustomed to patriarchal authority. Although the Stalin cult lacked the spirituality of religion, his persona was elevated to almost mythical status; the ritualistic singing of his praises became a form of political theater.

Stalin's quasi-sacred image permeated every aspect of people's lives, yet Stalin himself maintained a certain distance from the Soviet people. Unlike Hitler, he did not speak on radio or appear in newsreels; rather, he relied on the printed word. Stalin's justification for each and every policy shift also had a quasi-religious aspect to it; as the high priest of Marx-ism-Leninism, only the omniscient, wise, and just Stalin could bring salvation—a superior, socialist civilization—to the Soviet people. "Stalin's life is our life, our beautiful present and future," editorialized *Pravda* in 1936. When he died 17 years later, millions cried. In a fitting coda to his life, hundreds were crushed by the crowds wanting to get a last look at the corpse of the only leader many of them had ever known.

Despite Stalinism's promises of a better life, living standards for most people plummeted in the early 1930s thanks to the wastefulness of the capital investment program and the disaster of collectivization. The real wages of workers in Moscow—where living standards were always the highest—fell by more than half between 1928 and 1932, and meat and dairy consumption fell as rationing was introduced at the end of the 1920s. After five years of deprivation in anticipation of the promised socialist paradise, a corner was turned in 1933, and when rationing ended two years later, the authorities could proudly announce, "Life has become better, com-rades. Life has become happier." However, in order to meet the material needs of the Soviet people, the promise of an egalitarian order had to be sacrificed. Although the Industrial Revolution offered millions of Soviet citizens unprecedented social mobility, shortages and queues for scarce goods persisted, and housing in Soviet towns remained scarce; mean-while, for the privileged few—the party elite—there were cars, servants, special closed shops, and private flats.

The implementation of a two-tiered system of rewards in the mid-1930s was just one aspect of what has been called "the Great Retreat"—the grad-ual and surreptitious abandonment of revolutionary social and cultural practices in favor of traditional, prerevolutionary values. In art and lit-erature, the avant-garde was condemned and replaced by Socialist Real-ism, the peculiar Soviet form of realism. Reversing its earlier laissez-faire approach to sex and the family, in 1936 the regime outlawed abortions and made divorces more difficult to obtain. Perhaps the most significant aspect of the Great Retreat was the rehabilitation of the Russian nation, which Lenin had derided for its arrogance toward the country's other nationalities. From Lenin's day until about 1933, the Soviet Union had embraced the basic principle of unity through diversity. As Commissar of Nationalities from 1917 to 1924, Stalin had initially supported and over-seen this policy, which promoted non-Russian languages and national elites with the expectation that national identity would eventually be depoliticized. In the mid-1930s, however, Stalin reversed course. Now promoting the "Friendship of the Peoples," the Stalinist regime began to emphasize the status and unifying role of Russian culture throughout the entire Soviet Union. The Russian people became the "first among equals" and the "elder brother" to the Soviet Union's other nations and nationalities, and Russian was made an obligatory second language in non-Russian schools. Stalin's famous postwar toast to the Russian people, in which he acknowledged their leading place among the Soviet peoples, further cemented their elevated status.

Policies regarding Soviet nationalities remained a work in progress throughout the Stalin era: not only were ethno-national boundaries subject to constant tinkering, but additionally, the opprobrium once reserved for "great-power chauvinists" was transferred to "bourgeois nationalists" living in the Soviet Union's sensitive border areas. The battle with the Ukrainian peasantry—sometimes called a genocide—reached its peak in the early 1930s, and during the second half of the decade, other diaspora nationalities living in the Soviet Union—Germans, Poles, Finns, Balts, Koreans, Chinese, Estonians, Latvians, Kurds, and Iranians—were labeled "enemy nations" (a term whose explanation called for considerable ideological gymnastics) and were subjected to ethnic cleansing. The most lethal period for enemy nations was 1939–1941, when Stalin, having acquired a large swath of eastern Europe thanks to the Nazi–Soviet Non-Aggression Pact of August 1939, deported hundreds of thousands of Poles, Ukrainians, Lithuanians, Latvians, and Estonians to the Soviet interior. Accused of collaboration with the invading Germans, the entire Chechen nation, as well as Crimean Tatars, Ingushi, and others, were deported to Central Asia in 1943–1944. The repression of non-Russian nationalities continued into the postwar era, when Ukraine was again pacified, and collectivization was brought to the Baltic republics; hundreds of thousands more people, deemed guilty not for what they *did* but for who they *were,* were deported to the Soviet interior.

During the period of "high Stalinism," or the post–World War II years, Soviet Russia was practically a barracks state. The heroic figure of Stalin may have stood taller than ever, but an atmosphere of suspicion, heightened by Cold War tensions, darkened the Kremlin once again. In his last years, Stalin's authority was so absolute that between 1939 and 1952, not a single party congress was held; the emasculation of party bodies that had begun in the early 1930s was quite thorough by 1950. In the area of culture, Andrei A. Zhdanov presided over a Stalin-initiated campaign against alien influences and "cosmopolitanism" (Soviet-speak for Jews), and a pseudo-science called Lysenkoism—so named for the crackpot geneticist Trofim D. Lysenko—characterized the Kremlin's drive to direct scientific and intellectual life. In the early postwar years, all things Russian were praised, whereas Western science and culture were regarded with disdain and suspicion. With the exception of the horrific war period, these were the Soviet Union's darkest years; the dynamism of the 1930s was absent, and the popular hopes of the immediate postwar years for a more liberalized society were crushed. By the end of the 1940s, Stalin's paranoia focused once again on Leningrad, where yet another "conspiracy" was uncovered; many believe that it was only Stalin's death in 1953 that prevented the unleashing of another terror—one that would have fallen hardest on the country's remaining Jews.

When Stalin finally passed away at age 74, the number of prisoners in the Gulag was at its peak. Perhaps nothing better captures the essence of the Stalin era than this dreadful institution, through which as many as 18 million people passed between 1929 and 1953 (another 6 million were exiled to Siberia or Kazakhstan). Although the existence of the labor camp system had been well known to outsiders since the 1930s, it took the publication in the 1970s of Alexander I. Solzhenitsyn's three-volume *Gulag Archipelago* for readers in the West to come to terms fully with the scale and intensity of this phenomenon. Solzhenitysn emphatically stated that the Gulag was not simply a phenomenon of Stalinism, but had its origins in the earliest days of the Soviet state, when camps were first set up in the Arctic Circle's Solovetsky monastery. Utilizing their access to Soviet archives and unpublished camp memoirs, Western researchers have confirmed and amplified Solzhenitsyn's allegations. Perhaps the most significant revelation is the Gulag network's centrality to Soviet economic planning.

If Lenin was the Gulag's father, then Stalin was its emperor. During the Stalin era, there were all together 476 camp complexes, each of which contained several camps. Any redemptive purposes—"reformation through forced labor"—the Gulag might have had in the 1920s and early 1930s disappeared as the Gulag became linked with the Soviet Union's industrial and military needs. Perhaps 170,000 slave laborers were used to build the useless Belomor Canal; of these, about 25,000 died. The terror of 1937–1938, followed by mass arrests in the sensitive borderlands before and during the war, provided the regime with still more slave labor. By 1938, there were approximately 1.8 million prisoners in the Gulag, plus another million people who had been sentenced to exile in Siberia or Central Asia. Special colonies were set up for children, who beginning in 1935 could be charged with crimes as adults at age 12.

Although life in the Gulag was harshest for political prisoners—people charged with "counterrevolutionary activities" according to Article 58 of the Soviet criminal code—most who passed through the Gulag in the 1930s and 1940s were not "politics," but people with criminal sentences.

Immediately after the war, however, the number of political prisoners, often ordinary people who had no political views but who happened to be swept up in mass arrests, reached as high as 60 percent. They were joined by hundreds of thousands of prisoners of war and Soviet soldiers whose only crime was to have seen, and therefore been contaminated by, the West. Although convictions for counterrevolutionary activities rapidly fell after 1946, the overall number of prisoners in the Gulag camps and colonies continued to grow during Stalin's final years. Although profitability mattered more than ever after the war, even the sadistic former secret police chief Lavrenty D. Beria, who remained responsible for the Gulag empire until 1953, realized that the camps were corrupt, wasteful, and in the final analysis, unprofitable.

In many ways, the Gulag was the symbol and the essence of Stalinism: it was inhumane, lethal, and economically unsound. It also highlighted the appalling cruelty of the Stalin era. Although numbers do not tell the whole story, they can be illustrative. In 1916, the last year before the revolution that forever transformed Russia, 28,600 prisoners were serving forced labor sentences. When Stalin died 37 years later, the Gulag held approximately 2.5 million prisoners, many of whom greeted news of Stalin's death with open rejoicing.

SELECTED BIBLIOGRAPHY

Applebaum, Anne. *Gulag: A History.* New York: Doubleday, 2003.
     The most complete history of the origins and evolution of the Soviet labor camp system.
Brooks, Jeffrey. *Thank You, Comrade Stalin! Soviet Public Culture from Revolution to Cold War.* Princeton, NJ: Princeton University Press, 2000.
     A study of popular culture, especially the cult of Stalin, through a comprehensive examination of the early decades of the Soviet press.
Bullock, Alan. *Hitler and Stalin: Parallel Lives.* New York: Knopf, 1992.
     A weighty but compelling dual biography of the two most powerful and destructive leaders of the mid-twentieth century.
Conquest, Robert. *The Great Terror: A Reassessment.* New York: Oxford University Press, 1990.
     This is an updated version of Conquest's 1968 classic. It argues Stalin's central role in the terror of the 1930s.
———. *The Harvest of Sorrow: Soviet Collectivization and the Terror-Famine.* New York: Oxford University Press, 1986.
     Examines Stalin's assault on the Soviet peasantry, focusing in particular on the atrocities committed in Ukraine.
Davies, Sarah. *Popular Opinion in Stalin's Russia: Terror, Propaganda, and Dissent, 1934–1941.* Cambridge: Cambridge University Press, 1997.
     Deals with the response of ordinary Russians to the upheavals of the 1930s.

Fitzpatrick, Sheila, ed. *Everyday Stalinism: Ordinary Life in Extraordinary Times: Soviet Russia in the 1930s*. New York: Oxford University Press, 1999.
    A pioneering account of urban life in Stalin's Russia that illuminates how ordinary people tried to live normal lives under the extraordinary circumstances of the 1930s.
———. *Stalinism: New Directions*. New York: Routledge, 2000.
    A collection of articles, mostly by younger scholars, on topics such as social identity, consumerism, the terror, and nationality.
———. *Stalin's Peasants: Resistance and Survival in the Russian Village after Collectivization*. New York: Oxford University Press, 1994.
    This is the major study of the post-collectivization settlement.
Getty, J. Arch. *Origins of the Great Purge*. New York: Cambridge University Press, 1985.
    A revisionist account of the Great Terror that places the focus on the activities of Stalin's underlings.
Getty, J. Arch, and Roberta T. Manning, eds. *Stalinist Terror: New Perspectives*. Cambridge: Cambridge University Press, 1993.
    A series of essays by scholars, mostly revisionists, such as Getty, Manning, Lynne Viola, Robert Thurston, and Gábor T. Rittersporn. Especially noteworthy is Alec Nove's essay "Victims of Stalinism: How Many?"
Getty, J. Arch, and Oleg V. Naumov. *The Road to Terror: Stalin and the Self-Destruction of the Bolsheviks, 1932–1939*. New Haven, CT: Yale University Press, 1999.
    In some ways a corrective to Getty's earlier accounts; it allows the documents to tell the story of the terror.
Gorlizki, Yoram, and Oleg Khlevniuk. *Cold Peace: Stalin and the Ruling Circle, 1945–1953*. New York: Oxford University Press, 2004.
    Depicts Stalin's postwar relationship with his inner circle, focusing on his drive to preserve his dictatorship in old age as he pressed his country's claims as a global power. This study argues that Stalin's postwar ruling style was characterized by its fundamental rationality.
Kotkin, Stephen. *Magnetic Mountain: Stalinism as a Civilization*. Berkeley: University of California Press, 1995.
    An ambitious study of the Magnitogorsk steelworks, which was heralded in the 1930s as one of the great achievements of Soviet industrialization.
Martin, Terry. *The Affirmative Action Empire: Nations and Nationalism in the Soviet Union, 1923–1939*. Ithaca, NY: Cornell University Press, 2001.
    A massive study of the evolution of Soviet nationalities policy before World War II. Its central thesis is that prior to 1933, the USSR was an "affirmative action empire" that promoted national elites as well as national languages and cultures.
Medvedev, Roy. *Let History Judge: The Origins and Consequences of Stalinism*, rev. ed. New York: Columbia University Press, 1989.
    Written by a famous semi-dissident, this hefty book argues that Stalinism deformed the state created by Lenin. Whether or not one agrees with its Marxist thesis, it is a moving account of the horrors of Stalinism.
Montefiore, Simon Sebag. *Stalin: The Court of the Red Tsar*. New York: Knopf, 2004.

Highly readable account of Stalin's inner life. Although there is little on Stalin's policies, it vividly describes his relationships and the environment in which he lived.

Service, Robert. *Stalin: A Biography.* New Haven, CT: Yale University Press, 2005.
The most recent in a long line of Stalin biographies, its principal strength is that it draws upon sources that were unavailable to earlier biographers such as Robert Tucker and Isaac Deutcher.

Siegelbaum, Lewis, and Andrei Sokolov. *Stalinism as a Way of Life: A Narrative in Documents.* New Haven, CT: Yale University Press, 2000.
A collection of annotated documents drawn from the Russian archives, this text allows the people who lived through the 1930s to speak for themselves.

Talbott, Strobe, ed. *Khrushchev Remembers.* Boston, MA: Little, Brown, 1971.
Between Khrushchev's lies there is much revealing gossip about Stalin's personality and his inner circle.

Tucker, Robert C. *Stalin in Power: The Revolution from Above.* New York: Norton, 1990.
In the second volume of his massive biography of Stalin, Tucker takes a psychological approach to his subject and compares the Soviet leader to the tsars Ivan the Terrible and Peter the Great.

Viola, Lynne. *Peasant Rebels under Stalin: Collectivization and the Culture of Peasant Resistance.* New York: Oxford University Press, 1996.
Focusing on "voices from below," this is a study of resistance and accommodation to collectivization.

Volkogonov, Dmitri. *Stalin: Triumph and Tragedy.* New York: Grove Weidenfeld, 1991.
Written by a general in the Soviet Army, this biography, along with those of Lenin and Trotsky, caused a sensation in Russia when it was published at the end of the Soviet era.

Zubkova, E. *Russia after the War: Hopes, Illusions, and Disappointments, 1945–1957.* Armonk, NY: M. E. Sharpe, 1998.
Focusing on the relatively neglected era of "high Stalinism," this book examines public opinion in Russia from the end of the war to the beginning of the "thaw." Of particular interest are the chapters that detail the suffering and famine of the early postwar years.

Zubok, Vladislav M., and Constantine Pleshakov. *Inside the Kremlin's Cold War.* Cambridge, MA: Harvard University Press, 1995.
A compelling account by two Russian historians of Soviet diplomacy during the early years of the Cold War. Their research places particular focus on the motives and behavior of the top Soviet leaders.

8

World War II, 1941–1945

INTRODUCTION

On January 30, 1933, Adolf Hitler came to power in Germany. Although the major states of Europe found this turn of events to be less than inspiring, Hitler's ascendancy was not cause for immediate alarm in the Soviet Union. Despite his virulent anti-Communism, it seemed unlikely that Hitler would upset the relatively cordial relations between Germany and the Soviet Union, or at least that was Joseph Stalin's assessment. However, Hitler had his own ideas, and as German leader, he not only intensified his anti-Communist rhetoric and downgraded relations with the Soviet Union, but also declared openly that he wished to expand Germany eastward at the expense of the Soviet Union.

Hitler's truculence forced Stalin to revisit his options. Throughout 1933 and 1934, Stalin gradually came to the conclusion that Hitler presented a real and present danger to the Soviet Union. In order to counter this threat, the Soviet dictator changed course and began to seek rapprochement with the capitalist nations of western Europe in order to counter Nazi Germany. In 1934 the Soviet Union joined the League of Nations, and Soviet foreign minister Maxim Litvinov became an eloquent spokesman of collective security. At the same time, the Comintern (Communist International)—on orders from Moscow—called for all "progressive forces" to oppose fascism, and in 1935 the Soviet Union allied itself with both France and Czechoslovakia. The policy of the "Popular Front," which demanded a united stance in the face of fascist aggression, was in full bloom.

Joseph V. Stalin and German Foreign Minister Joachim v. Ribbentrop look on as Soviet Foreign Minister Viacheslav M. Molotov signs the August 23, 1939, Nazi–Soviet Non-Aggression Pact. This agreement kept the Soviet Union out of World War II for almost two years and allowed the Soviet Union to add considerable territory on its western borders. (Reproduced from the Collections of the Library of Congress.)

However, Stalin's would-be Western partners viewed him with suspicion, and the agreements that he reached with them did not include an ironclad commitment to defend the Soviet Union against Nazi aggression. Moreover, when France and Great Britain did nothing in the face of Hitler's March 1936 remilitarization of the Rhineland—a clear violation of the Treaty of Versailles—Stalin had to think twice about his Popular Front policy. Nevertheless, as German hostility toward the Soviet Union increased, Stalin had nowhere else to turn.

Stalin's concern grew when Britain and France allowed a fascist takeover in Spain and then sat passively by as Hitler's Third Reich annexed Austria in March 1938. If Stalin had not already given up on the West and the Popular Front, the 1938 Czech crisis certainly convinced him that he had to move in a new direction. In that year, Hitler demanded that Czechoslovakia hand over to Germany its Sudetenland region, where many ethnic Germans lived. When Hitler threatened war, the British and French panicked. They agreed to a hastily called conference in Munich, where at the end of September 1938, they signed the Munich Agreement, which gave Hitler all that he had demanded. This high-water mark of appeasement came despite the Soviet Union's offer (which may or may not have been sincere) to defend Czechoslovakia against Nazi aggression.

The Czech crisis and Munich Agreement clearly demonstrated to the Soviet Union just how isolated it was, how little the West thought of it, and how much the policy of the Popular Front was a failure. In fact, given Hitler's hatred of Communism, Russians, and the Soviet Union, it appeared to some observers as though the West—in order to save its own skin—was encouraging Hitler to move against the Soviet Union.

At this juncture, practical considerations intervened to produce a cynically expedient result. On one hand, Stalin desperately wanted to avoid war, especially one in which he would have to stand alone against the Nazi hordes. On the other hand, the German dictatorship knew that Poland would be its next target and that its aggression was likely to provoke war with France and Great Britain. In that case, the Nazis did not want to repeat the mistake of World War I of having to fight on two fronts. Like two lost souls in the night, the Nazis and the Soviets ineluctably drifted toward each other. After a few preliminary gestures, the two mortal enemies opened serious but secret talks. These negotiations bore fruit on August 23, 1939, with the signing of the Nazi–Soviet (sometimes referred to as the Hitler-Stalin) Non-Aggression Pact.

This unexpected agreement contained two parts, one public and one secret. The public protocol pledged each side to remain neutral toward the other in the event of war. This ensured that the Soviet Union would remain on the sidelines if war broke out between Germany and the West and that Hitler could now attack Poland without having to worry about the possibility of the Soviet Union entering the conflict. The secret protocol called for the Soviet Union and Nazi Germany to divide much of East Central Europe. The Nazis were to receive the lion's share of Poland, and the Soviets were to establish spheres of influence in Estonia, Latvia, Lithuania, Finland, the Romanian province of Bessarabia, and eastern Poland. On September 1, 1939, Hitler started World War II in Europe with an unprovoked attack on Poland. Two and one-half weeks later, on September 17, the jackal-like Soviet Union, pausing to confirm that Germany would, indeed, overwhelm Poland, declared war on the hapless Poles and seized their eastern territories as per the Non-Aggression Pact's secret provision.

Having finished with Poland, Hitler now turned westward, where he met with great success against France and Great Britain. Meanwhile, Stalin strengthened his grip on the Soviet Union's share of the spoils. In November 1939, he attacked Finland when that country refused the Soviet Union's demands for a border revision favorable to Moscow. Although the Red Army performed miserably during the so-called Winter War, the hopelessly outmanned Finns eventually bent to Stalin's will. In July 1940 the Soviet Union absorbed Estonia, Latvia, and Lithuania and seized both Bessarabia and northern Bukovina from Romania.

Nazi relations with its Soviet ally had never been especially smooth, and Hitler, brimming with self-confidence after his easy triumphs in western Europe, once again cast a covetous eye to the east. On December 18, 1940, he ordered that preparations begin for "Barbarossa," a massive attack on the Soviet Union. As Germany shifted troops and equipment from the west to the east, Stalin stubbornly ignored warnings of what was to come. Consequently, when the Nazi blow fell on the night of June 21, 1941, the Soviet Union was completely unprepared.

Fortunately for Stalin, he had already concluded a nonaggression pact with Japan, thereby freeing him of worries about having to fight a two-front war and enabling him to shift significant numbers of troops from the east to the west. And those troops and their equipment were sorely needed as the Nazi juggernaut mauled the Red Army in the opening days of the campaign. Numbering 154 divisions, the Nazis and their allies struck along a 1,200-mile front stretching from the Baltic to the Black Seas. The devastated Red Army fell back in disarray as the Germans successfully employed their blitzkrieg tactics once again. Within a matter of weeks, the Germans captured more than a million Soviet soldiers; by the beginning of December, they were at the gates of Moscow, had virtually surrounded Leningrad, and in the south had taken Kiev and moved well across the

Dnieper River. In all, Germany had seized 500,000 square miles of the Soviet Union with a population of 65 million.

Meanwhile, Stalin had disappeared, resurfacing only on July 3, when he addressed the nation. Using a style and vocabulary usually associated with the Russian Orthodox Church, Stalin called upon Russians to repel the invader, defend the motherland, and exhibit the highest level of Russian patriotism. Gone were the trite Communist slogans, the glorification of a revolutionary Lenin, and the claims of infallibility for Karl Marx.

Faced with annihilation, the Soviet Union rallied in December 1941 at the Battle of Moscow. Nazi forces drove to within 20 miles of the city and were poised to take the capital and, perhaps, drive the Soviet Union from the war. However, Soviet resistance stiffened when the defeated Red Army regrouped and received significant reinforcements from Siberia. As for the Germans, their forces were overextended, exhausted, and exposed to horrible weather featuring temperatures dropping to 30 and 40 degrees below zero. In a desperate struggle, the Soviets stopped the Nazis in the Moscow suburbs and drove them back. The significance of the Battle of Moscow cannot be overestimated. Germany's hopes of a quick victory were shattered; the war would become one of attrition, and Germany could not possibly hope to win such a war.

Nor was the Soviet Union left standing alone. On the day the Nazi invasion commenced, British Prime Minister Winston Churchill voiced his determination to stand with the Soviets against Hitler despite his frequent denunciation of Communism. In July the United States sent a mission to Moscow that established Lend-Lease, a supply program that during the course of the war provided more than 15 million tons of supplies valued at more than 11 billion dollars to the beleaguered Soviets. After Germany declared war against the United States in December 1941, the Soviet Union, the United States, and Great Britain joined together in the wartime Grand Alliance.

During 1942, the Soviet Union continued to be the site of the most widespread, intense, and brutal combat of World War II. In the spring, a large Soviet counterattack failed, and the Germans again went on the offensive as the weather improved. Hitler, content with besieging Leningrad and leaving Moscow in Soviet hands, turned his attention to the Caucasus and the large oil reserves there. He ordered the German Sixth Army under the command of General Friedrich Paulus to take the strategically situated city of Stalingrad (once Tsaritsyn and now Volgograd) and interdict the main routes from the south to Moscow. What ensued was the Battle of Stalingrad, the most important clash of World War II.

Facing Paulus was General Basil I. Chuikov and the newly created 62nd Army. In bitter house-to-house fighting that began in late August 1942, the Red Army slowly drained the life from the Germans. The fate of the Sixth Army was sealed when Hitler ordered Paulus not to retreat under any circumstances, and the Soviets, under General George K. Zhukov, the Deputy Supreme Commander, smashed Romanian and Italian units guarding the German rear and encircled their opponents. When Paulus finally surrendered on February 2, 1943, only 91,000 Germans remained of his original command. Estimates are that German forces suffered 850,000 casualties and that the Soviets lost upward of one million. Moreover, the psychological consequences of this largest battle in history were enormous for both Germany and the Soviet Union.

Despite the terrible losses at Stalingrad, Germany still had the strength for one more major offensive. In summer 1943, the Nazis assembled a huge force consisting of perhaps 500,000 men. Seventeen armored divisions boasted 2,000 tanks and 2,000 airplanes. The Germans planned to break out of the Kursk salient where the central and southern sectors of the front intersected and to move forward to seize Moscow. The Soviets anticipated the German offensive and massed their soldiers to meet the threat. In July 1943, the Battle of Kursk, the greatest tank battle in history, began. After the Germans achieved some impressive initial gains, the superior Russian tank, the T-34, began to take a deadly toll. At the close of the battle, the Red Army had virtually destroyed the German force. Kursk was the last significant Nazi offensive; henceforth, the Soviets would be on the offensive, and the Germans would be relegated to fighting a bitter but ultimately fruitless defensive action.

Throughout 1944, the Red Army rolled westward, driving the Nazis from the Soviet Union. However, in their wake, the Germans left incredible human and physical destruction. Governed by Hitler's pathological hatred of Communism, Jews, and Slavs, German forces deliberately and systematically destroyed as much as they could both on their way into and their way out of the Soviet Union.

One of the short-term consequences of the Nazi invasion was a distinct relaxation of Stalinist controls. In particular, the Soviet campaign to discredit religion ceased, and the various religious bodies, but especially the Russian Orthodox Church, were rehabilitated and enlisted in the struggle against Germany. Moreover, patriotism rather than Marxism became the guiding principle for Soviet life—hence, the designation of World War II as the "Great Patriotic War," or "Great Fatherland War."

During the course of the war, the Grand Alliance survived, but not without papering over a number of serious problems. In addition to the general distrust that existed because of ideological differences, Great Britain and the United States still smarted from the Nazi–Soviet Non-Aggression Pact. More importantly, the two Western allies harbored real concern about how far the Red Army intended to go as it pursued the retreating Germans and what it intended to do with the territory and peoples it liberated, especially Poland and the Poles. For their part, the Soviets never fully accepted Western promises not to conclude a separate peace with Germany. Most importantly, the failure of their Western allies to open a second European front against the Nazis until 1944 outraged the Soviets. This failure made it appear as though the Western allies were content to see the Nazis do as much damage as possible to the Soviet Union. During the war, the leaders of the Grand Alliance came together for conferences at Teheran (November 1943) and Yalta (February 1945). Churchill and Stalin met separately at Moscow in October 1944.

As 1945 opened, the Red Army crossed into Germany proper and drove toward Berlin, the capital. At the same time, Anglo-American forces moved into the western reaches of Germany. The Red Army began the final assault on the Nazi capital on April 16, 1945. Sixteen days later, Hitler was dead, and Berlin was in Soviet hands. The formal unconditional surrender of Nazi Germany occurred on May 8, 1945. A few months later, the Soviet Union declared war on Japan just in time to gather some of the spoils as the United States vanquished its Pacific rival. No reliable figures exist to delineate the true cost of World War II for the Soviet Union. However, there can be no question that millions upon millions died, at least half of whom were civilians.

INTERPRETIVE ESSAY
Martin J. Blackwell

The Soviet Union's victory in World War II was its greatest moment. But even as this victory solidified the rule of a one-party dictatorship over that country, the Soviet people's experience of "total war" during 1941–1945 fostered a desire for political change that would eventually contribute to the collapse of Communism. Now, as the peoples of the former Soviet Union engage with the wider world in the early twenty-first century, the most important question that emerges from the Soviet Union's World War II experience is how it changed that country's political structure after the propagandized social mobility for the masses and the use of terror against its elites had solidified it in the 1930s. Because of the arduous victory achieved by the Soviet people, the society that emerged from the conflict could no longer be ruled in totalitarian fashion if its leaders were to hold onto power. Although the Soviet Union was to remain an authoritarian dictatorship for decades to come, the war placed the Stalinists throughout the land on the defensive, for they were now forced to take the people's real interests into account if social harmony was to be maintained.

It was Germany's remarkable economic and political turnaround in the 1930s under the leadership of the Nazi Party that allowed Adolf Hitler to attempt to create a powerful empire abroad. Above all, Hitler was animated by his desire to provide the "living-space" (lebensraum) necessary for his "master-race." A product of the pessimistic culture of early twentieth-century Europe, he believed history was the story of struggle between human cultures to determine which of them would survive and prosper. Accordingly, the "backward" peoples on the lands to Germany's east were to face enslavement and extermination as the Germans began their efforts to conquer the world. At the same time that Hitler's economic success and political terror made dissent an unattractive option for Germany's elites, his propaganda convinced many Germans that if the Nazi order crumbled, their so-called cultured and comfortable way of life would disappear with it.

Another reason such fantasies were allowed to come to fruition was the inability of the capitalist democracies to Germany's west and Stalin's Communist dictatorship to its east to work together to prevent aggression. There is little doubt that British and French fear of another world war and their preference for Hitler's version of capitalism to Stalin's socialism allowed Hitler to begin "gathering up the Germans" in central Europe in the latter half of the 1930s. British Prime Minister Neville Chamberlain, for example, ultimately claimed in 1938 that the fate of Czechoslovakia meant little for the average Englishman because Czechoslovakia was a country "far away that we know little about." Meanwhile, Stalin's revolutionary rhetoric that it was best to let the capitalists destroy each other also helped to undermine any chance for cooperation between East and West. Thus, when the Germans unexpectedly approached the Soviets in August 1939 about the possibility of negotiating a nonaggression treaty, Stalin agreed to listen.

Hitler sought an agreement because he wished to avoid a two-front war similar to the one that had contributed significantly to Germany's loss in World War I. Stalin endorsed the Nazi–Soviet Non-Aggression Pact (sometimes known as the "Hitler-Stalin Pact") because he wished to avoid war when his country was militarily unprepared. The Soviets had long understood the threat of an attack from Hitler; however, the Red Army's traditional plan for defense "in breadth" along the country's western border called for a massive defensive force that in practice did not exist. Thus, one week after the nonaggression treaty was signed, Hitler attacked Poland on September 1, 1939, and France and Great Britain rather reluctantly declared war on Germany. It seemed that Stalin had analyzed the situation correctly, for now what Leninists considered the inevitable fight to the death among the imperialists was seemingly underway.

But the Nazi–Soviet Non-Aggression Pact was hardly an act of peacemaking. Its secret protocols contained Stalin and Hitler's agreement to divide up East Central Europe. For his part, Stalin moved quickly to incorporate eastern Poland into the Soviet Union's Belorussian republic, and his police force (the People's Commissariat of Internal Affairs, or NKVD) deported more than a million "problematic" Poles to points east in the process. There, and in western Ukraine, the Soviets also staged fake "celebratory reunions" between the formerly divided peoples of these borderland nations. Finally, in 1940, Stalin annexed the three independent Baltic states of Estonia, Latvia, and Lithuania, a process that featured its own deportations and contrived elections where Baltic peoples "voted" to become new republics of the Soviet Union. Although Finland's fate had not been discussed, Stalin soon took advantage of a distracted Hitler to demand strategic concessions from that Baltic nation too. When the Finns balked, war ensued. Although the Soviet Union ultimately triumphed, the effectiveness of the Finnish fighters demonstrated to both the Red Army and Stalin's armament industries how much work lay before them.

By summer 1940, Hitler had finished off the French, leaving only Great Britain to battle on resolutely. Because of Britain's resistance, Stalin could not believe Hitler would attack the Soviet Union and thus initiate the dreaded two-front war. But crucially, Hitler feared that his own people could not stomach the domestic sacrifices necessary to win a "total war" lasting many years. Thus, the fateful decision was made to deliver a quick "knockout blow" to Stalin's Soviet Union using the same blitzkrieg methods that had destroyed the Poles and the French. Recently, evidence has surfaced that Stalin knew as early as December 1940 about the Nazi plan to attack the Soviet Union. This knowledge may explain efforts made during the first half of 1941 to prevent the Nazi attack while armament "in breadth" along the Soviet frontlines was being prepared. One of these efforts, the Soviets' diplomatic aggrandizement in the direction of the Turkish straits and Romanian oil fields, provoked the Germans to invade southeastern Europe in spring 1941. This pushed the Nazi invasion of the Soviet Union back into the summer, and that, of course, meant that the Russian winter was upon the Germans sooner than they expected. It remains a mystery why Stalin at this critical moment took so little notice of the German threat. All he would say to his generals and advisors in May and June of 1941 was, "We don't want to alarm the Germans," and he stubbornly held to the idea that Hitler would back down from opening a two-front war. But fatefully for the Soviet people, this was not to be the case.

The unprovoked Nazi attack against the Soviet Union came on the night of June 21, 1941, and it led to disaster along the unprepared Soviet frontlines and to a severe crisis in Moscow. The Soviet Union was poorly prepared for war because defense "in breadth" had long been Stalin's unimaginative response to Hitler's rise to power. The generals who had disagreed with him and called for Soviet blitzkrieg tactics to be developed had been destroyed in the Great Terror of the 1930s. Thus, the Germans easily blasted their way through the Soviet lines and moved to conquer the western Soviet Union quickly. Left reeling from such blows, the Red Army began a chaotic retreat that saw many of its frontline forces surrounded. Meanwhile, the NKVD killed the prisoners it held in the western cities in a murderous frenzy, and the local Communist Party cadres desperately worked to organize volunteers, carry out the draft, and build defenses in cities further to the east such as Leningrad and Kiev.

Back in Moscow, it was the foreign minister, Viacheslav M. Molotov, not Stalin, who now called on the Soviet people to resist the Germans. Stunned by Hitler's decision to attack, Stalin went into seclusion. By the end of June, news of the Soviet armed forces' mounting losses led the crude Stalin to tell his Politburo subordinates, "Everything's lost. I give up. Lenin founded our state and we've screwed it up." Stalin retired to his county house at Kuntsevo on the outskirts of Moscow, and the Politburo members were left to decide what course of action to follow. Their response to the Nazi attack was to create a General Staff *(Stavka)* to command the armed forces and a State Committee of Defense *(GKO)* to coordinate the war effort at home, with Stalin, the party's general secretary, as the leader of both new entities. Although Stalin feigned surprise when his colleagues visited Kuntsevo to inform him of these plans, it is doubtful that political stability in the Soviet Union could have been guaranteed without his presence as leader. With war now upon them, the Soviet leadership decided to increase the political centralization of the state; for the next four years, nothing would happen within the Soviet Union without a resolution from the five-man GKO.

It was up to Stalin, meanwhile, as the public face of Soviet power, to propagandize why the Soviet people should fight. In short, defeating the Nazis became the animating force for everything in Soviet society for the next four years. The need to defend Mother Russia became everyone's duty in the face of Hitler's barbarism, and the building of socialism, so long trumpeted on the pages of the Soviet press, faded away. The result was the rapid development of a mosaic of moods among the Soviet peoples. Russian historians have recently argued that the events of June 1941 awoke in the Soviet people the ability to think about variants, to critically evaluate a situation, and not to take the existing order as immutable. The effort to repel the Nazis also meant that, at least at the local level of Soviet life, the democratic centralism of Lenin and Stalin's party was no longer tenable. The key criterion for becoming a Soviet leader was no longer a person's party loyalty, but rather his or her contributions to the work of the front. Out in the provinces, the Communist leaders were told to train their subordinates in the following fashion: the party is interested in having people think, and stop instructing the masses and learn from them. That life in the Soviet Union would now be shaped by the real interests of ordinary people was a big change from the 1930s, when life had been shaped by their imaginary desires, and Stalin's terror squads had made sure the elites worked to meet them.

Meanwhile, Hitler's armies were well on their way toward Leningrad, Moscow, and central Ukraine by July 1941. Leningrad was soon surrounded and would be under siege for the next three and a half years as 1.5 million Leningrad residents starved to death in the process. The main reason Moscow did not suffer the same fate was Hitler's decision to concentrate his efforts on capturing Ukraine with its fertile fields, coal mines, ferrous metals resources, and strategic access to the oilfields of the Caucasus. Although the Red Army's successful counterattacks were another major reason for this diversion to the south, there can be little doubt that Ukraine was also the area that Hitler prized most as the perfect lebensraum for the German people. And such strategic and racial motivations also help explain why Hitler did not take advantage of his being greeted as a liberator by the peoples of western Ukraine, Belorussia, and the Baltic states who had suffered so much from the Nazi–Soviet Non-Aggression Pact.

Although the Nazis treated these peoples as "lesser-beings" *(untermenschen)* from the start and would not allow them any rights whatsoever, what really convinced the Ukrainians and others of Hitler's malevolent intentions toward the Soviet people was the German army's treatment of its Red Army POWs and the occupied Jewish population. In places such as Kiev, where 650,000 Soviet troops were surrounded in September 1941 after a spirited defense of the Ukrainian capital and the Dnieper River region, perhaps two-thirds of the Soviet POWs died of hunger in Nazi captivity. It was amid the euphoria of such victories in fall 1941 that the Hitlerites devised their Final Solution to rid these captured areas of their "great misfortune"—the Jews. In the end, almost half the Jews who died in the Holocaust (some 2.5 million people) were Soviet citizens. Importantly, some of these people died in ways more ghastly than the gas chambers of Poland—mass machine gunning was the most popular method used—as the Nazis, the Wehrmacht (or German army), and a still unknown number of local collaborators experimented with methods of killing to find the most efficient way to achieve genocide. Meanwhile, the vast majority of the surviving Ukrainian and Belorussian civilian populations could only hope for the return of the Stalinists and an authoritarian rule that they understood and might be able to manipulate to their advantage.

In the face of such calamities, Stalin's effort to maintain control over the Russian rear certainly did not show any relaxation of his coercive methods. Red Army men who surrendered, for example, were said to be traitors and were liable to court-martial. Meanwhile, Communist Party members who remained behind on occupied territory were automatically suspect, and if for some reason they crossed back into Soviet-held territory, they were subject to a rigorous check of their backgrounds. Workers who violated the 1940 labor legislation on tardiness, absenteeism, or the prohibition of movement from one job to another could be hauled before a military tribunal. And the same eventually became true for those civilians who ignored compulsory labor mobilizations, responsibilities that impacted everyone but the elderly and the mothers of young children.

Stalin's epic mistakes on the battlefield were soon overshadowed by Hitler's own bungling, and the Soviets found themselves with a second chance. The Nazi leader's earlier decision not to take Moscow ensured that fighting for the Russian capital would take place in the winter, only after the Soviets had had enough time to prepare their defenses. Nevertheless, it was mainly the desperate resistance and simple patriotism of rapidly enlisted men and rearguard troops that saved Moscow in winter 1941–1942 from the Wehrmacht's "Army Group Center." But the GKO's incredibly centralized, command-and-administer system also allowed for the Ural and western Siberian economies to be quickly mobilized to meet the needs of the front. This was particularly important in winter 1941–1942 because the strategic Lend-Lease aid from the Soviet Union's new American ally would not substantively help the Soviet war effort for another year. Even so, Stalin's refusal to let his more able generals lead the efforts at the front resulted in yet more devastating defeats in spring 1942, with the Nazis now occupying all of Ukraine and moving toward their strategic goal of taking southern Russia and the Caucasus.

Here again, though, the Soviets were saved from themselves by Hitler's hubris. The Nazi leader's greatest strategic mistake came with his decision to try to destroy the besieged city of Stalingrad in fall 1942 in order to deal a public relations blow to the "man of steel." Hitler could have concentrated his efforts on occupying the Caucasus and Kuban (Russia's own breadbasket) and exploiting their petroleum and agricultural resources in order to solidify his rule over his new eastern empire. But he went after Stalingrad in an effort to inflict a decisive blow against the Kremlin leader's omnipotent presence in Soviet society. Stalin recognized the stakes too, and after a year of terrible retreat, he finally decided to listen to his generals and make a stand at this city lying along the Volga River. The crucial point here is that the Wehrmacht was spread too thin by this time; Hitler did not have the resources necessary to continue his blitzkrieg. The Wehrmacht's supply lines, for example, were stretched to the breaking point. Thus, the Soviets were eventually able to surround the German Sixth Army at Stalingrad and destroy it after Hitler stubbornly refused to let Field Marshal Friedrich von Paulus retreat. This was the beginning of the end for the Germans—the crucial turning point in the war—where the logistics of what they were doing caught up with them. Hitler's refusal to fully mobilize his own people and his murderous treatment of the *untermenschen* now meant the fighting initiative went over to the Soviet side.

Meanwhile, Hitler's refusal to demand sacrifice from his own population resulted in anger and embitterment among the occupied Ukrainians and Belorussians as their sons and daughters were shipped to Germany to become slave laborers *(Ostarbeitery)*. As the Soviets loomed on the eastern horizon, the Germans liberalized their agricultural policy by dissolving Stalin's hated collective farms; however, at the same time, they were also stripping these areas of anything of value. Not only did the Germans seize raw materials, but they also took tools and machines from factories and valuables from the republics' museums and private apartments as well. One result of all this was a huge expansion in the forest-based anti-Nazi guerilla movement during 1943. True, many of these partisan fighters were motivated by a desire to curry favor with the advancing Red Army; but in the westernmost regions of the Soviet Union's post-1939 borders, many partisans were there to fight sincerely for their nation's political independence as Europe's two totalitarian empires clashed. These "forest brothers," many of whom were as hostile to Moscow as they were to Berlin, would eventually be crushed by the NKVD after war's end. However, their bravery and unhappy end deepened the hostility that many subject peoples felt toward Moscow.

In February 1943, the Red Army started to push the Germans out of the Soviet Union. By that summer, Soviet armed forces had won the biggest tank battle in history at Kursk in central Ukraine, and the Nazis had begun to retreat across the Dnieper. Beginning with the recapture of Kiev in November 1943, the Soviets started a push to the west that would change the face of European politics for the next half century. It was these military successes that finally brought about political agreements between Stalin and his Western allies that went beyond the increasingly important Lend-Lease aid already mentioned. Stalin had always voiced his concern for the opening of a "second front" against the Germans in western Europe. But although his allies, Franklin D. Roosevelt and Winston Churchill, had agreed that they were fighting for the establishment of basic freedoms across Europe, the question of just how Stalin's dictatorship would contribute to this cause had long put off serious discussions of military cooperation. Now, however, the Red Army was moving west, and there was no doubt that its soldiers were highly motivated following the raping and pillaging of their homeland by the Nazis.

At the Teheran Conference of November 1943, the members of the so-called Grand Alliance truly began to work together. Here the decision to open the second front during 1944 was finally made. Here also one can see the birth of the United Nations as each side thought it might eventually use this organization to extend its influence over the world. And most importantly, the decision to control Germany jointly was made at this time too. No surrender from Hitler would be accepted for this was now a fight to destroy fascism once and for all. There can be little doubt that all members of the Grand Alliance understood that because the Soviet people had almost single-handedly turned back the Nazi onslaught, the Stalin regime was going to play a major role in Europe's political life for a long time to come.

The results of this were clear long before World War II ended. During 1944, the siege of Leningrad was broken, the Baltic nations were "liberated," and the country of Poland was taken from the Nazis only after the Germans had been allowed to destroy the local pro-democratic resistance first. These Soviet victories, along with the entrance of Great Britain and the United States into the European Theatre of Operations that summer, made the fate of East Central Europe paramount to each member of the Grand Alliance. The Red Army's presence on the ground in many of these areas proved decisive. In no way were British and American leaders prepared to sacrifice their men for the independence of Poles, Romanians, Yugoslavs, and others in the region. Thus, when Churchill and Stalin met in October 1944, the former scrawled on a paper napkin his ideas about how the lands stretching from the Balkans to the Baltic should be divided upon percentage terms into spheres of influence for the East and the West. This outrageously cynical approach to the fate of so many millions of people remains a remarkable fact.

By the Yalta Conference of February 1945, Stalin's forces were bearing down on Berlin, and for the Grand Alliance, East Central Europe's fate was already sealed. At Yalta, the representatives of the Grand Alliance made important decisions about Germany's future. They decided to create zones of occupation for each of the members of the Grand Alliance—including the newly freed French—and to hold jointly the capital, Berlin. For the economically devastated Soviet Union, Stalin convinced his allies to allow German reparations to his country to take the form of Moscow's plundering of its former enemy's industrial infrastructure. Although Stalin did promise to allow "free and fair elections" to take place in East Central Europe, many people there already realized that having been on the right side of history during the Soviets' sweep through the east was about as much as their nations could be thankful for at this time. The other issue decided at Yalta concerned the United Nations. Stalin finally accepted the idea of a world body in return for his inclusion in the alliance's effort to occupy and destroy imperial Japan and the spoils that might generate. Only the dropping of the atomic bomb—and the new geopolitical era it inaugurated—prevented the Soviet leader from thoroughly enjoying the fruits of his people's victories over Nazi Germany.

The end for the Nazis came in April 1945 as the Red Army, led by George K. Zhukov and Ivan S. Konev, used a two-pronged attack to take Nazi-occupied Hungary and Czechoslovakia from the south while attacking eastern Germany from the north. During these events, Stalin did not object to the news of his soldiers raping German women and pillaging the property of those they came across on enemy turf. Because of this, any chance for a later rapprochement between the Soviet authorities and the newly occupied German people was destroyed. Meanwhile, by late April, Zhukov had won the race to Berlin, and a few days later, after Hitler committed suicide, the Grand Alliance declared victory.

For four horrendous years, defeating the Nazis had been the modus operandi for Stalin's people. At the center of Soviet life, the front became the sole concern of Stalin and his Stavka and GKO cohorts, and meeting the needs of the military was what held the country together from 1941 to 1945. Meanwhile, on the periphery, it was the job of local Communist Party members to make sure the people they ruled over were physically able to do the work necessary to fulfill the military-related orders contained in the myriad of resolutions handed down from the center. Stalin's terrible pronouncements and the NKVD's killing of those considered harmful to the Soviet cause were evident in 1941, so the question that needs to be answered here is how exactly did Stalin's local party men make certain that the people in the Soviet rear remained committed to fulfilling Moscow's plans after that fateful year?

Although it is true that a simple patriotic desire to help defend one's homeland and support one's kin in the fight against a loathsome and barbaric enemy was probably reason enough for the people's support of Stalin's wartime plans, it cannot be forgotten that 20 million Soviet citizens died in the fight against Hitler. And it was that huge demographic loss that eventually caused major changes in how Moscow governed the Soviet Union. Most importantly, perhaps, are indications that the NKVD became more involved in the frantic search for reinforcements for the front as the war continued than it was in randomly terrorizing the Soviet population as it had done in the 1930s. In addition to this fundamental change in Stalin's system, a large number of Red Army soldiers and their surviving dependents—a massive chunk of the Soviet population as whole—were now given the titles of privilege holders that previously had been the exclusive preserve of Stakhanovite shock-workers and the cowering professional classes during the Great Breakthrough. As for those Soviets working in the country's factories, the temptation to move—despite the prohibitions against doing so—to the command economy's enterprises that provided the best housing and nourishment amid a harsh wartime regime was irresistible. It was against these politicized social currents that the local Communist captains had to navigate their ships of state in an effort to ensure both that Moscow's needs were met and that their careers were not dashed against the rocks of Soviet political reality.

The ability of these local Communist Party officials to perform this delicate balancing act was most enhanced in the Volga, Urals, and western Siberian regions where the Stalin regime's military-industrial complex was rapidly reformed during the war years. But problems arose in several areas, particularly the European part of the Soviet Union that had been occupied by the Nazis. Here, the local Communist Party leadership found itself dealing with people whose inadequate material conditions hardly translated into support for whatever harebrained reconstruction plans the local leaders had on tap. Perhaps Stalin's liberalization of the cultural realm, which now allowed writers to compose tracts in relative freedom and granted the Orthodox Church a reprieve from the murderous actions taken against it during the prewar years, were part of his regime's effort to overcome this situation in the European part of the Soviet Union. Only in the Caucasus, where some of that area's Muslim peoples were accused of having treasonously supported the occupying Nazis and were then exiled en masse to Soviet Central Asia, does one see a repeat of the terrible events of the 1930s.

Satisfying the interests of these various local populations in order to meet Moscow's present and future desires obviously required a good deal of political flexibility on the part of the Communist Party members in question. But such flexibility did not mean that organized dissent against Stalin's regime would emerge at this time. The horrors of the war on top of the social atomization brought about by Moscow's terror campaigns of the 1930s made cooperation among the peoples of the Soviet Union unthinkable at this time. However, there can be little doubt that the alternative reality of the 1930s—a situation in which the regime's propaganda about the masses' supposed interests shaped the Soviet elites' social psychology and in which the elites supported the building of socialism in order to achieve advancement for themselves—had been destroyed by the Nazi attack of 1941. Simply put, much of the Soviet ruling class, including the local Communist Party members, now asked themselves how the building of socialism could exist when the country and its people had lost so much after Hitler's move east. The result was not only that local leaders were no longer wracked by self-doubt when it came to the true interests of the masses as they had been in the 1930s, but also a realization that the masses' now plainly evident post-conflict needs would have to be satisfied if reconstruction was to begin and the economy was to be rebuilt.

Thus, the main result of the Soviet Union's wartime experience was the shifting to the people of the initiative for political change, following the death blow dealt by Hitler's blitzkrieg to the state's animating ideology of "building socialism." However, the people were now also horribly divided among themselves. It was still up to the local Communist Party members to devise ways to get them to work, and it was in these processes that the seeds of political change for the Soviet Union's future were sown. The fact that two-thirds of the Communist Party's members were themselves new to that organization in 1945 and knew little if anything about Marx and Engels is perhaps the best reason for further examination of how they satisfied the interests of the Soviet people as World War II came to an end. Although the Soviet Union was now a superpower on the world stage, the efforts of these Communists to build successful careers for themselves probably laid the groundwork for the Soviet Union's subsequent destruction from within.

SELECTED BIBLIOGRAPHY

Barber, John, and Mark Harrison. *The Soviet Home Front, 1941–1945: A Social and Economic History.* New York: Longman, 1991.
    Still the most comprehensive account of the different forces influencing the ordinary people's understanding of their country's life during a time of "total war."

Bardach, Janusz. *Man is Wolf to Man: Surviving the Gulag.* Berkeley: University of California Press, 1998.

An almost unbelievable memoir by a man from Soviet-occupied Poland who fought for the Red Army only to be accused of treason and sent for a torturous journey through Stalin's wartime camps deep in the Siberian rear.

Bartov, Omer. *The Eastern Front, 1941–1945, German Troops and the Barbarization of Warfare.* New York: Palgrave, 2001.

A pathbreaking history that argues that ordinary German army men—not just the shock troops of Hitler's SS—were "true believers" in Nazi racist ideology and that this was a main reason behind Germany's ultimate failure on the eastern front.

Beevor, Antony. *Stalingrad: The Fateful Siege, 1942–43.* New York: Viking, 1998.

An extraordinary account of the ordinary Russian soldier's experience at the Battle of Stalingrad using sources made available after the fall of Communism.

Berkoff, Karel. *Harvest of Despair: Life and Death in Ukraine under Nazi Rule.* Cambridge, MA: The Belknap Press of Harvard University Press, 2004.

The definitive account which argues that the Nazis were only interested in exploiting the Ukrainians and that the latter soon longed for the return of a totalitarian regime they could at least understand and possibly manipulate to their advantage.

Bonwetsch, Bernd, and Robert Thurston, eds. *A People's War: Popular Responses to World War II in the Soviet Union.* Champaign-Urbana: University of Illinois Press, 2000.

A collection of articles, some of which explain the "mosaic of moods" that overcame the Soviet people as they tried to rationalize their life situations amid the Nazi attack and the sudden end of Stalin's 1930s aura of infallibility.

Gitelman, Zwi. *Bitter Legacy: Confronting the Holocaust in the USSR.* Bloomington: Indiana University Press, 1997.

This work examines the unknown histories of events that became a taboo subject in a postwar Soviet Union where ethnic groups were not allowed to particularize their suffering at the hands of the Nazis.

Glantz, David, and Jonathan M. House. *When Titans Clashed: How the Soviet Union Stopped Hitler.* Lawrence: University of Kansas Press, 1995.

The standard military history of World War II's eastern European front argues that the Soviets' dwindling reserves of fighting men forced their General Staff and commanders in the field to become better battlefield tacticians as time passed.

Gorodetsky, Gabriel. *Grand Delusion: Stalin and the German Invasion of Russia.* New Haven, CT: Yale University Press, 1999.

This definitive account of why Hitler's attack in June 1941 came as a surprise to the Soviet Union argues that Stalin mistakenly believed the Nazis would seek to defeat Great Britain first before heading to the east.

Moskoff, William. *The Bread of Affliction: The Food Supply in the USSR during World War II.* Cambridge: Cambridge University Press, 2002.

A work that examines what happened after local authorities in the Soviet Union were delegated the task of keeping their subjects alive through the war years with little, if any, assistance from the center.

Naimark, Norman, *The Russians in Germany: A History of the Soviet Occupation of Germany*. Cambridge, MA: The Belknap Press of the Harvard University Press, 1996.

A pathbreaking and comprehensive work that argues in part that the Soviets' treatment of women in occupied Germany undermined Moscow's sizeable effort to establish a positive relationship with the new "East Germans."

Nekrich, Alexander. *The Punished Peoples: The Deportation and the Fate of the Soviet Minorities at the End of the Second World War*. New York: Norton, 1978.

An early but accurate account by an exiled Russian dissident about Stalin's ethnic cleansing of the Crimean Tatars and Muslim peoples of the North Caucasus after they were accused of collaboration with the Nazis.

Overy, Richard. *Russia's War: A History of the Soviet War Effort, 1941–1945*. New York: Penguin, 1998.

A recent work of synthesis that integrates much of the post-1991 research done on the war years and that is particularly strong on sorting out the historiographic debates of the past surrounding Soviet wartime foreign policy.

Rigby, Theodore H. *Communist Party Membership in the USSR, 1917–1967*. Princeton, NJ: Princeton University Press, 1968.

A work that contains vital chapters on how World War II fundamentally changed the social makeup of the only legally active political institution in the Soviet Union.

Simmons, Cynthia, and Nina Perlina. *Writing the Siege of Leningrad: Women's Diaries, Memoirs and Documentary Prose*. Pittsburgh, PA: University of Pittsburgh Press, 2002.

Complete with a historical introduction and the critical commentary necessary to provide context, this volume succeeds in providing a definitive understanding of daily life amid Leningrad's extraordinary circumstances.

Stites, Richard, ed. *Culture and Entertainment in Wartime Russia*. Bloomington: Indiana University Press, 1995.

A collection of articles that captures the wartime rebirth of artistic freedom in the Soviet Union, which Moscow believed was necessary for keeping up morale in the face of the Nazis.

Tumarkin, Nina. *The Living and the Dead: The Rise and Fall of the Cult of the War*. New York: Basic Books, 1994.

A unique work that tracks how the image of a supposedly unified Soviet people's victorious effort in World War II was resurrected in the 1960s and 1970s to become a propagandistic myth used by the Communist Party to help hold an already fractious society together.

Weiner, Amir. *Making Sense of War: The Second World War and the Fate of the Bolshevik Revolution*. Princeton, NJ: Princeton University Press, 2001.

The first monograph based on archival research about the aftermath of the war experience in the Soviet Union; it argues that one's contributions to victory became the all-important "social capital" needed to advance in postwar Ukrainian society.

Werth, Alexander. *Russia at War, 1941–1945*. New York: Avon, 1964.

The leading journalistic account of World War II in the Soviet Union written by a British correspondent who witnessed the war from such places as the diplomatic corridors of Moscow, the streets of the rearguard cities, and the lands just liberated from the Nazi occupiers.

Zubkova, Elena. *Russia after the War: Hopes, Illusions, and Disappointments, 1945–1957.* Armonk, NY: M. E. Sharpe. 1998.
    A Russian historian recounts why the Soviet people were unable to mount a challenge to the Stalin regime following the latter's horrendous wartime mistakes and its own wartime exposure to the world outside its borders.

9

The Cold War, 1945–1991

INTRODUCTION

Unlike many conflicts, it is difficult to pinpoint a precise date for the start of the Cold War, although most observers agree that it began shortly after the close of World War II. In a broad sense, the Cold War represented the culmination of conflicting viewpoints tracing back to the early nineteenth century. With the onset of the Industrial Revolution, mankind's relationship to the forces that produce wealth, or the means of production, once again took center stage. The eighteenth century generated a model, perhaps best articulated by Adam Smith, that enshrined the sanctity of private property, blessed the profit motive, and elevated the free market to almost infallible status. As a political corollary, the supporters of what came to be called laissez-faire capitalism endorsed the features of nascent liberal democracy, including constitutions, restricted suffrage, minimalist government, and civil liberties.

Reacting to the horrors of the Industrial Revolution's early stages, a growing number of nineteenth-century intellectuals, led by the German émigré Karl Marx, rejected laissez-faire capitalism. Although some advocated reform and regulation, others such as Marx envisioned class warfare and called for capitalism's complete destruction. In capitalism's place they would erect a system based on the collective ownership of the means of production and an equal sharing of its obligations and bounties. According to Marx, the state, before "withering away," would act as an agent for the workers, carrying out the wishes of the "dictatorship of the proletariat."

In July 1959, U.S. Vice President Richard M. Nixon angrily confronted Soviet leader Nikita S. Khrushchev during the famous "kitchen debate" at a U.S. exhibition in Moscow. The Cold War was the defining event of the post World War II era for both countries. (Reproduced from the Collections of the Library of Congress.)

Throughout the nineteenth century, these two irreconcilable visions competed; however, both also fractured. Among the capitalists, some gradually drifted away from the laissez-faire position and came to embrace—with varying degrees of enthusiasm—a model that called for some regulation of the free-market economy in the name of the common good. Among socialists, a split occurred when some embraced revisionism, the view that socialism could be achieved in a peaceful, evolutionary manner through the ballot box and the labor union. The revisionists clashed with orthodox Marxists, or Communists, who insisted on the primacy of class warfare to achieve socialism's goals.

Several months after the rickety Russian Empire collapsed in March 1917, the Bolsheviks, or Russian Communists, under the leadership of Vladimir I. Lenin, seized power. This development alarmed capitalists, and their fear and revulsion played a role in dispatching Western troops to intervene in the Russian civil war that followed the Bolshevik triumph. The Bolsheviks defeated their Russian opponents, but this Western attempt to "strangle socialism in its cradle" was not forgotten. Conversely, the Bolsheviks confirmed the West's worst suspicions by imposing a bloody and brutal Communist dictatorship on Russia and trying to export their revolution.

During World War II, the Soviet Union, the United States, and Great Britain united against the common Nazi enemy. However, this Grand Alliance was truly a marriage of convenience; its cracks were barely papered over. Beyond the unbridgeable ideological differences, the two sides differed over both prewar policies and wartime actions. The Soviet Union condemned the West's failure to join it in forming an anti-Nazi popular front during the 1930s, whereas the Western countries criticized the Soviet Union for having signed a nonaggression pact with Hitler on the war's eve. During the war, the refusal of the Western allies to open a second front against Germany until June 1944 outraged the Soviets, who concluded that the West was intentionally letting Germany bleed the Soviet Union white. Meanwhile, the West looked askance at Soviet behavior in East Central Europe, where, in the guise of liberators, the Soviets were imposing their will and extending the reach of Marxism. In retrospect, it should have come as no surprise that the Grand Alliance broke up almost immediately after Nazi Germany's defeat.

The opening "shots" of the Cold War occurred in occupied Germany when it became clear that the Soviet Union on one hand and the Anglo-American combination on the other hand fundamentally disagreed on how to deal with their defeated adversary. The reparations question posed a particular problem. The Soviet Union demanded extensive reparations to compensate for the massive damage done to the Soviet homeland by the German armies. Suspecting the Soviet Union's ultimate intentions, the Western allies rejected these demands.

Beginning in summer 1945, East–West relations gradually deteriorated. In May 1945, the United States startled the Soviet Union when it announced a cessation of Lend-Lease. A few months later, the dropping of atomic bombs on Japan signaled to the Soviets that the United States not only possessed a weapon of unusual destructive power but also was willing to use it. Meanwhile, the Soviet Union continued to tighten its grip on East Central Europe despite pledges to the contrary and remained uncooperative on German issues.

Early in 1946, rhetorical blasts revealed an increasing level of hostility between East and West. In February, Soviet leader Joseph V. Stalin publicly denigrated the West's contribution to the recently ended war and warned that the Soviet Union remained locked in a life-and-death ideological struggle with capitalism despite its victory over Germany. The West's response came a month later when former British prime minister

Winston Churchill, with U.S. President Harry S Truman at his side, declared, "From Stettin in the Baltic to Trieste in the Adriatic, an iron curtain has descended across the continent."

In the following year, the Soviet Union, having installed Communist regimes in the East Central European countries that it had liberated, now destroyed any real or potential opposition to its supremacy and cemented Stalinist systems into place. Furthermore, a wave of Soviet-instigated labor unrest swept over western Europe. In response to a Communist-inspired civil war in Greece, President Truman promulgated the Truman Doctrine whereby the United States promised to "support free peoples who are resisting attempted subjugation by armed minorities or outside pressures." A few months later, the U.S. Congress approved the European Recovery Act, or Marshall Plan, which provided billions of dollars for Europeans to rebuild their economy and, by implication, resist the lure that Communism had for the downtrodden.

In February 1948, the Soviet Union strengthened Communist control over Czechoslovakia, thereby prompting the Western allies to announce their intention to unify their German zones of occupation, an obvious step toward resurrecting a German state. Any sort of independent Germany was anathema to Stalin, and in June 1948 he retaliated by interdicting land access to occupied Berlin. The West countered with an airlift that supplied Berlin's western zones for almost a year. Stalin's Berlin Blockade hastened the creation of the Western-sponsored Federal Republic of Germany, or West Germany, in May 1949. The Soviet Union then turned its zone of occupation into the German Democratic Republic, or East Germany, in October 1949.

Moreover, in 1949 the West created the North Atlantic Treaty Organization (NATO), a defensive military alliance clearly directed against the Soviet Union. The Soviets responded with a de facto military alliance of their own that was not formally inaugurated until 1955 as the Warsaw Treaty Organization (WTO). In September 1949, the Soviet Union exploded its own atomic bomb, but the United States was already working on a much more powerful hydrogen bomb. A runaway arms race soon became a hallmark characteristic of the Cold War.

Cold War economic competition took place as well. As western Europe moved toward greater economic unity, in 1949 the Soviet Union created the Council of Mutual Economic Assistance (CMEA or COMECON) to coordinate economic matters for those countries under its control.

By the late 1940s, the Cold War was moving from its European origins to a global stage. In 1949 Communists triumphed in China after a prolonged civil war, and one year later, Communists launched a war on the Korean peninsula. Although the Soviet role remains complicated and open to interpretation, the West at that time had no doubt that Moscow had orchestrated both events.

Stalin's death in March 1953 signaled a change in the Cold War's nature. Henceforth, East–West relations would no longer be hopelessly frozen. Rather, although the underlying animosity driving the relationship remained constant, the Cold War came to resemble a roller coaster featuring a series of ups and downs—periodic warmings followed by renewed crises. Perhaps most importantly, the new Soviet leader, Nikita S. Khrushchev, abandoned Stalin's belief in the inevitability of a violent confrontation and decreed instead a policy of "peaceful coexistence." Realizing that a nuclear exchange would benefit no one, Khrushchev said that henceforth the East and West would compete in every imaginable manner while striving to avoid a shooting war. This was a position that the West had already taken, and the post-Stalin Soviet readjustment was welcomed.

During the 1950s, several events pointed to a warming in East–West relations: Khrushchev and his entourage visited both Great Britain and the United States; the Austrian State Treaty provided for the creation of an independent but neutral Austria; the Soviet Union sought greater international trade and marginally opened itself to scholars and tourists; and Khrushchev and Dwight D. Eisenhower, the U.S. president, met cordially at Geneva, Switzerland, in 1955. However, there were also serious Cold War issues during the decade, including a burgeoning arms race, the Soviet Union's attempts to thrust itself into Middle Eastern matters, continual tension over the status of Berlin, and in 1956 the brutal and bloody Soviet suppression of the Hungarian Revolution.

In the early 1960s, a series of Cold War crises returned East–West relations to the deep freeze and brought the world to the brink of nuclear holocaust. In May 1960, the U-2 spy plane incident shattered the rapport between Khrushchev and Eisenhower. A year later, the failed U.S. attempt at the Bay of Pigs to overthrow Fidel Castro, the successful Cuban revolutionary, provided the Soviet Union with an entree into the western hemisphere. A few months later, Khrushchev met the new U.S. president, John F. Kennedy, at Vienna and came away convinced that Kennedy was weak and could be bullied. In August, in order to protect the German Democratic Republic from a growing exodus of educated and skilled people, Khrushchev authorized the erection of the Berlin Wall, which divided that city in two. In the fall of 1962, the Soviet Union overreached when it tried to place missiles in what had become its Cuban satellite. Kennedy responded with a naval blockade of the island, and war seemed imminent.

As the world held its breath, the Soviets chose not to run the blockade, and the crisis eased. However, the thought of nuclear missiles falling from the sky once again reminded the world of the seriousness of the Cold War. In 1963 a series of agreements between the Soviet Union and the United States seemed to promise a less dangerous if no less hostile future.

During the 1960s, both the Soviet Union and the United States experienced problems that momentarily distracted them from the Cold War. The former had to contend with Khrushchev's 1964 ouster and his replacement by Leonid I. Brezhnev, with China's challenge to Soviet supremacy within the global Marxist movement, and with an invasion of Czechoslovakia in 1968 to restore an orthodox Marxist regime. At the same time, the United States had to deal with the discord inherent in the U.S. civil rights movement; a spate of assassinations that took the lives of Kennedy, his brother Robert, and Martin Luther King Jr.; and its growing involvement in the Vietnam War, itself an outgrowth of the Cold War.

Somewhat surprisingly, in the early 1970s, East–West relations improved perceptibly under what came to be called "détente," or a relaxation of tensions. President Richard M. Nixon, who had made his mark as a strident anti-Communist, met Brezhnev several times, producing agreements to limit the arms race, including a Strategic Arms Limitation Treaty (SALT I) and the Anti-Ballistic Missile (ABM) Treaty. Détente peaked in 1975 with the joint Apollo-Soyuz space mission and the signing of the Helsinki Accords, which, among other things, legitimized Europe's post–World War II borders and the Soviet gains they reflected.

Détente crashed in the late 1970s when the Soviet Union invaded Afghanistan to prop up a puppet regime; crushed Solidarity, Poland's independent trade union and a threat to Soviet control there; and supported more actively Marxist-oriented revolutionary movements in the Caribbean, Central America, and Africa. One consequence of this was the 1980 U.S. election victory of the staunch anti-Communist Ronald Reagan, who significantly increased the U.S. military's budget, pushed for the deployment of missiles in Europe to counter Soviet missile deployment, and advocated a missile defense shield to protect the United States from Soviet missiles while leaving that country vulnerable to a U.S. attack. In 1983 Reagan publicly referred to the Soviet Union as an "evil empire." The frostiest days of the Cold War had returned.

The Cold War's end caught everyone by surprise. Brezhnev's passing in 1982 initiated a generational change among the Soviet Union's leadership. In March 1985, Mikhail S. Gorbachev headed the Communist Party and continued to replace antiquated veterans with younger, reform-minded officials. Determined to revitalize his stagnant country, Gorbachev inaugurated a number of fundamental but not well-thought-out or well-executed reforms. In order to concentrate on his domestic reforms, Gorbachev sought a return to détente-like conditions. Subsequently, Gorbachev and Reagan held productive summits, and in December 1987 they signed the important Intermediate-Range Nuclear Forces (INF) Treaty. Meanwhile, Gorbachev's reforms were spinning out of control, and the Soviet leader deemed it prudent to undertake a global retrenchment. A major watershed occurred in 1989 when Gorbachev refused to employ military might to preserve unpopular Communist regimes in East Central Europe, and the Soviet Union's post–World War II satellite empire disappeared. As it turned out, the Soviet Union itself was on its last legs. Centrifugal forces pulled the country apart, and on December 31, 1991, it officially closed up shop. With the death of the Soviet Union, the Cold War came to an end.

INTERPRETIVE ESSAY
Jerry Pubantz

A simple vignette captures the beginnings of the Cold War. On April 23, 1945, Soviet Foreign Minister Viacheslav M. Molotov met President Harry Truman at the White House. Truman's predecessor, Franklin D. Roosevelt, had died less than two weeks earlier. The war in Europe was ending, and Adolf Hitler's regime was disintegrating. Molotov's visit came as he was en route to San Francisco for the organizing conference of the United Nations, another apparent product of cooperation among the United States, the Soviet Union, and Great Britain. However, when the two men met in the Oval Office, Truman immediately raised the subject of events in Poland and the U.S. government's intention to withhold recognition of any Polish government imposed by the Soviet Union that was not the product of free elections. As Molotov began to explain the Soviet Union's national security interests in Poland, Truman cut him off, saying that he did not want to hear any propaganda. The president's response signaled a new adversarial tone that the Soviet government had not experienced during the Roosevelt years. A letter from Stalin the following day reiterating Soviet national interests in Poland proved to be, in Truman's own words, "one of the most revealing and disquieting messages" Truman received in the early days of his presidency. A new era of confrontation was at hand.

Poland was not the only bone of contention in the early stages of the Cold War. The sides had disputes over United Nations membership and the use of the veto. Additionally, Stalin's demands for German reparations went unheeded by his former Western allies. Also, in the spring of 1945, Soviet troops remained in northern Iran, apparently violating an earlier promise to the United States and Great Britain to vacate that territory.

As World War II concluded, the wartime alliance frayed. This is not an unusual occurrence in international affairs. Coalitions during wartime are often held together by little more than a common enemy. Once the war ends, differing national interests, values, and older animosities destroy allied comity. What proved unusual in this case were the length, severity, and consequences of the emerging divisions between the Soviet Union and its former allied democracies. Over the next 45 years, the early confrontations deepened into a global struggle between East and West.

The Cold War came and went in stages, with each period marked by intricate foreign policy engagements between the two superpowers and their respective allies. But when one surveys the full sweep of confrontation between the United States and the Soviet Union, the observer is struck by the overriding sense that this long era was, in fact, far more dangerous for the interests and survival of the Soviet Union than for the United States. It proved to be the final crisis of the 70-year Soviet experiment, culminating in the collapse of the Soviet political, ideological, and economic system in 1991. Furthermore, by providing the catalyst for the Soviet Union's implosion, the Cold War brought to an end centuries of Russian autocracy and empire and ushered in a difficult transition to democracy.

From the perspective of Russian domestic and foreign policy, the Cold War can be divided for useful discussion into four distinct periods: the era of Stalinist imperial expansion and virulent ideological orthodoxy (1945–1953), peaceful coexistence and ideological revision (1953–1962), détente (1962–1979), and atrophy and ideological rejection (1980–1991). Each of these periods had its unique East–West policy confrontations and broader implications for international affairs. Each era was produced in significant part by internal Soviet politics, and each era in turn dramatically affected the Soviet state, ideology, and economy. Finally, these segments of the Cold War, to the extent that they were the outcomes of Soviet foreign policy, reflected the continuing strains between Marxist-Leninist ideology, which served as the legitimizing authority for Communist Party rule, and Soviet national interests.

Three factors motivated Soviet policies in the immediate postwar era: a strategic interest in defending the Soviet state from another war of aggression such as it had experienced twice in the twentieth century at the hands of Germany; the reimposition of Stalinist ideological orthodoxy at home and in its newly acquired empire; and Stalin's paranoia. Having lost tens of millions of Soviet citizens to the German war machine, Stalin was adamant about creating a buffer zone of satellite regimes in East Central Europe. As it became clear that the U.S. military, economic, and political commitment to Europe would not be withdrawn, as had been the case following World War I, Stalin moved to secure tight Soviet control over the border nations reaching from the Baltic Sea in the north to the Adriatic Sea in the south. In each of these countries, Stalin began a common process of first claiming key positions in the provisional government for Communist Party leaders, then undermining scheduled all-party elections, and finally imposing Soviet-style Communist regimes.

Soviet actions in the early stages of the Cold War were presented as the natural outcome of the laws of history, first identified by Karl Marx and refined by Vladimir I. Lenin, the architect of the Bolshevik revolution. Following Lenin's death in 1924, all future Soviet leaders couched their domestic and foreign policies in "Marxist-Leninist" terms. It was essential to demonstrate the compatibility of their actions with orthodox Communist teachings. Ideology provided the legitimacy required for the regime's existence, tying subsequent leaders' decisions to the revolutionary past and supposedly to the future course of history to which they were uniquely privy. In the context of post-1945 international conditions, the Soviet government defined both its foreign and domestic Cold War policies in terms of two critical theories: inevitable war and the two-camp doctrine.

Inevitable war was central to both Lenin's and Stalin's worldviews. Lenin asserted the inevitability of intercapitalist war in *Imperialism: The Highest Stage of Capitalism* (1916). He argued that in the era of finance capitalism, the world literally had been divided up among the major capitalist states. In the future, only redivision would be possible, and that could happen only by way of imperialist war. After the Bolsheviks' seizure of power in 1917, the relationship between the first socialist state and the capitalist world had to be understood in this context of the capitalist proclivity for war. Lenin fully expected a bourgeois attack on the new Russian state. In 1919 he told the delegates to the Eighth Party Congress that "the existence of the Soviet Republic side by side with the imperialist states for a long time is unthinkable. One or the other must triumph in the end. And before that end supervenes, a series of frightful collisions between the Soviet Republic and the bourgeois states will be inevitable." Stalin also saw war as inevitable. In 1928 he argued that at best, an inevitable capitalist attack on the Soviet Union could only be postponed. Thus, the intervening period must be used for the massive industrialization and military preparation of the Soviet Union. Much of Stalin's draconian domestic program—forced collectivization of agriculture, the rapid building of an industrial society through overly optimistic five-year plans, the imposition of the terror and the purges—was rationalized by the need to build "socialism in one country" before the capitalists launched their aggressive assault.

In the mid-1930s, Stalin blurred the doctrine of inevitable war. This was occasioned by the rise of Hitler in Germany and the need to forge a "United Front," or "Popular Front," with capitalist states against the fascist threat. Stalin, however, did not see the avoidance of war with capitalism as a permanent possibility. Following World War II, the Soviets quickly returned to orthodoxy. The emerging Cold War with the United States and its allies, particularly those that joined the North Atlantic Treaty Organization (NATO) in 1949, demonstrated to the Soviets the hostile intent of the capitalist bloc.

The return to ideological confrontation with the West, with its frightening prospect of global war, accompanied the imposition of ideological purity and economic isolation at home. The era of Andrei A. Zhdanov (*Zhdanovshchina*) took hold. Zhdanov was the Communist Party secretary for Leningrad and Stalin's chief subordinate in the campaign to return to Communist orthodoxy. Zhdanov condemned all flirtations with Western ideas, art, or social life, calling them "vile obscenities," "philistinism," and "anti-party" treachery. He endorsed complete economic and scientific autarky. The postwar rebuilding of the Soviet Union had to be done under strict quarantine from outside capitalist influence. Stalin rejected Marshall Plan funds and barred Soviet satellite regimes from economic ties with Western Europe. Particularly after Tito's Yugoslavia deserted the Communist fold in 1948, Stalinist repression at home and abroad reached the levels of the mid-1930s. Reasonably moderate Communist regimes in East Central Europe were replaced with hard-line governments; show trials and purges occurred throughout the Soviet bloc; and in the Soviet Union, Stalin insinuated that the fourth Five-Year Plan (1946–1950), which was already austere, would be followed by even more difficult economic times. The persistent presentation of the West in threatening Cold War terms made this strategy more palatable.

Theoretically, Stalin's inevitable war theory demanded the existence of two irreconcilable camps in world affairs; it envisioned a group of socialist states surrounded by an implacable foe. The U.S. policy of containment that emerged after President Truman's 1947 assertion of an American commitment to defend free states from Communist aggression or subversion seemed to demonstrate the truth of a capitalist encirclement, defeatable only by absolute ideological solidarity of all segments of socialist society and by the expansion of the socialist bloc whenever the opportunity presented itself.

The two-camp doctrine provided rationalization for the creation of a Soviet trading bloc separate from the world economy. This bloc, the Council of Mutual Economic Assistance (COMECON or CMEA), redirected the traditional trading patterns of the East Central European states away from the West and toward the Soviet Union. The camp theory also provided an ideological rationale for the rapid advancement of Soviet science to catch up to and surpass the United States in the burgeoning nuclear arms race and to root out all symptoms of corrosive bourgeois influence inside the socialist camp.

The camp theory also imposed limits on Soviet Cold War policy. In the growing global confrontation with the United States, it would have been advantageous for Soviet foreign policy to break the capitalist encirclement by reaching out to the newly liberated states of Africa and Asia. These former European colonies had achieved national independence and were likely to hold anti-Western sentiments. Many of the new national-liberation governments espoused socialist economic programs and sought friendly relations with Moscow. But without a clear declaration of loyalty by these nations to the Stalinist model of development and to the Soviet bloc, Stalin expressed little interest in developing ties to those states. One opportunity of special value was Egypt, which experienced a revolution in 1952 led by Gamal Abdel Nasser. However, Stalin believed Nasser to be an agent of the West because his regime could not be defined as "socialist" with a one-party Communist state in place. Soviet foreign policy would have to await Stalin's passing before new leadership would revise Communist ideology to make closer ties with Egypt and other developing countries possible.

The ideological prism through which Joseph Stalin interpreted world affairs cemented his paranoia. "Enemies" had threatened Stalin's political survival from the earliest days of the Bolshevik regime. After surviving the succession crisis following Lenin's death, banishing his most serious rival, Leon D. Trotsky, to foreign exile, and securing his dominant position in the party in 1929, Stalin had turned to eliminating any remaining potential competitors. In the 1930s he used the secret police and show trials to purge the party even of loyal Old Bolsheviks who might emerge as contenders for his power. In the lead-up to World War II, Stalin also saw treachery in the policies of the powers that had won World War I and crafted the Versailles Treaty. As Hitler successively tore up the terms of that treaty, Western governments stood by and did little to rein in Germany. Stalin concluded that the capitalists were playing a cynical game to draw the Nazi regime into a war with the Soviet Union. When Czechoslovakia was carved up with British and French consent in the fall of 1938, Stalin made it clear he would not save Europe from Hitler, and then he made his deal with the devil in the 1939 Nazi–Soviet Non-Aggression Pact. Even during the war, Stalin remained highly suspicious of his allies, particularly as they postponed opening a second front against Germany in the west.

Thus, the suspicion and distrust that characterized Stalinist foreign policy after the war was not novel. The unwillingness of his allies to make good on promised reparations, Truman's offhand remarks to Stalin at the Potsdam Conference in July 1945 that the United States had developed a new and extraordinarily powerful bomb, and the U.S. president's dispatch of an American warship to the eastern Mediterranean in March 1946 to pressure the Soviets to withdraw from Iran all demonstrated to Stalin that the United States and the Western alliance were intent on undermining his government. What were essentially defensive moves in the West against perceived Soviet expansionism were understood in exactly the opposite way by Stalin.

In East Central Europe, Stalin's paranoia resulted in the imposition of totalitarian regimes on millions of people. It is not unusual for Great Powers to seek friendly buffer states on their borders. However, in those cases where a major power has insisted that surrounding states maintain cooperative domestic and foreign policies, it normally has not demanded that the satellite regimes duplicate the Great Power's political and economic system. Stalin provided the exception. Fearful that any deviation from the Soviet model would endanger socialist solidarity in the face of the Cold War, East Central European governments were expected to be governed by Communist parties that organizationally paralleled the Communist Party of the Soviet Union. They were expected to impose collectivized farming and planned economies. Each was expected to employ an extensive secret police, which, in turn, was to be integrated with the Soviet police system. Each government was also expected to insist on ideological conformity in the arts, education, and social life.

Stalin's paranoia extended to the domestic front. The *Zhdanovshchina*— or Zhdanov's vicious attack on Western culture and ideas carried out at Stalin's behest—was central to Stalin's efforts to find spies and infiltrators of the socialist camp. In his last years, Stalin seemed intent on another round of purges. In January 1953 the Soviet press announced the arrest of nine Kremlin doctors. The state charged them with working on behalf of a U.S. Jewish organization and using their medical access to senior party leaders to murder Zhdanov and other Soviet officials. The "Doctors' Plot" seemed similar in style to the strategy used by Stalin to launch the Great Purge in the 1930s. Fortunately for other Soviet politicians, this final act of Stalin's paranoia was cut short by the dictator's death in 1953.

All successor Soviet governments had the challenge of adapting the Stalinist model to contemporary Cold War conditions. This task aggravated the already difficult but permanent need to balance ideology against national interest. The Stalinist system overburdened the Soviet economy with military expenditures and excessive administrative control from the central ministries. It saddled the Soviet Union with the maintenance of an untenable empire, particularly in East Central Europe. Stalin's legacy forced the Soviet Union to compete with the United States on a global stage and to confront a superpower far better suited to that competition in nearly all arenas of policy-making.

Stalin's death inaugurated "collective leadership" in the Soviet Union and a power struggle that culminated in the emergence of Nikita S. Khrushchev at the 1956 Twentieth Party Congress as Stalin's successor. Even before that important meeting, however, it was clear the new Soviet leaders were trying to find ways to adjust official ideology and Stalinist policies to meet the challenges of the Cold War.

The first step was to ease the two-camp doctrine to recognize an expanding "peace zone" that included the Soviet Union, the socialist states of East Central Europe, the People's Republic of China, and those states of the Third World that were following, in Soviet Marxist-Leninist jargon, "the non-capitalist path of development." This last group included states that Stalin had previously labeled collaborators with the West, but that in the new leadership's view were anti-Western in perspective and socialist in orientation, making them likely allies in the Cold War struggle. Soviet leaders reached out particularly to India and Egypt. Jawaharlal Nehru of India and Egypt's Nasser were leaders of the emerging nonaligned movement, and by befriending both, as well as repairing relations with a third leader of that movement, Josep Broz Tito of Yugoslavia, the Soviet government sought an advantage in the Cold War diplomatic competition with the United States. Africa and Asia soon became major battlegrounds in the East–West struggle. In order to move in this direction, however, it was essential for the Soviet Union to undercut the rigid camp doctrine Stalin had decreed.

Other Cold War developments required jettisoning the Marxist-Leninist theory of inevitable war. Such an ideological revision, however, was far more problematic than altering the two-camp doctrine, given that the belief in unavoidable conflict with capitalism dated to at least Lenin. The achievement of the final stage of history as predicted by Karl Marx—scientific Communism—turned on a world proletarian revolution, something inconceivable without a global confrontation with the major capitalist powers. Yet the birth of the nuclear age and the massive arms race underway in the 1950s made inevitable war unthinkable. This dilemma raised the question of how past ideology could be wrong yet continue to be controlling.

The problem in Nikita Khrushchev's mind was solved by the theory of peaceful coexistence *(mirnoe sosushestvovenniye)*. The doctrine brought back echoes of the New Economic Policy (NEP) period (1921–1929) in Soviet history. During the earlier era, the state had sought a temporary relaxation of relations with capitalist European countries in hopes of solving some of its serious economic difficulties through expanded trade. To accomplish this, elements of free-market mechanisms had been introduced in Soviet life. There had also been a liberalization of cultural expression. Now Khrushchev proposed peaceful coexistence as a form of permanent but peaceful struggle between the two world systems, in which cooperation and conflict would be viewed as interpenetrating, dialectically compatible phenomena.

Khrushchev's program of peaceful coexistence was part of his broad de-Stalinization campaign. He accused Stalin of crimes against the party, state, and population. He rejected the use of terror and Stalin's cult of personality. He tried to argue that Stalin had eclipsed the Communist Party with a police state. Consequently, Khrushchev argued it was critical to dismantle the Stalinist system and to introduce liberal reforms. The government eased censorship, and new efforts were made to revitalize the Soviet economy.

De-Stalinization carried with it deep threats to the Soviet system. It suggested that the inerrant party that knew the laws of history had produced Stalin and had pursued fallible and dangerous policies in the past. The obvious conclusion was that it could do these things again. Khrushchev's conservative critics within the party charged that his reforms might well get out of hand, and forces were likely to emerge to challenge the Communist Party system. Khrushchev's condemnation of Stalin undermined the Stalinist leaders in East Central Europe as well. The steady criticisms of Stalin and the pursuit of peaceful coexistence also made an enemy of Mao Zedong, the leader of Communist China and arguably the most Stalinist of rulers in the global Communist camp.

Khrushchev was forced to follow a peripatetic course, sometimes seeking better relations with the United States—he visited the United States in 1959, establishing with President Dwight Eisenhower the "spirit of Camp David"—and at other times confronting Washington in terms that suggested likely war. Crises arose over Berlin, the Congo, the Suez Canal, and U.S. spy flights over the Soviet Union, but there were also initiatives toward disarmament discussions, the purchases of Western agricultural goods, and better relations with Western European states. Khrushchev believed that peaceful confrontation with the West, liberalization at home, and defense of socialism within the Soviet bloc would ultimately produce the global victory of socialism over the capitalist system without resorting to nuclear war.

Perhaps the most dangerous encounter between the superpowers occurred during the Cuban Missile Crisis in October 1962. The confrontation challenged Khrushchev's basic thesis that the two superpowers could compete in every arena and still avoid the ultimate confrontation. In a humiliating defeat for the Soviet Union, it was forced to withdraw its missiles from Cuba. The incident seemed to have a deep impact on the rival leaders in the Cold War—President John Kennedy and Khrushchev—who, in mid-1963, agreed to sign a nuclear test ban treaty.

Because his policies seemed to undermine party control at home and within the bloc, while providing little tangible improvement in the domestic economy, Khrushchev had to fend off efforts to remove him from office. Party bureaucrats, old Stalinists, and conservatives who were worried about unrestrained liberalization attacked the Soviet leader. When Khrushchev moved to reorganize the party and to stack it with his supporters, an internal party revolt led to his political demise. In 1964 Khrushchev's closest colleagues in the Politburo ousted him, charging him with "hare-brained schemes." With Khrushchev's departure, a new "collective leadership" assumed control.

Foreign policy is always based on perceptions that may or may not conform to reality. Peaceful coexistence was no exception. The expectation that ideological struggle could continue and even lead to a global socialist victory without inevitable nuclear confrontation was shattered by the events of the Cuban Missile Crisis. Yet a return to Stalin's prescriptions for fighting the Cold War was inconceivable. In fact, the lesson of the 1962 crisis was that some permanent accommodation with the West must be secured, or another confrontation could lead to the unthinkable. The task of achieving that accommodation without allowing the internal unraveling of the Soviet system of one-party rule fell to the new leadership, increasingly under the direction of Leonid I. Brezhnev, the new party general secretary.

Brezhnev, while continuing to espouse the doctrine of peaceful coexistence, promoted a relaxation of tensions and a pragmatic diplomacy, even cooperation, with the United States and its allies that came to be known as détente. The movement in this direction had begun even in the last months of Khrushchev's rule when the United States and the Soviet Union signed the Nuclear Test Ban Treaty in August 1963. The Brezhnev years witnessed the signing of several agreements with Washington, the most important being the Nuclear Non-Proliferation Treaty (1969), a settlement on Berlin (1971), and the Strategic Arms Limitation Treaty

(SALT I) (1972). The height of the normalization of U.S.–Soviet relations occurred with the May 1972 Moscow summit between Brezhnev and President Richard Nixon, during which the two leaders recognized the parity between the two states and agreed to resolve issues on the basis of mutual benefit.

The desertion of permanent struggle with the imperialist camp, which détente in essence recognized, marked the death of ideology as the theoretical foundation of the Soviet state. Having given up the worldview that had brought the Bolsheviks to power in 1917 and that had legitimized the right of the party to rule for the previous 60 years, Brezhnev and his colleagues had three options for maintaining one-party rule. First, they could continue the relatively popular liberalization that Khrushchev had inaugurated with de-Stalinization in hopes that it would significantly improve the domestic economic situation. However, this strategy would likely lead to more demands for democratic reform, to the end of empire throughout the Soviet bloc, and to growing secessionist sentiments among non-Russian nationalities at home. Second, the leadership could reverse course and reimpose Stalinist repression, which would curtail the forces of liberal change, but which would also make nearly impossible the continued improvement of relations with democratic states in the West, undercutting any meaningful value to détente. In the end, the Brezhnev regime opted for a third course, that of conservative repression that guaranteed dominance by the existing party bureaucracy, along with tepid and temporary experiments at economic reform.

The Brezhnev strategy produced an ossifying political system in which a decreasing percentage of the Soviet population had any belief, an eroding economy that diminished the standard of living and undermined the basic social contract of support for the authoritarian regime in return for long-term improvement in economic conditions, and an inability to keep up with the technological and scientific revolution underway in the West. Following the Cuban Missile Crisis, the Soviet government made an irrevocable commitment to enhance its military capability so that it would never again find itself in the strategically inferior position to the United States that occurred in October 1962. The steady increase in military spending meant that by the mid-1970s, the Brezhnev government was financing the largest military-industrial complex in the world, sapping needed resources for domestic economic programs.

The worsening economic conditions coupled with the normalization of relations with the West encouraged centrifugal forces throughout the Soviet bloc. East Central European governments sought their own détente with the West. The improved European atmosphere led to demands for domestic change and challenges to Communist Party rule. The most serious threats to the Soviet empire came in Czechoslovakia (1968) and in Poland (1980). In the former, a reform government under liberal Communist Alexander Dubcek promised the end of Stalinism. Egged on by East Germany, the Soviets concluded that Dubcek's experiment threatened their control over East Central Europe, and Brezhnev ordered troops into Czechoslovakia despite serious negative effects on Soviet rapprochement with the West. The Soviet leader issued the "Brezhnev Doctrine," asserting the obligation of all socialist states to maintain socialism and to defend it when it came under attack in a fraternal country. In Poland, the challenge was different but just as threatening. The emergence of an independent workers' movement within a supposed workers' state endangered the Polish Communist Party's hold on power. Only the imposition of martial law stayed the prospect of another Soviet intervention.

The elderly Brezhnev launched the Soviet empire's last imperial adventure with the 1979 invasion of Afghanistan. Faced with the rising threat of radical Islam on the Soviet Union's southern, non-Russian border, the Soviets moved to support a friendly secular government in Kabul. Sapping the last elements of the political and economic system's vitality, the invasion also ended détente with the United States. The election of Ronald Reagan in the 1980 U.S. presidential contest brought to office an advocate of confronting the "evil empire." The Cold War deepened, and neither ideology nor national interest suggested an effective plan of action for the Soviet leaders.

There is a seamlessness to Russian history that is not evident in other national histories. Dating from the eighteenth-century Enlightenment, every era of reform has endangered the regime. Liberalization has tended to threaten autocracy's survival by releasing forces that demand more change and that in the end question the legitimacy of the ruling government. And in each case, except the last, Russian tsars and succeeding Soviet rulers responded with a return to repression and with economic and social retreat. Catherine the Great's flirtations with reform were reversed after the Pugachev Rebellion. Tsar Alexander I gave up his reform agenda after the Napoleonic Wars. Alexander III's reign was a return to universal oppression after the more liberal era of Alexander II. In the Soviet era, Stalin's totalitarian rule succeeded NEP. Khrushchev's liberalization in the face of possible nuclear Armageddon gave way to Brezhnev's conservatism. The sole exception to this Russian strategy was the regime of Mikhail S. Gorbachev.

Gorbachev came to power in March 1985, two and a half years after Brezhnev's death. The interregnum, managed by Yuri A. Andropov and

Constantine U. Chernenko, had only continued Soviet paralysis in the face of growing U.S. Cold War superiority. The youngest member of the Politburo at the time of his elevation to party general secretary, Gorbachev had come to political consciousness during Khrushchev's thaw. He was a problem-solver, not an ideologue. His policies of *perestroika* ("restructuring" of the economy), *glasnost* (openness), and "new foreign policy thinking" emulated the liberalization of both the NEP and the Khrushchev periods. However, the policies were not accompanied by new rationalizing ideological doctrines. Constantly tacking in the political wind, Gorbachev was pushed toward greater reforms by rivals such as Boris N. Yeltsin and public opinion. Yet he also faced growing conservative demands for a halt to perestroika and glasnost; party stalwarts feared, and rightly so, that reform would unravel the Soviet Union.

At the United Nations, in December of 1988, Gorbachev made an important gesture toward bringing the Cold War to an end. After a genial meeting with outgoing President Reagan, the Soviet leader addressed the General Assembly, insisting that it was now "high time to make use of the opportunities provided by this universal organization." By the time of the Iraqi invasion of Kuwait in 1990 and the Gulf War in 1991, Gorbachev's anticipation of an effective United Nations seemed prescient as Moscow and Washington cooperated within the Security Council in ways that would have astonished an earlier generation of diplomats in both countries.

At home, when faced with disappointing economic results from perestroika, in large part because of bureaucratic sabotage, and rising dissent against party rule and Russian domination of non-Russian nationalities, Gorbachev rejected Stalinist tactics to secure his position. Instead, he proposed a revolutionary break with the past—the "democratization" of the one-party state.

The ancient Greek historian Thucydides once noted that democracy is incompatible with running an empire. The logic of the Cold War, built on the threat of nuclear war between the two camps, coupled with a Soviet legitimizing ideology of global struggle, meant that no Soviet leader could fully embrace democratic reform and expect to maintain either the empire of the Soviet-controlled states in East Central Europe or the internal empire of non-Russian nationalities. Events moved quickly in the period from 1988 to 1991. First, the non-Russian nationalities demanded independence. Then the East Central European regimes faced unrest. In the case of the latter, Gorbachev counseled liberalization and reform. The result was the fall of the Berlin Wall in November 1989 and the subsequent collapse of all East Central European Communist governments. Within the Soviet Union, after a brief show of force in the Baltic and the Caucasus, Gorbachev acknowledged that repression would mark the defeat of his reform program. But more democracy threatened the rationale for the party's rule. Reactionary party leaders made their last stand in a coup attempt in August 1991 as Gorbachev prepared to sign a new Union Treaty that would effectively end the unified Soviet state. With the coup's collapse, the Soviet Union disintegrated. In the nuclear shadow of the Cold War, the Soviet 50-year effort to craft a reasonable foreign, domestic, and imperial policy that simultaneously met ideological and national interests proved the undoing of the Marxist-Leninist empire. It brought to a close not only the Soviet experiment, but also the 400-year-old Russian, or Soviet, autocracy.

SELECTED BIBLIOGRAPHY

Allison, Graham T. *The Essence of Decision: Explaining the Cuban Missile Crisis.* New York: Longman, 1999.
> Allison's book is the accepted classic analysis of the foreign policy process that occurred during the Cuban Missile Crisis.

English, Robert D. *Russia and the Idea of the West: Gorbachev, Intellectuals, and the End of the Cold War.* New York: Columbia University Press, 2000.
> This volume describes the ideas Gorbachev and his closest advisors developed in the 1950s and how those ideas became policy during his regime.

Gaddis, John Lewis. *The Cold War: A New History.* New York: Penguin, 2005.
> Gaddis is recognized as one of the seminal Cold War historians, and this is his latest analysis of that era.

———. *Cold War Statesmen Confront the Bomb: Nuclear Diplomacy Since 1945.* New York: Oxford University Press, 1999.
> This is a history of the negotiations surrounding one of the critical issues of the Cold War.

———. *We Now Know: Rethinking Cold War History.* Oxford: Clarendon Press, 1997.
> Using sensitive Soviet materials previously not available, Gaddis is able to assess the thinking of Soviet leaders during the early Cold War era.

Gorbachev, Mikhail S. *On My Country and the World.* New York: Columbia University Press, 2000.
> This is a collection of essays by the former Soviet leader on Russian domestic and foreign affairs.

———. *Perestroika: New Thinking for Our Country and the World.* New York: Harper & Row, 1987.
> Published during his term as CPSU general secretary, *Perestroika* outlines the revolutionary changes in Soviet foreign policy proposed by Gorbachev.

Holloway, David. *The Soviet Union and the Arms Race.* New Haven, CT: Yale University Press, 1984.
> Holloway's book is the classic work on Soviet arms policy and arms-control negotiations.

Hough, Jerry. *Russia and the West: Gorbachev and the Politics of Reform.* New York: Simon and Schuster, 1988.
> Hough presents a careful description of the Gorbachev reforms as they were happening.

Khrushchev, Nikita S. *Khrushchev Remembers.* Boston, MA: Little, Brown, 1974.
    Smuggled out of the Soviet Union while he was still alive, Khrushchev's
    memoirs proved an embarrassment to the Brezhnev regime and a gold
    mine for researchers on Soviet policy-making.
Levering, Ralph B. *The Cold War: A Post–Cold War History.* 2nd ed. Wheeling, IL:
    Harlan Davidson, 2005.
    This is the latest and a somewhat revisionist history of the Cold War.
Matlock, Jack F., Jr. *Autopsy of an Empire: The American Ambassador's Account of the
    Collapse of the Soviet Union.* New York: Random House, 1995.
    Present when historic events were happening, Ambassador Matlock gives
    an excellent analysis of the forces destroying the Soviet empire at the time.
Nogee, Joseph L., and Robert H. Donaldson. *Soviet Foreign Policy since World War
    II.* 4th ed. New York: Macmillan Publishing, 1992.
    Now in its fourth edition, Nogee's text is one of the generally accepted
    authoritative overviews of Soviet foreign policy.
Petro, Nicolai N., and Alvin Z. Rubenstein. *Russian Foreign Policy: From Empire to
    Nation-State.* New York: Longman, 1997.
    Alvin Rubenstein is an authority on Soviet foreign policy, and this is his
    analysis on how Russia's foreign policy has changed as a product of the
    collapse of the Soviet Union.
Remnick, David. *Lenin's Tomb: The Last Days of the Soviet Empire.* New York: Vintage
    Books, 1994.
    A best seller at the time of its publication, Remnick's book describes the
    internal political struggle within the highest levels of the political system as
    the Soviet Union disintegrated.
Seabury, Paul. *The Rise and Decline of the Cold War.* New York: Basic Books, 1967.
    This is an early work that assesses the important implications of the nuclear
    age on the Cold War.
Stoessinger, John G. *Nations at Dawn: China, Russia, and America.* 6th ed. New York:
    McGraw-Hill, 1994.
    This is the sequel to Stoessinger's *Nations in Darkness,* which was written
    during the depths of the Cold War.
Thompson, Kenneth W. *Cold War Theories: Volume I, World Polarization, 1943–1953.*
    Baton Rouge: Louisiana State University Press, 1981.
    Thompson has written an excellent analysis of the various explanations for
    the beginnings of the Cold War.
Ulam, Adam B. *The Communists: The Story of Power and Lost Illusions, 1948–1991.*
    New York: Scribner's, 1992.
    One of the grand old men of Sovietology, Ulam explains here what hap-
    pened to the Communist movement during the Cold War.
———. *Expansion and Coexistence: Soviet Foreign Policy, 1917–1973.* New York:
    Praeger, 1974.
    Ulam has written in this book a panoramic history of Soviet foreign policy.
Zubok, Vladislav, and Constantine Pleshakov. *Inside the Kremlin's Cold War: From
    Stalin to Khrushchev.* Cambridge, MA: Harvard University Press, 1997.
    Zubok and Pleshakov's work was the first Russian post–Cold War history
    of the Soviet period using formerly classified materials.

The Collapse of the Soviet Union, 1991

INTRODUCTION

When Soviet leader Leonid I. Brezhnev died in 1982, virtually no one could imagine that within 10 years, the Soviet Union itself would collapse and subsequently disappear. Since its founding by Vladimir I. Lenin and the Bolsheviks in November 1917, the Soviet Union had survived numerous blows, including a brutal civil war, the murderous regime of Joseph V. Stalin, and the cataclysmic World War II. By 1980, the Soviet Union was the world's largest country and its third most populous, with 265 million people spread across 11 different time zones. The Soviet Union produced more steel, coal, and petroleum than any other state; regularly placed manned satellites in orbit around the earth; possessed a large, modern military that could project its might well beyond the country's borders; controlled most of East Central Europe; had established spheres of influence in the Middle East, Asia, Africa, and the Caribbean; and appeared to be the living embodiment of a set of ideas and values (Marxism-Leninism) that appealed to millions throughout the world.

Nevertheless, the Soviet Union faced daunting problems that defied easy solutions. Perhaps none was greater than a stagnating economy. The era of computers and "high-tech" fueled spectacular growth among Western, capitalistic countries, but hardly registered in the Soviet Union except for the military sphere. Consequently, the Soviet Union could send cosmonauts into space but could not provide adequate food, shelter, and clothing for its population. Capital expenditures were routinely allocated to obsolete industries such as steel and coal, while new ventures were ignored.

Soviet leader Mikhail S. Gorbachev looks on in befuddlement as he tries to comprehend the collapse of Communism and the disintegration of the Soviet Union. Realizing the need to revitalize an increasingly stagnant Soviet Union, Gorbachev introduced a number of ill-conceived and poorly executed policies that proved fatal to his cause. (Reproduced from the Collections of the Library of Congress.)

Economic backwardness also harmed the average Soviet citizen. Even though the Soviet standard of living in 1980 was higher than ever, it still was not very high. Housing was cramped and shoddily constructed; every year, millions of rubles were spent to import enough food to sustain the population; and store shelves were either empty or filled with poorly made goods that no one would purchase. Furthermore, a slow but steady stream of visitors from the West made obvious the substandard nature of Soviet material life.

Soviets became increasingly disillusioned and cynical. Virtually all leisure-time activities, ranging from high culture to the most mundane, were controlled by the Communist Party for the benefit of the party. Party propaganda was ubiquitous. For example, *Pravda* and *Izvestia*, the country's two major newspapers, ran story after story about workers or collective farm members who heroically advanced the cause of socialism or about productive units that exceeded their assigned quota. Frequently, they featured panegyrics about party leaders past and present.

The discrepancies between theory and reality also demoralized many Soviets. The fundamental principle of Marxism-Leninism is collectivism; yet, as in George Orwell's *Animal Farm*, it was painfully obvious that some Soviets were "more equal" than others. Party membership bestowed a range of perks that ordinary citizens could only dream about. Furthermore, corruption was rampant, and men and women on the take filled the ranks of the ubiquitous, unmovable bureaucracy. Bribery was an accepted way of life. Finally, a seemingly unquenchable thirst for vodka gave rise to a nation of unproductive, sickly alcoholics.

Beyond unhappy individuals, large groups also resented the status quo. The Soviet Union was a multinational state composed of well over 100 different nationalities. Soviet leaders had labored to destroy traditional national sentiments and to substitute in their place a loyalty to the Soviet Union, but a number of these nationalities yearned to be free. They included Estonians, Latvians, and Lithuanians, who were violently incorporated into the Soviet Union in 1940, and Ukrainians, who in 1980 totaled 43 million, or about 16 percent of the entire population.

Globally, the Soviet Union also faced serious challenges, the most important being a determined Western alliance led by the United States. In comparison with the Soviet Union, the West was wealthier, more populous, more economically vibrant, and more militarily advanced. Furthermore, it practiced containment, pledging to resist global Communist expansion.

In competing with the West, the Soviet Union had badly overextended itself during the 1960s and 1970s. It simply lacked the resources necessary to retain its global position in places such as Africa and Latin America. East Central Europe presented a particular problem. Forcibly brought under Soviet control after World War II, the satellite countries of East Central Europe continuously drained Soviet resources.

In 1980, the Soviet leadership facing these serious problems was singularly uninspiring. Headed by a decrepit Brezhnev, the Soviet leadership has rightly been termed a gerontocracy lacking energy and creativity. The Politburo, the Soviet Union's policy-setting body, consisted of 13 men, 11 of whom were more than 65 years old.

When Brezhnev died, he was succeeded first by Yuri V. Andropov and then by Constantine U. Chernenko, both of whom were old and sick. When Chernenko died early in 1985, a generational change got underway with the elevation of 54-year-old Mikhail S. Gorbachev to the post of general secretary of the Communist Party, or leader of the Soviet Union. Gorbachev came from Stavropol, where his father had worked on a collective farm.

Coming of age after Stalin's death, as a young man, Gorbachev had shared in the early enthusiasm for Nikita S. Khrushchev's reforms. He was highly educated, holding a law degree from Moscow State University, and he was aided by his sophisticated, chic, and likewise highly educated wife, Raisa. The story of the Soviet Union's collapse is very much the story of Gorbachev's failed efforts at reform.

Gorbachev was (and remains) a committed Communist. However, he understood that the Soviet Union desperately needed reform, and he possessed the energy and confidence to attempt that formidable task. However, before Gorbachev could implement reform, he had to master the party and, thus, the state. During his first months in office, Gorbachev dismissed the remnants of the old gerontocracy and brought in fresh new faces, including Boris N. Yeltsin, a young, reform-minded maverick Communist from Siberia.

In the meantime, during the early 1980s, new problems were added to the old ones. The Soviet Union now found itself bogged down in a costly and bloody guerilla war in Afghanistan, and its client states continued to squander Soviet money at an astonishing rate. Furthermore, in 1980 the United States had elected Ronald Reagan, a strident anti-Communist who took an adversarial approach to East–West relations. At home, the military continued to monopolize scarce capital, and the antiquated industrial sector revealed obsolescence, corruption, and stunning mismanagement. The agrarian sector was no better off, with the Soviet Union importing staggering amounts of food. Economic growth slowed to almost zero, and a shrinking economy loomed on the horizon. Moreover, an increasing number of Soviets had grown tired of the incessant propaganda, stagnant standard of living, mind-numbing boredom, and lack of civil liberties. An even greater number turned to vodka, and the rate of alcoholism—already high to begin with—skyrocketed.

Gorbachev possessed no master plan to remedy the Soviet Union's ills; rather, he wanted to "tweak" a system that he considered fundamentally sound. He envisioned the creation of a "market socialism" that would result in a growing economy, greater efficiency, and renewed popular support for Marxism-Leninism. All this was to occur under the banner of *perestroika*, a Russian word meaning rebuilding, reconstruction, reorganization, or reorientation. Perestroika called for a retreat from the highly centralized economy, a devolution of decision-making powers to individual factory managers, competition for securing raw materials and labor, an expanded right for factory managers to hire and fire, the institution of quality control (which was unknown in the Soviet system), competitive pricing for final products, greatly expanded foreign trade and foreign investment, the formation of small, capitalistic cooperatives to provide consumer goods and services, and encouragement of collective farmers to produce at least some foodstuffs on a market rather than command basis. However, perestroika proved troubling; not only were its elements implemented in an uncoordinated and confused manner, but they also ran counter to decades of Soviet experience, especially the rigid economic model developed by Stalin.

Perestroika required large amounts of scarce capital, and this forced Gorbachev to end the Soviet Union's global overextension. The subsequent retrenchment included a withdrawal from Afghanistan, a drastic reduction of subsidies to Communist allies such as Cuba and North Vietnam, and a drastic lowering of the Soviet Union's profile in Africa, the Middle East, and Central America.

In order to facilitate perestroika, Gorbachev also embraced *glasnost,* or "openness." Glasnost called for openness and honesty with the Soviet people in order to reinvigorate the population, reverse the downward spiral of demoralization, and unleash pent-up creativity. Gorbachev believed that if the Soviet people knew the true nature of the country's condition and were given reassurances that they could make constructive criticism without fear of Stalinist retribution, they would rally to his reform efforts.

Gorbachev also needed a break from the Cold War's unrelenting pressures. As long as this struggle absorbed much of the Soviet Union's limited resources, his reform efforts would almost certainly fail. Gorbachev opened a dialogue with a skeptical United States that resulted in several startling agreements, including the 1987 INF Treaty, which greatly reduced the number of Soviet intermediate-range nuclear missiles aimed at Western Europe, and the 1991 Strategic Arms Reduction Treaty (START I), which drastically cut the number of long-range nuclear missiles. Gorbachev coupled these concrete steps with a "charm" offensive. He held several summit meetings with U.S. presidents Ronald Reagan and George H. W. Bush; traveled to Western Europe, where he mingled with the crowds; lifted harsh restrictions on the emigration of Soviet Jews to Israel; addressed the United Nations; and publicly declared his support for a "common European house" stretching from the Atlantic Ocean to the Ural Mountains.

In 1989 the Soviet Union's post–World War II satellite empire in East Central Europe rose in largely peaceful revolution. Instead of rolling in Soviet tanks to prop up the unpopular but subservient Communist regimes, Gorbachev let them collapse under popular pressure. The climax was the dramatic (and televised) destruction of the Berlin Wall, long the symbol of the Cold War.

Not surprisingly, Gorbachev's reforms sparked opposition within the Soviet Union. Those who found their ox being gored—party conservatives, the managerial class, the officer corps, the *apparat*, or bloated, corrupt, incompetent bureaucracy—challenged Gorbachev. In order to strengthen his grip on an increasingly unhappy Communist Party, Gorbachev instituted *demokratizatsiia*, or democracy. Although the Communist Party remained the only legal political party, henceforth, there would be more than one candidate for each office. Restricted though it might have been, demokratizatsiia gave the electorate a choice, a radical departure from the Soviet past.

Meanwhile, instead of revitalizing the sagging Soviet economy, the reforms spread confusion and chaos. Four years into the Gorbachev era, the Soviet economy had shrunk to 1970s levels. Although most Soviets liked their newfound freedoms, fewer and fewer were eager to maintain them at the cost of their standard of living. Gorbachev's conservative enemies criticized him for going too far too fast; the reformers, such as Yeltsin, castigated him for not going far enough fast enough. With his confusing and poorly implemented reforms rapidly spinning out of control, Gorbachev vacillated. First, he tried to mollify the reactionaries, and then he sought to placate the progressives; in both instances, he failed while earning for himself a reputation as weak and indecisive.

With his reforms failing, Gorbachev now faced a new challenge that Soviet authorities had suppressed for decades—nationalism. By early 1991, Estonians, Latvians, and Lithuanians were openly demanding independence, and the Ukrainians increasingly indicated their desire to follow the lead of the Baltic peoples.

The climax to the Gorbachev era occurred in August 1991, when a cabal of disgruntled conservatives drawn from the party, secret police, and army placed him under house arrest as a prelude to seizing power, destroying the reforms, and returning the Soviet Union to its pre-Gorbachev days. Even though Gorbachev had lost all popular support, many Soviets, especially those living in the cities, had no desire to return to the Brezhnev era, and they took to the streets. In Moscow, they were led by Yeltsin, the now democratically elected president of the Russian Republic, who climbed atop a tank to shout his defiance. Meanwhile, the conspirators proved to be an incompetent, cowardly lot, and troops refused to follow their orders.

The coup quickly collapsed, but it had dealt a fatal blow to both Gorbachev and the Soviet Union itself. In the wake of the failed coup, Gorbachev came across as naïve and spineless, and upon his return to Moscow, he was publicly humiliated by Yeltsin, the man of the hour. As for the Soviet Union, the coup attempt revealed it to be a lifeless corpse.

On December 1, 1991, the Ukrainians voted overwhelmingly to become independent, thereby joining the Baltic peoples, Moldovans, Azerbaijanis, and Belorussians, who had already seceded. This final straw preceded the dissolution of the Soviet Union by only a few weeks. At year's end, the Soviet Union ceased to exist.

INTERPRETIVE ESSAY
Charles E. Ziegler

Why did the Soviet Union collapse? The Soviet state was extremely powerful and, if not really "totalitarian," at least strongly authoritarian. The Communist Party and state bureaucracy had penetrated every facet of Soviet life, from agriculture and industry to education and the media. Political opposition was not tolerated. The Committee on State Security (the KGB) routinely quashed any unsanctioned political activities, rounding up dissidents and incarcerating them in labor camps or psychiatric hospitals. Television, radio, and newspapers were all heavily censored; history was distorted and falsified; travel was restricted. Most knowledgeable observers agree that the system could have muddled along for decades. So what factor, or combination of factors, led the Soviet Union to disintegrate in the closing days of 1991?

In trying to explain fundamental political changes such as the collapse of the Soviet Union, it is useful to think in terms of what social scientists call structure and agency. Structure refers to patterned sets of relationships that are generally very difficult for individuals to affect. Major structures in societies include collective entities such as economic systems, social and religious organizations, governmental bureaucracies, and cultural networks. Agency refers to individual political actors, who may work either to effect or to obstruct change. The question then, in studying the collapse of the Soviet Union, is to what extent the changes that took place in 1985–1991 can be explained by structural factors such as the inherent weakness of the centrally planned economy and growing ethnic discontent, or by agency, through the decisions of individual actors such as Mikhail S. Gorbachev and other reformers in the Communist Party. Analysis shows that structure and agency each played a key role in the Soviet demise.

Most close observers of the Soviet Union agree that economic problems were a major factor leading to the start of the reform process in the mid-1980s. All the countries with centrally planned economies— the Soviet Union, East Central Europe, and the client states of Cuba and Vietnam—were lagging well behind the dynamic capitalist world in technological developments and in the simple ability to provide a decent standard of living for their populations. The centrally planned economy had worked moderately well during the extensive growth phase of industrialization, but could not develop and produce high-tech goods in the more competitive postindustrial phase. The one Communist country that had adopted extensive market reforms—the People's Republic of China, in 1978—had seen its economic growth rates increase dramatically.

One problem confronted Soviet leaders with both an economic and an ideological challenge. Communist systems had been established in accord with Marxist theory, to benefit the working class, which Karl Marx claimed had been oppressed under capitalism. At first, this appeal rang true for many, considering the abuses of workers by the industrializing capitalist systems of the nineteenth and early twentieth centuries. By the 1970s and 1980s, however, workers in the capitalist West had secured relatively short workdays, good pay, and extensive benefits. Worker productivity was high in comparison with the level of productivity in the workers' states, just the opposite of what one might suppose. Soviet workers were inefficient, often absent from their jobs, and frequently drunk. Poland's Solidarity movement of 1980–1981 challenged the entire Communist system because it was a workers' revolt against a workers' state. One prominent Soviet sociologist, Tatiana Zaslavskaia, presented an influential paper (the Novosibirsk Report) to Soviet officials arguing that workers under Communism were alienated from their jobs no less than workers in capitalist countries. This was a telling indictment of the Soviet system, and it attracted the attention of the younger, more reform-minded generation of Soviet officials.

Soviet leaders in the mid-to-late 1960s had experimented cautiously with economic reforms, but to little effect. Many in the leadership feared the political demands that might accompany economic change, as happened in Czechoslovakia in 1968, and so they resisted genuine reform. Consequently, the Communist states relied on domestic subsidies and foreign borrowing to keep their economies limping along. The Soviet economy had been buoyed in the 1970s by the high price of oil (and newly discovered fields in West Siberia), together with high levels of production—12.6 million barrels per day, about a third more than Saudi Arabia produced in 2005. Moscow provided extremely cheap, subsidized oil to its East Central European allies and other client states, but by the mid-1980s, oil production was dropping. Declining levels of production meant higher effective internal prices together with reduced export earnings, both of which contributed to an impending economic crisis.

The Soviet Union had become partially integrated into the world economy via energy exports in the1970s and 1980s, which had a major impact on domestic affairs. By the mid-1980s, energy exports accounted for 80 percent of Soviet hard currency income. The mid-1980s drop in world prices combined with rising marginal production costs and declining output placed severe strains on the Soviet system. The elderly, infirm leaders of the late Brezhnev era did not address these problems adequately. One expert on Soviet natural resources, Thane Gustafson, contends that the Soviet Union was in the midst of a severe energy crisis by the 1980s. The Soviet Union was not running out of oil, but it was experiencing runaway costs, abysmal inefficiencies in production and distribution, and repeated shocks and surprises. Gustafson concluded that of all the difficulties facing the command economy, energy policy was the single most disruptive factor in Soviet industry.

Adopting a broad historical approach, Princeton University historian Stephen Kotkin has observed that the developed nations of the West—Britain, the United States, France, Germany, and Japan—underwent a wrenching transition following World War II, as their older industrial economies evolved into more high-tech service economies. The Soviet Union experienced similar stresses, but the inflexible, centrally planned economy and the absence of any real market mechanisms meant that the Soviet economy could not readily adapt to changing conditions. Moreover, the aging Soviet leadership was extremely conservative in dealing with social and economic issues and valued stability over efficient governance. Leonid I. Brezhnev, the general secretary of the Communist Party, was never very imaginative, and in any case, he suffered a major stroke in 1974 that left him virtually incapacitated. Boris N. Yeltsin, in his memoirs, relates how as party first secretary from Sverdlovsk (now Ekaterinburg), he once visited Moscow to secure funding for a subway. Brezhnev was vegetative, and his secretary literally had to guide his hand to sign the paperwork.

By the early 1980s, it was clear to many of the younger generation of Soviet leaders that the country was falling behind the advanced Western countries and was quickly losing ground to the newly industrializing states of East Asia. In the Khrushchev era, a popular slogan had exhorted Soviets to "catch up and overtake the United States." But now the Soviet economy was being overtaken even by South Korea and Taiwan. When Brezhnev died in November 1982, his successor, Yuri V. Andropov, former head of the KGB, was well aware of the problems facing the socialist world and was at least willing to consider some modest reforms. But Andropov soon died, to be replaced by Constantine U. Chernenko, a sickly nonentity and protégé of Brezhnev who accomplished nothing. When Chernenko died in March 1985, the youngest member of the Politburo (at 54), Mikhail Gorbachev, was chosen by his colleagues to become general secretary of the Communist Party. Gorbachev believed he had a mandate for change.

Gorbachev, a former party first secretary from Stavropol who had studied law at the prestigious Moscow State University, moved quickly to criticize the Brezhnev period as an "era of stagnation." Initially, the new Soviet leader pursued a cautious line, promoting symbolic and largely ineffectual measures such as "acceleration" of economic production and advocating greater labor discipline. One of his most unpopular early schemes was an anti-alcohol campaign, which consisted of cutting back production, destroying vineyards, limiting hours for serving liquor, and imposing heavy taxes. The result was a steep decline in revenue (taxes on alcohol were a major source of revenue for the state) and shortages of sugar, as thirsty Russians bought up all they could find to make moonshine (*samogon*).

Realizing that the secrecy and the heavily bureaucratized Soviet party-state system was a brake on progress, the new general secretary advocated *glasnost* (greater openness) in order to open the moribund economy and encourage efficiency. This new policy received a boost in April 1986 with the Chernobyl nuclear disaster, which Moscow initially sought to cover up. Over the next few years, the secret society was pried open. "Blank spots" in history were filled in—the bloody purges of the 1930s, Stalin's failings during World War II, the vast prison-camp system (the Gulag Archipelago). Information on elite privileges, bureaucratic waste and corruption, environmental destruction, military spending, and foreign policy adventures became public, fueling discontent and cynicism. Even Vladimir I. Lenin, the founder of the Soviet state who had become a virtual deity, came under criticism. Newspapers and magazines that had been closely censored for years vied with each other to present the most sensational stories, to the delight of their readers. Long-banned novels were published, Western rock bands were invited to tour the country, and Russian satirists attacked the government with a vengeance.

Soviet intellectuals had known or suspected much of what was revealed by glasnost, although no one had understood the full extent of the system's failings. Official Marxist-Leninist ideology no longer motivated heroic sacrifices, as it had in the early Soviet era, but average Soviets accepted the system or at least assumed it was the best they could expect. Many were proud of their country's accomplishments, including defeating Germany in World War II, being the first in space, and becoming a superpower equal to the United States. Glasnost, however, exposed Soviet propaganda about the superiority of socialism as a lie. Gorbachev expected that the new openness would convince the Soviet people of the party's sincerity about reforming Communism. Instead, the litany of failings, which had in the past been suppressed by the censors, undermined the legitimacy of Communist Party rule.

One of the system's major flaws that became apparent early in the glasnost era was its disastrous record on environmental protection. As in most other areas, the party had long asserted that socialism was far more environmentally benign than capitalism. In reality, the emphasis on industrialization at all costs and the wasteful approach to production had polluted rivers and lakes, fouled the air, destroyed the forests, and irradiated large areas. Environmental degradation had reached such levels that some authors termed the Soviet collapse "death by ecocide." As Soviet society liberalized, small localized but vocal ecology groups emerged, many of which demanded that the government call a halt to building projects, clean the air spewing out of factories, close military bases, or shut down nuclear power stations. Some of the most visible environmental disasters were the desiccation of the huge Aral Sea in Central Asia (caused by diverting water to irrigate cotton crops); the pollution of Lake Baikal, the largest body of fresh water in the world; and of course the explosion at the Chernobyl nuclear reactor in April 1986. Women predominated in these groups because children's health was an issue of great concern. Over time, many of the ecology movements assumed a nationalist character, reflecting popular discontent with Moscow's exploitative approach to the non-Russian regions.

Although most Soviet specialists agree that internal factors are crucial in explaining the collapse of the Soviet Union, the international context of the late twentieth century also played a role. Some analysts have argued that the impact of the international system was indirect, that the more efficient, productive, and humane Western democracies illustrated by their existence a better alternative to the Communist model. Some credit pressures generated by the international energy market, into which the Soviet economy had gradually been drawn. Others claim the West impacted the reform process more directly.

Conservatives in the United States, for example, credit President Ronald Reagan's confrontational policies and high levels of military spending with bringing about the collapse of the Soviet state. Officials in the Reagan administration started from the premise that the Soviet economy was extremely weak and the Soviets globally overextended. Their strategy included supplying the mujahedin in Afghanistan with advanced weaponry, supporting the Solidarity movement in Poland, embargoing sensitive technology exports to the Eastern bloc, and funding anti-Communist movements throughout the world. Reagan and his advisors were concerned that a natural gas pipeline from the Soviet Union to Western Europe would prop up the Soviet economy and encourage an unhealthy dependence on Soviet energy resources; they lobbied hard against the pipeline. Additional pressure consisted of ratcheting up U.S. defense expenditures and launching expensive, high-tech military projects, most notably the Strategic Defense Initiative (SDI), with the idea of further straining the Soviet defense burden. Anatoly F. Dobrynin, who served as ambassador to the United States from 1962 to 1986, confirms in his memoirs that Reagan's plan to erect a defensive barrier against ballistic nuclear missiles did indeed preoccupy the Soviet defense establishment in the 1980s.

During the late 1960s and throughout the 1970s, the United States had suffered defeat in Vietnam, withdrawn from many of its commitments in the Third World, and recognized Soviet parity through Richard Nixon's détente policy. The 1980s, however, were a time of serious reversals in foreign policy for the Soviet Union. Afghanistan became a type of Soviet Vietnam, a "bleeding wound," as Gorbachev called it, which siphoned off men and resources. Supplying cheap fuel and weapons to client states—Vietnam, Cuba, North Korea, and East Central Europe—became increasingly expensive and seldom bought Moscow the sort of political influence it sought. The Communist socioeconomic model became increasingly discredited as the planned economies stagnated while free market states saw their growth rates soar. Poland's Solidarity movement, repressed by General Wojciech Jaruzelski in response to Soviet pressure, likewise eroded much of the remaining legitimacy of the Communist model.

Ideas and ideology matter a great deal in politics. The Cold War was in many respects a war of ideas, one in which the Western liberal democratic world was victorious. Francis Fukuyama, a former U.S. State Department official and Soviet specialist, provoked a great deal of controversy in 1989 when he published an article suggesting that Communist ideology, like fascism before it, had been discredited by its performance in the twentieth century. Liberal democratic values, Fukuyama argued, had proved superior to these rival ideologies and offered the only realistic alternative for the future. In this sense, Fukuyama said, history as a great clash of "isms" had ended with the collapse of Marxism-Leninism.

Abstract notions of democracy likely influenced a relatively small number of intellectuals in the Soviet Union. More attractive to the average person was the mix of popular music, culture, films, and news distributed by the BBC, Voice of America, Radio Liberty, and various European outlets. Most foreign broadcasts were jammed, but listeners found ways to get around the problem. Illegal publications were painstakingly retyped (copying machines were not available for general use) and circulated to trusted friends. Soviet viewers marveled at the level of affluence depicted in the few Western films approved for distribution. Jazz and rock music found a wide audience among young people. Pavel Palazchenko, Gorbachev's personal translator, relates in his memoirs that the obsession that he and his friends had with the Beatles was a subtle way to reject the stifling conformity of Soviet life.

Western governments frequently urged Moscow to respect the rights of dissidents and religious believers. Political scientist Daniel Thomas suggests that the European Community (now the EU) contributed to the fall of Communism through its consistent emphasis on human rights as a norm in European politics. U.S. foreign policy prior to Jimmy Carter's presidency paid scant attention to human rights in international affairs. Richard Nixon and Henry Kissinger were realists who appreciated political and military power in foreign affairs; promoting democratic norms and values was not part of their foreign policy repertoire. The Europeans endorsed human rights through the Helsinki process, formally known as the Conference on Security and Cooperation in Europe. They convinced the Eastern bloc to accept provisions committing Communist states to acknowledge a liberal democratic definition of human rights in exchange for security agreements and acceptance of the postwar territorial status quo (the Soviet East Central European empire) and promises of economic and technological cooperation.

"Basket Three" of the Helsinki Accords, signed in 1975, provided for the free flow of ideas, information, and people. By signing on to the accords, the Soviet Union and East Central Europe openly and legally accepted European norms. In this sense, they became part of the "common European home" well before Gorbachev began to use that language. Emboldened by international legal support for their cause, dissidents in East Central Europe and the Soviet Union began to push the boundaries of what was politically acceptable. Some examples of democratic movements that emerged subsequently were the Moscow Helsinki Group (which included such notable dissidents as Andrei D. Sakharov, Anatoly B. Shcharansky, and Alexander I. Ginzburg), Charter 77 in Czechoslovakia, and of course Solidarity in Poland. The Communist regimes persecuted these activists, but police forces were often held in check by accusations that they were violating international laws that their leaders had accepted. The United States now provided support for these movements in the form of human rights campaigns initiated by presidents Carter and Reagan, congressional hearings, and the formation of a U.S. Commission on Security and Cooperation in Europe. The Helsinki process was neither directly nor solely responsible for the collapse of Communism, but it did catalyze a small but vocal opposition that challenged the party's monopoly over political expression.

Gorbachev's initiatives, as might be expected, produced a major split between those who favored the reform process and conservatives who were offended by attacks on the fundamentals of the Soviet system. In part this was a generational difference. The older cadre of Soviet leaders had moved into positions of power under Joseph V. Stalin, often replacing officials who had been imprisoned or executed in the Great Terror, the purges of the 1930s. This generation had found their positions threatened by Nikita S. Khrushchev's experiments of the 1950s and were reassured by the cautious policies pursued under Brezhnev. The younger generation of leaders was better educated and more willing to take chances in order to reinvigorate Soviet socialism. Neither group, however, seriously considered the wholesale abandonment of Communism as a goal, at least not at the start.

Communist systems prohibited the normal articulation of political interests and differences through mechanisms found in democratic societies such as parties and interest groups. Political conflicts existed, but were played out over policy differences (whether to invest in consumer goods or heavy industry, for example) and were generally hidden from the public. Whereas Brezhnev's strategy had been to avoid internecine disputes by ignoring problems and avoiding hard decisions, Gorbachev's innovative reforms led to serious and relatively open conflicts between conservative and reformist factions in the leadership. These political battles, which were not channeled into institutionalized forms of competition as happens in democracies, contributed to chaotic political struggles and the ultimate disintegration of the Soviet Union.

The pattern of political struggle from 1985 to 1991 is roughly as follows. In the first year after becoming the Communist Party's general secretary, Gorbachev consolidated his position by retiring many of the old guard (Foreign Minister Andrei A. Gromyko, for example) and replacing them with reformers with whom he could work (Eduard A. Shevardnadze). These personnel changes gave Gorbachev a free hand in foreign policy, and he quickly implemented his own more accommodative "new thinking." The Reagan administration initially resisted Gorbachev's overtures, suspecting the usual Communist duplicity, but Reagan and Gorbachev soon found common ground. The Intermediate-range Nuclear

Forces (INF) agreement of 1987 was a major breakthrough in arms talks; it stood in clear contrast to the endless rounds of fruitless negotiations that had preceded it. Glasnost gained strength, pushed by the Chernobyl disaster and by intellectuals challenging the boundaries of acceptability. By 1987–1988, reform of the state enterprises had been proposed and cooperatives (small private businesses) legalized. The accelerating pace of reform frightened many in the party and government.

By the middle of 1988, a conservative reaction led some observers to suggest that Gorbachev's program was in trouble, but he countered with a political move. Couching his proposals as a return to true Leninism ("all power to the Soviets!"), the general secretary proposed the creation of several new institutions—a Congress of People's Deputies, to be chosen through competitive elections; a powerful Supreme Soviet (to replace the rubber-stamp parliament of the Brezhnev period); and an indirectly elected Soviet Presidency. His strategy was to emasculate the Communist Party's monopoly over all-important decision making in the Soviet Union by shifting real power to the state. Although the elections of March 1989 did not follow the principle of one person, one vote, they did introduce genuine competition into the political process. Soviets were mesmerized by the televised proceedings of the congress that met in May, as deputies heatedly argued about a range of topics, from pollution and historical repressions to the rights of ethnic minorities and the future of the country.

Since 1922, the Soviet Union had been a federative state, a grudging concession to nationalism. The Bolsheviks preferred a centralized unitary state, but they maintained the fiction of a decentralized system in order to placate the many nationalities who were not ethnically Russian. By the 1970s, nearly half the population was made up of non-Russian ethnic groups—including Ukrainians, Georgians, Belorussians, Moldovans, Lithuanians, Uzbeks, Kazakhs, Tatars, and Buryat Mongols—more than 100 in all. According to the 1977 Soviet constitution, the major nationalities were represented by union republics, with somewhat smaller groups having autonomous republics, autonomous regions, and national areas within and subordinate to the union republics. The liberalization of Soviet politics and society unleashed forces of nationalism that had long been suppressed by the Communist Party. The Baltic states (Latvia, Lithuania, and Estonia) had consistently held that their forcible incorporation in 1940 was illegal, and they were the first to demand sovereignty. But many other Soviet nationalities also held grudges against the Russians, and national identity was the most potent dimension along which large numbers of people could be mobilized. The U.S. political scientist Mark Beissinger presents data showing that in the late 1980s, far more demonstrators took to the streets to advocate ethno-nationalist demands than to condemn environmental pollution, demand political liberalization, or protest economic conditions.

Nationalist demands did not start the liberalization process, but they accelerated the pace of the reform movement and, along with the economic crisis of 1990–1991, must be counted as one of the most important factors contributing to the collapse of the Soviet Union. Nationalism combines both structure and agency. Although few Soviet nationalities felt the immediacy or intensity of opposition to Russian rule that the Baltic peoples did, most resented their second-class status. In Central Asia, for example, ethnic Russians and other Slavs (Ukrainians and Belorussians) migrated into the region and held the most prominent economic, political, and cultural positions. Russians and their Slavic "younger brothers" were deemed the most reliable politically and so tended to dominate sensitive positions in the security and military communities. Russians often assumed an attitude of colonial superiority toward the national minorities. They seldom learned the indigenous languages, and education was designed to bring Russian civilization to these "less developed" peoples. The history and accomplishments of the minority peoples were consistently slighted in favor of "Soviet" (usually Russian) heroes. And Moscow's developmental priorities skewed the economies of the republics by making them dependent on a single crop, such as cotton in the case of Uzbekistan, or by forcing them to abandon nomadic herding practices, as happened with the Kazakhs.

And yet national consciousness remained quiescent among most Soviet minority peoples until, in the context of Gorbachev's liberalization, nationalist "entrepreneurs" stepped forward to mobilize national identity and direct it into political channels. Popular leaders in the Baltic republics (lawyers, journalists, economists, and eventually defecting Communist Party functionaries) provided the intellectual capital for organizing national movements in that region and consciously played an important role in supporting the creation of nationalist movements throughout the Soviet state. Boris Yeltsin aligned his cause—Russian independence from the Soviet state—with that of the Baltic nationalist leaders against Gorbachev's efforts to hold the union together when, in 1990, Soviet troops attempted a crackdown in the republics' capitals. Widespread opposition to the use of force in Russia and throughout the Western world caused Gorbachev to back off and strengthened the Baltic independence movements.

Nationalism in the Soviet Union received a real boost when Gorbachev signaled in his 1988 speech to the United Nations that the Brezhnev

Doctrine (reserving for Moscow the right to preserve socialism in East Central Europe) was no longer policy. Democratic forces in East Central Europe moved quickly, and in the course of a single year Poland, Hungary, Czechoslovakia, Bulgaria, Romania, and Albania all abandoned Communism. Multinational Yugoslavia, which had been independent of Moscow since 1948, began to fragment as nationalist firebrands like Slobodan Milosevic played the ethnic card. Surmounting tremendous opposition from the military and Russian nationalists, Gorbachev and his foreign minister, Eduard Shevardnadze, negotiated the integration of Communist East Germany into the liberal democratic and capitalist Federal Republic of Germany. These developments encouraged separatists in the Soviet Union. Moscow had accepted the loss of the external empire, so independence for the "internal empire" (the union republics) now seemed within the realm of possibility.

During 1989–1991, various forces converged to promote the fragmentation of the Soviet Union. In addition to the movements for national sovereignty in the Baltics, Ukraine, and the Caucasus, many of the constituent units of the Russian Federation began to agitate for greater autonomy. Yeltsin understood that decentralization would undercut Gorbachev's authority, so he urged Russia's regions to "take as much sovereignty as they could swallow." At the same time, a growing Russian nationalist movement composed of conservatives within the Communist Party articulated their grievances against the Soviet system, charging that the policy of national equality promoted by the party had disadvantaged ethnic Russians, who were by history and culture entitled to a leading role. The effect of their campaign was to strengthen the case for Russia's separation from the Soviet Union, a goal that meshed nicely with the liberal objectives of Yeltsin and the reformers.

To keep the country intact, Gorbachev in early 1991 proposed a new Union Treaty, based on a genuine federal—almost confederal—constitution that would grant a significant degree of autonomy to the republics. Nine of the 15 republics agreed on the outlines of the new constitution, with the Baltic states, Armenia, Georgia, and Moldova refusing to participate. Conservatives realized this devolution of power would undermine the fundamental nature of the Soviet system, and on August 19, 1991, representatives of the KGB, Interior Ministry, Communist Party, and Soviet military, together with Gorbachev's vice president, Gennadi I. Yanaev, took power from Gorbachev in a bloodless coup. The leadership of the "State Committee on the State Emergency," as it was called, was made up of weak, indecisive, heavy-drinking mediocrities, and the coup collapsed in three days. Yeltsin, who had boldly rallied the forces for democracy during the coup, emerged much stronger than Gorbachev, who was held responsible for placing his conservative opponents in power and who had ignored warnings from Foreign Minister Shevardnadze that reactionaries were threatening to overturn the reform program (Shevardnadze resigned in December 1990).

The Baltic states had declared their formal independence during the coup; over the course of the next four months, the remaining republics seceded from the Soviet Union. When on the first of December, Ukraine voted overwhelmingly in favor of independence, it was clear that the grand Soviet experiment had failed. One week later, the leaders of the Slavic republics of Russia, Ukraine, and Belarus (Boris N. Yeltsin, Leonid M. Kravchuk, and Stanislav S. Shushkevich, respectively) met in Minsk to announce the dissolution of the 1922 Union Treaty and the formation of a new confederal entity, the Commonwealth of Independent States. On December 25, 1991, Mikhail Gorbachev resigned his position as president of the Soviet Union, effectively turning over power to Yeltsin, president of the successor state of the Russian Federation.

The collapse of the Soviet Union in 1991 in some respects signaled a return to the prerevolutionary social and political order. For over 70 years, Marxist-Leninist ideology had served as a state religion, above challenge or even criticism, protected by the political monopoly of the Communist Party. The new Russian Federation was far more Russian than the former Soviet Union—80 percent ethnic Russian, in comparison with barely 50 percent on the eve of the breakup. After a great deal of spiritual searching, Russian Orthodoxy emerged as something close to a state religion, with chaplains serving in the military and Orthodox clergy blessing government functions. Russians became more nationalistic, even chauvinistic, rejecting purely Western political values as inconsistent with Russian traditions. President Vladimir V. Putin reflected the evolving nature of Russian society. He reined in the powerful oligarchs while preserving the basic principles of a market economy, emasculated the power of the national legislature and the regional governors, re-centralized the Russian state, extended controls over a nascent civil society, and carved out an independent foreign policy that made the most of the country's weakened international posture.

The collapse of the Soviet Union cannot be explained easily. As we have seen, scholars have attributed the collapse to various causes, some internal to the Soviet Union and others external. Structural factors appeal the most to political scientists, whereas historians generally stress the impact of individual leaders. The inflexibility and inefficiency of the centrally planned economy was probably the single most important structural factor that made reform imperative. Another structural factor, generational change, shifted the dominant leadership tendency from conservative to reformist, but the efforts of a few individuals—Mikhail Gorbachev, Boris Yeltsin, Eduard Shevardnadze—must also be counted as critical. Once the reform process was underway, social forces in the form of nationalist organizations accelerated the pace of change, and these movements were central in dismantling the Soviet state. But once again, key actors at critical turning points made all the difference. Had the leaders of the Baltic states and Ukraine proved as loyal to the system as those in Central Asia, the Soviet Union might well have survived much longer than it did. Finally, the international context is another structural component that must be considered. Individual Western leaders may not have had much control over the world oil market or the shift to a postindustrial global economy, but they did make conscious decisions to challenge the Soviet Union militarily, culturally, and ideologically.

SELECTED BIBLIOGRAPHY

Beissinger, Mark R. *Nationalist Mobilization and the Collapse of the Soviet State.* Cambridge: Cambridge University Press, 2002.
> This book describes how the collapse of the Soviet Union can be attributed to a tide of nationalism that transformed the critical actors in Soviet politics during the final two years of the country's existence.

Brown, Archie. *The Gorbachev Factor.* Oxford: Oxford University Press, 1997.
> This leading British political scientist makes the case that Gorbachev's leadership was critical in transforming the Soviet system and ending the Cold War.

Dobrynin, Anatoly. *In Confidence: Moscow's Ambassador to America's Six Cold War Presidents, 1962–1986.* New York: Random House, 1995.
> This insider's account of U.S.–Soviet relations from the Cuban Missile Crisis through the early years of Gorbachev's reforms provides keen insights into the motivations of leaders on both sides.

Feshbach, Murray, and Fred Friendly Jr. *Ecocide in the USSR: Health and Nature under Siege.* New York: Basic Books, 1992.
> A leading demographer and prominent correspondent chronicle the many environmental disasters of the Soviet period.

Fukuyama, Francis. "The End of History?" *The National Interest 16* (1989): 3–18.
> Fukuyama generated vigorous debate with his contention that liberal democratic ideals had bested other major ideologies through a process of Hegelian dialectical struggle resulting in the "end of history."

Gustafson, Thane. *Crisis Amid Plenty: The Politics of Soviet Energy under Brezhnev and Gorbachev.* Princeton, NJ: Princeton University Press, 1989.
> Gustafson focuses on energy in the late Soviet period as an example of a critical industrial sector resistant to reform because of systemic failings and, at least until Gorbachev appeared, because of an absence of innovative leadership.

Hosking, Goeffrey. *The Awakening of the Soviet Union.* Cambridge, MA: Harvard University Press, 1990.

This British historian concentrates on the social and cultural developments of the reform period, including civil society, religion, and nationalism.

Kotkin, Stephen. *Armageddon Averted: The Soviet Collapse, 1970–2000.* Oxford: Oxford University Press, 2001.

Kotkin argues that a 30-year perspective shows how the Soviet Union's inflexible command economy and stagnant governmental system were unable to adapt to changes that faced all the other industrial powers.

Kotz, David M., with Fred Weir. *Revolution from Above: The Demise of the Soviet System.* London: Routledge, 1997.

An economist and a journalist argue that the ruling party and government elite, motivated by the potential for acquiring wealth and power, voluntarily dismantled the Soviet system.

Lo, Bobo. *Soviet Labour Ideology and the Collapse of the State.* London: MacMillan, 2000.

The author, a former Australian diplomat turned academic, argues that as early as Andropov's tenure, the Soviet regime focused on the problem of declining labor productivity, which in turn led to an ideological transformation and was the major factor in the collapse of the state.

Lockwood, David. *The Destruction of the Soviet Union: A Study in Globalization.* London: MacMillan, 2000.

The author uses a Marxist approach to argue that although globalization affects all states, in Communist systems, the state controls the dominant production relationship, and so global economic changes lead to social upheavals and political crises that do not impact capitalist states as severely.

Palazchenko, Pavel. *My Years with Gorbachev and Shevardnadze: The Memoir of a Soviet Interpreter.* University Park: Pennsylvania State University Press, 1997.

Palazchenko served as chief interpreter for Gorbachev from 1985 through 1991, and his memoirs are filled with fascinating insights into high-level diplomacy of the period.

Reynolds, Douglas B. "Soviet Economic Decline: Did an Oil Crisis Cause the Transition in the Soviet Union?" *Journal of Energy and Development* 24 (1998): 65–82.

Reynolds suggests that a decline in oil production in the late 1980s caused the economic decline and final breakdown of the Soviet economy.

Sakwa, Richard. *Gorbachev and His Reforms, 1985–1990.* New York: Prentice Hall, 1990.

This British scholar examines the Soviet reform process as the interaction of individuals, institutions, ideas, groups, and nations, with special attention to the leadership of Mikhail Gorbachev.

Schweitzer, Peter. *Victory: The Reagan Administration's Secret Strategy That Hastened the Collapse of the Soviet Union.* New York: Atlantic Monthly Press, 1994.

Schweitzer, a Senior Fellow at the Hoover Institution, draws on interviews with major figures in the Reagan administration to detail a range of confrontational policies designed to bring down the Soviet empire.

Strayer, Robert. *Why Did the Soviet Union Collapse? Understanding Historical Change.* Armonk, NY: M. E. Sharpe, 1998.

The author uses a broad-based historical approach to examine alternative explanations for the Soviet Union's collapse.

Thomas, Daniel C. *The Helsinki Effect: International Norms, Human Rights, and the Demise of Communism.* Princeton, NJ: Princeton University Press, 2001.

Thomas contends that the Conference on Security and Cooperation in Europe (Helsinki Accords) gave dissidents in Communist systems the backing of international law and the force of international public opinion in their struggle for human rights, constraining the Communist regimes' repressive tactics.

Zaslavskaia, Tatiana. "Novosibirsk Report." *Survey: A Journal of East & West Studies* 28 (1984).

Pathbreaking article by a Soviet sociologist arguing, in light of the Solidarity movement and unpublicized labor protests in the Soviet Union, that workers under Communism were alienated from their work very much like workers in capitalist countries.

Ziegler, Charles E. *Environmental Policy in the USSR.* Amherst: University of Massachusetts Press, 1990.

The author examines the political, legal, philosophical, administrative, and foreign policy aspects of ecology and environmental policy in the late Soviet era.

Appendix A

Glossary

barshchina. Under serfdom, a peasant usually discharged his obligation to his master by providing his uncompensated labor to work the master's land. This form of serf service was called *barschina.*

Berlin Wall (1961). The Berlin Wall physically separated the already divided city of Berlin. Designed to prevent citizens of the Soviet satellite state of East Germany from fleeing to the West, the wall came to symbolize the Cold War. Its destruction in 1989 signaled the liberation of East Central Europe from Soviet control and the coming end of the Cold War itself.

Bukharin, Nicholas I. (1888–1938). Bukharin first surfaced as an important Bolshevik in 1908. After the 1917 Russian Revolution, he held several important posts, including editor of *Pravda* and membership in the Politburo. A Marxist theorist with a cautionary streak, Bukharin incurred Stalin's wrath when he opposed the dictator's policy of forced industrialization. He was executed during the Great Purge.

Chernobyl. The village of Chernobyl was the site of a major ecological disaster when a nuclear reactor at the power plant located there exploded in April 1986. The Soviet Union's attempt to hide this calamity outraged the world community.

Comintern. Officially known as the Third International, or Communist International, the Comintern was established by the Bolsheviks in 1919. The Comintern attacked less radical socialists, promoted world revolution, and served the interests of the Soviet state. Joseph Stalin abolished the Comintern in 1943 as a concession to his World War II allies, the United States and Great Britain.

Congress of Berlin (1878). This grand diplomatic gathering, hosted by Germany's chancellor, Otto von Bismarck, followed on the heels of the Russo-Turkish War. Disturbed by the significant expansion of Russian influence in the Balkans, the European states at the Congress of Berlin forced an unhappy Russia to cede some of its gains.

Crimean War (1853–1856). This almost accidental war featured Russia fighting Great Britain and France over the question of influence in the declining Ottoman Empire. Russia's poor battlefield performance helped to convince a reluctant Alexander II that fundamental reform was required if Russia hoped to keep abreast of her European competitors.

Democratic Centralism. Democratic Centralism was the organizing principle of the Communist Party of the Soviet Union. In theory, wide-open debate was encouraged; however, once a decision had been reached, the result was binding on everyone. In practice, the party was highly centralized, with authority emanating from the top and filtering downward. Those in lower positions were obligated to obey the dictates of their superiors without question, or even debate for that matter.

General Secretary. This was the title employed by the leader of the Communist Party of the Soviet Union (CPSU) and, hence, leader of the country. Officially, the general secretary was the first secretary of the Central Committee of the CPSU. He also served as chairman of the Politburo.

Ginzburg, Alexander I. (1936–2002). One of the better known dissidents of the 1960s and 1970s, Ginzburg is frequently given credit for initiating a form of publishing known as *samizdat,* or self-publication, which consisted of individuals typing out their manuscripts in several carbon copies and then circulating them privately from friend to friend because the Soviet government refused to allow official channels for the publication of anything that did not meet its prior approval. Arrested for his activities, Ginzburg spent significant time in labor camps before Soviet authorities exiled him to the West.

Great Power. Throughout the nineteenth century, several European states, including Great Britain, France, Austria, Germany (Prussia), and Russia, ruled Europe and dominated the globe. Collectively, these five countries were known as the Great Powers.

Great Terror. The Great Terror is sometimes known as the Great Purge. Beginning in late 1934, Soviet dictator Joseph Stalin began to persecute both real and imaginary enemies within the Communist Party. Eventually, Stalin's sweep grew to massive proportions and engulfed the entire country. Estimates are that 8 to 10 million Soviet citizens were arrested and executed or sent off to forced labor camps before the Great Terror tapered off in early 1939.

Helsinki Accords (1975). The Helsinki Accords were the culmination of several years of negotiation by the Conference on Security and Co-operation in Europe, which included representatives from all the European countries and the United States. In effect, the Helsinki Accords represent the peace treaty ending World War II. According to the agreement, the West recognized the de facto post–World War II boundaries of East Central Europe, and the Soviet Union promised to expand civil liberties and human rights, although neither term was ever defined, and no enforcement mechanism was included in the agreement.

hooliganism. A term widely employed in the Soviet Union to describe antisocial behavior, especially on the part of young people. Soviet authorities believed that hooliganism, such as public drunkenness, undermined social order and reflected poorly on the workers' state.

Hungarian Revolution (1956). Following Nikita Khrushchev's "secret speech" denouncing the crimes of Joseph Stalin, the Hungarian nation rose in revolt against its Soviet overlords and their Hungarian stooges. After some hesitation, the Soviet Union sent in the tanks, brutally crushing the revolution and executing its leader, Imre Nagy.

Jacobin. This historical term is derived from the French Revolution and is used to designate extreme revolutionary political movements or their supporters.

Market socialism. As Communism faltered at the end of the twentieth century, market socialism appeared as a popular solution to the difficulties presented by the failure of Marxist economics. Market socialism proposes that the means of production remain under collective ownership but that the principles of the free market system be employed in other aspects of economic life, such as wages, acquisition of raw materials, and the pricing and distribution of goods.

Kamenev, Leo B. (1883–1936). One of the early leaders of the Bolsheviks, Kamenev (real name Rosenfeld) stood with Lenin during the 1917 Russian Revolution even though he disagreed with some of Lenin's tactics. Kamenev held a number of important positions, including membership in the Politburo; however, eventually he was tried and executed by Stalin during the Great Terror, or Great Purge.

Kremlin. The word "kremlin" is Russian for fortress. Practically every medieval Russian town had a kremlin, although the one located at Moscow has gained the greatest fame. In a more modern and general sense, the Kremlin meant either the leadership cadre of the Soviet Union or the country itself.

kulak. Translated literally, *kulak* means fist. The term came to denote peasants who were better off than the average. During his rule, Joseph Stalin took dead aim at the kulaks and during the 1930s eliminated them as a class.

Lend-Lease. After the June 1941 Nazi invasion of the Soviet Union, the Grand Alliance of the Soviet Union, the United States, and Great Britain came into existence for the duration of the conflict. As part of this arrangement, the United States extended Lend-Lease, a program that sent significant amounts of food, clothing, and military equipment to the Soviet Union. Many think that the abrupt cessation of Lend-Lease aid in summer 1945 contributed to the coming of the Cold War.

Lysenko, Trofim D. (1898–1976). Lysenko was a prominent agrobiologist and geneticist under Joseph Stalin. He attacked mainstream ideas about genetics and claimed that by means of a controlled environment, new genetic traits could be created overnight and then passed on to subsequent generations. His hare-brained schemes destroyed serious biogenetic research in the Soviet Union and brought disaster when applied to the country's agrarian sector.

Marshall Plan. First outlined in 1947 by U.S. Secretary of State George C. Marshall and enacted by the U.S. Congress a year later, the Marshall Plan, or the European Recovery Act, called for a massive infusion of U.S. capital into a war-torn Europe in order to revive its lagging economy. The Marshall Plan proved to be an effective blow in the Cold War because the Soviet Union and its satellites refused to participate while the Western Europeans who took advantage of the offer saw their economies recover and, with the return of prosperity, saw the attractiveness of Communism in their countries disappear.

Marxism-Leninism. Marxism-Leninism is the collective wisdom of Karl Marx and Vladimir I. Lenin. For the Soviet Union, Marxism-Leninism provided the state's philosophical and intellectual foundation, although in practice there was much deviation from the ideal.

Nazi–Soviet Non-Aggression Pact (1939). Sometimes called the Hitler–Stalin Non-Aggression Pact, this agreement between Germany and the Soviet Union pledged each country to remain neutral in a conflict involving the other. Secret clauses called for the two countries to divide East Central Europe if war came. Germany's invasion of the Soviet Union in June 1941 effectively nullified the pact.

New Economic Policy (NEP). Following the nation's devastating civil war and the failed policy of War Communism, in 1921 Lenin convinced his fellow Bolsheviks to endorse the New Economic Policy (NEP). Noting that sometimes it is necessary to go "one step backwards in order to go two steps forward," under NEP, Lenin reintroduced a rudimentary form of capitalism, especially in the sprawling agrarian sector, in order to hasten the Soviet Union's economic recovery.

NKVD. The Russian initials for the People's Commissariat of Internal Affairs, the NKVD was one of several incarnations of the Soviet Union's secret police. Beginning with the Cheka, founded by Felix Dzerzhinsky in 1917, and extending through the KGB, the Soviet Union relied heavily on secret police organizations to maintain order, ferret out and crush opposition, operate forced labor camps, and do the bidding of the Communist Party's leadership.

Novikov, Nicholas I. (1744–1818). More than anyone else, Novikov is responsible for bringing the ideas and ideals of the Enlightenment to Russia. His voluminous writings emphasized reason, virtue, education, and humanitarianism. Eventually, Catherine the Great imprisoned Novikov for his allegedly subversive activities.

obrok. Under serfdom, *obrok* allowed the serf to discharge his obligations to his master by making a yearly cash payment or payment in kind rather than providing labor service.

Old Believers. In the middle of the seventeenth century, the Russian Orthodox Church fractured over the question of reforms to its rituals and liturgy. Those who refused to accept the mandated changes became known as the Old Believers. Over the centuries, the Old Believers were periodically persecuted. Many Old Believers belonged to the merchant class or were successful peasants.

Old Bolsheviks. This term refers to those who belonged to V. I. Lenin's faction of the Russian Social Democratic Party prior to the 1917 Russian Revolution that brought the Bolsheviks to power. Joseph Stalin always distrusted the Old Bolsheviks and eliminated most of them during the purges of the 1930s.

Oligarchs. With the collapse of the Soviet Union in 1991, there was a mad scramble to gain control of the fallen state's numerous resources. The Oligarchs, the successful—and often unscrupulous—victors in this free-for-all, became fabulously wealthy overnight and subsequently alienated many Russians with their ostentatious lifestyles.

Orgburo. The Orgburo, or Organization Bureau, was an important but not definitive department of the Communist Party of the Soviet Union. It was eliminated in 1952.

Politburo. Although its name had been changed from the Politburo to the Presidium and back, the Political Bureau, or Politburo, remained the center of Communist power from its establishment in 1917 until the end of the Soviet Union in 1991. Usually consisting of a dozen or so members, the Politburo was the Communist Party's executive committee, presided over by a general secretary such as Leonid I. Brezhnev or Mikhail S. Gorbachev who headed the party and set its agenda.

Pravda. "Pravda" is the Russian word for truth. It is also the name of the daily newspaper of the Central Committee of the Communist Party. During Soviet times, *Pravda* circulated widely throughout the Soviet Union.

Pugachev, Emelian I. (1726–1775). A Cossack peasant, Pugachev led a revolt that attracted as many as perhaps one million rebellious serfs and swept north through the valley of the Volga River toward Moscow. Although Pugachev was ultimately defeated and executed, his revolt left an indelible mark of fear on the minds of both the monarchy and the aristocracy.

Putin, Vladimir V. (1952–). At the end of 1999, Putin, a former member of the Soviet secret police, succeeded Boris N. Yeltsin as the second president of the Russian Federation. His tenure as president has been marked by increased prosperity resulting from higher oil prices, by a draining war against Islamic separatists in Chechnya, and by a slow but steady drift toward authoritarianism.

Radishchev, Alexander N. (1749–1802). Western Europe's Enlightenment deeply influenced this eighteenth-century intellectual and writer. In 1790 he published *A Journey from St. Petersburg to Moscow,* which was highly critical of serfdom and, by extension, the tsarina, Catherine the Great. Exiled to Siberia, Radishchev later returned to St. Petersburg and governmental work; however, his depression over Russian conditions was profound and led him to commit suicide.

Russification. A nineteenth-century tsarist policy that many argue continued under the Communists in a modified form, Russification sought to force the non-Russian nationalities of the empire to embrace the Russian language, culture, customs, and religion.

Sakharov, Andrei D. (1921–1989). A brilliant physicist, Sakharov is considered the father of the Soviet H-bomb. However, growing concern about nuclear proliferation and the possibility of a catastrophic nuclear exchange led Sakharov to become politically active. In 1975 he won the Nobel Peace Prize for his efforts; nevertheless, the Soviet leadership resented Sakharov's activism, and he was systematically harassed until Mikhail Gorbachev came to power shortly before Sakharov's death.

Socialist Realism. During the Soviet period, but especially under Stalin's rule, Socialist Realism provided the official guideline for all cultural, intellectual, and artistic activity. Socialist Realism demanded that all creative output serve the concrete purpose of promoting the construction of Communism among the masses as defined by Marx, Lenin, and Stalin.

Solidarity. A major challenge to Soviet domination of East Central Europe surfaced in 1980 when unhappy Polish shipyard workers formed Solidarity, the first independent trade union in a Soviet-controlled state. Very quickly, Solidarity captured the imagination of the Poles, who hated both Communism and the Russians. Although outlawed in 1981 when marshal law was declared, Solidarity recovered to play the key role in destroying the Soviet-sponsored regime in Poland in 1989. Its leader, Lech Walesa, not only received the Nobel Peace Prize in 1983, but also served as independent Poland's president from 1990 to 1995.

Solzhenitsyn, Alexander I. (1918–). Solzhenitsyn is perhaps the most famous Russian writer of the twentieth century. A courageous opponent of Russia's Communist rulers, Solzhenitsyn took advantage of the "thaw" after Stalin's death to publish *One Day in the Life of Ivan Denisovich*. He followed that with other critical works that earned him the Nobel Prize for Literature in 1970 and expulsion from the Soviet Union in 1974.

Stakhanovite. Named after the coal miner Alexis G. Stakhanov, who in 1935 far exceeded his daily production quota, the Stakhanovite movement featured industrial "shock workers" who set production records and provided models for other workers to emulate during the forced industrialization of the early Five-Year Plans.

Stolypin, Peter A. (1862–1911). Stolypin was perhaps the last competent figure to serve Nicholas II. As minister of the interior after the Revolution of 1905, Stolypin broke the back of resistance in the countryside and introduced agrarian reforms that emphasized capitalistic initiative and independence at the expense of the commune. His assassination in 1911 remains shrouded in mystery.

U-2 Incident (1960). The U-2 Incident was one of the many crises that delineated the Cold War. In May 1960, the Soviet Union shot down a U-2 spy plane as it flew over that country. The United States denied any intention to spy on the Soviet Union and claimed that the plane was a weather-research aircraft gone astray. However, when Soviet leader Nikita Khrushchev produced both the spy plane and its pilot, who confessed to spying, a major row ensued.

volost. A *volost* was the smallest administrative unit in tsarist Russia. Often a volost consisted of several peasant villages.

zemstvo. The basic unit of local self-government in the late tsarist period, the *zemstvos* were created in 1864 as part of Alexander II's Great Reforms. Over the next several decades, the zemstvos grew in stature and importance as a viable alternative to the corrupt and inefficient imperial bureaucracy. They were particularly important in promoting education, health, and agronomy.

Zhdanov, Andrei A. (1896–1948). Zhdanov rose from humble origins to become Leningrad's Communist Party boss and a staunch ally of Joseph Stalin. After World War II, Stalin ordered Zhdanov to restore strict Stalinist orthodoxy in the Soviet Union's cultural and intellectual spheres, and to root out and destroy any deviations.

Zinoviev, Gregory E. (1883–1936). Zinoviev (real name Radomyslsky) was one of the founding fathers of the Bolshevik faction of the Russian Social Democratic Labor Party. After the 1917 Russian Revolution, he held several important posts, and from 1919 to 1926, he led the Communist International (Comintern). An Old Bolshevik, Zinoviev ran afoul of Stalin, who executed him in 1936.

Appendix B

Timeline

1853–1856	Crimean War
1855–1881	Alexander II, Tsar of Russia
1856	Treaty of Paris ends Crimean War
1857	A. Herzen publishes *Koloko* (The Bell) in London
1861–1874	Era of the Great Reforms
1861	Emancipation of the serfs
	I. Turgenev, *Fathers and Sons*
1862	N. Chernyshevsky, *What Is to Be Done?*
1863–1864	Rebellion in Poland
1863	Higher-education reform
1864	*Zemstvo* reform
	Judicial reform
1865–1876	Central Asia brought under Russian control
1865	L. Tolstoy, *War and Peace*
1866	Failed attempt to assassinate Alexander II
	F. Dostoevsky, *Crime and Punishment*

	Moscow conservatory founded
1867	Alaska sold to the United States
1870	Municipal government reform
1873–1874	*V narod* (To the People) movement
1873	I. Repin, *The Volga Barge Haulers*
1874	Military reform
	M. Musorgsky, *Pictures at an Exhibition*
1876–1895	Rail system doubles in size
1876	Land and Freedom founded
1877–1878	Russo-Turkish War
1878	Congress of Berlin
	Russia's first industrial strike
1879–1881	People's Will terror campaign
1880–1905	C. Pobedonostsev serves as procurator of the Holy Synod
1881–1894	Alexander III, Tsar of Russia
	The era of counterreforms
1881–1886	N. Bunge serves as minister of finance
1881	Alexander II assassinated
1882	Legal restrictions on Jews expanded
	Factory legislation restricting child labor
1883	K. Marx dies
1884	Increased restrictions on the universities
1885	Strike at Morozov textile factory
1886–1892	I. Vyshnegradsky serves as minister of finance
1887	Reinsurance Treaty between Russia and Germany
1889	Office of land captain created
1890	Legislation limiting zemstvos

1891–1892	Famine
1891–1905	Construction of the Trans-Siberian railroad
1892–1903	S. Witte serves as minister of finance
1894–1917	Nicholas II, Tsar of Russia
1894	Franco-Russian Entente
1895	P. Tchaikovsky, *Swan Lake*
1897	First Russian census
	Russia moves to the gold standard
	Six-day workweek introduced
1898	Russian Social-Democratic Labor Party (SD) founded
1901	N. Boglepov, minister of education, assassinated
1902	Socialist Revolutionary Party (SR) founded
	D. Sipiagin, minister of the interior, assassinated
	M. Gorky, *The Lower Depths*
1903	Anti-Semitic pogroms
	Social Democratic Labor Party splits into Bolshevik and Menshevik factions; V. Lenin leads the Bolsheviks
	Workmen's compensation introduced
1904–1905	Russo-Japanese War
1904	V. Plehve, minister of the interior, assassinated
	A. Chekhov, *The Cherry Orchard*
	Strike at Putilov steelworks
1905	Bloody Sunday
	Grand Duke Sergei assassinated
	Battle of Mukden
	Battle of Tsushima Straits
	Mutiny on the battleship *Potemkin*
	Treaty of Portsmouth ends Russo-Japanese War

	Constitutional Democratic Party (Kadets) formed
	October Manifesto
	Moscow Soviet crushed
1906	Fundamental Laws
	First Duma called into session
	P. Stolypin, minister of the interior and president of the council of ministers, initiates reform of Russian agriculture
1907	Anglo-Russian Entente
1908	Bosnian crisis
1911	Stolypin assassinated
1912	Lena goldfields massacre
1913	I. Stravinsky, *The Rite of Spring*
	A. Bely, *Petersburg*
1914–1918	World War I
1914	Twin battles of Tannenburg and the Masurian Lakes
	St. Petersburg renamed Petrograd
1915	Poland lost to Germany
1916	Brusilov Offensive
	G. Rasputin murdered
	V. Lenin, *Imperialism: The Highest Stage of Capitalism*
1917–1921	Russian Revolution and Civil War
1917	Nicholas II abdicates
	Provisional Government
	Lenin returns to Russia, proclaims "April Theses"
	L. Trotsky returns to Russia
	July Days

	Bolsheviks seize power
	Cheka (secret police) established
1918	Constituent Assembly dissolved by Bolsheviks
	Treaty of Brest-Litovsk
	Outbreak of civil war
	Trotsky builds Red Army
	Nicholas II and family murdered
	Assassination attempt on Lenin
	War Communism
1919–1921	War with Poland
1919	Comintern (Communist International) created
1921	Bolsheviks win civil war
	Kronstadt Mutiny
	New Economic Policy (NEP) inaugurated
	Treaty of Riga establishes Polish-Russian border
	Widespread famine
1922	J. Stalin named general secretary of CPSU
	Treaty of Rapallo with Germany
	Union of Soviet Socialist Republics formed
1924	Lenin dies
	Petrograd renamed Leningrad
1924–1928	Power struggle to succeed Lenin
1925	Trotsky ousted from position of war commissar
	S. Eisenstein, *Battleship Potemkin*
1928	First Five-Year Plan announced
1929	Trotsky exiled from Soviet Union
	Forced collectivization begins

1930	V. Mayakovsky commits suicide
1932–1933	Severe famine in Ukraine
1932	Mandatory internal passports introduced
1933–1937	Second Five-Year Plan
1933	Hitler comes to power in Germany
	Diplomatic relations established with the United States
	I. Bunin awarded Nobel Prize for Literature
1934	S. Kirov murdered
	Soviet Union enters League of Nations
1935	Stakhanovite drive initiated
1936–1938	Height of Great Terror
1936	New Soviet constitution
1938–1941	Third Five-Year Plan
1938	Munich Conference
1939	N. Yezhov, head of the secret police, arrested and subsequently executed
	Nazi–Soviet Non-Aggression Pact
	Soviet Union seizes eastern Poland
1939–1940	Russo-Finnish "Winter War"
1940	Soviet Union absorbs Estonia, Latvia, and Lithuania
	M. Bulgakov, *The Master and Margarita*
1941–1945	Soviet participation in World War II
	Lend-Lease aid from United States
1941–1944	Siege of Leningrad
1941	Nazi Germany invades Soviet Union
	Battle of Moscow
	Formation of Grand Alliance (Soviet Union, United States, Great Britain)
1942–1943	Battle of Stalingrad

1942	D. Shostakovich, *Seventh Symphony* ("Leningrad")
1943	Comintern dismantled
	Battle of Kursk
	Kiev recaptured
	Teheran Conference
1945–1948	Soviet Union installs puppet regimes in East Central Europe
1945	Yalta Conference
	Red Army captures Berlin
	Potsdam Conference
	United States drops atomic bombs on Japan
1946–1950	Fourth Five-Year Plan
1946	Winston Churchill's "Iron Curtain" speech
1947	Cold War begins in earnest
	Truman Doctrine
	Marshall Plan
	Cominform established
1948	Coup in Czechoslovakia
	Berlin Blockade
	A. Zhdanov dies
1949	Council of Mutual Economic Assistance (CMEA or COMECON) created
	North Atlantic Treaty Organization (NATO) created
	West Germany founded
	Soviet Union explodes atomic bomb
	East Germany founded
	Communists triumph in China
1950–1953	Korean War
1950	Sino-Soviet alliance

1951–1955	Fifth Five-Year Plan
1953	Stalin dies
	N. Khrushchev named first secretary of CPSU
	L. Beria, head of the secret police, executed
1954	Virgin lands scheme
1955	Warsaw Treaty Organization established
	Geneva Summit, Khrushchev and U.S. President D. Eisenhower meet
	V. Nabokov, *Lolita*
1956–1960	Sixth Five-Year Plan
1956	Khrushchev denounces Stalin at Twentieth Party Congress
	Soviet Union crushes revolution in Hungary
1957	Sputnik launched
	B. Pasternak, *Dr. Zhivago*
1958	Pasternak awarded Nobel Prize for Literature
1959–1965	Seventh Five-Year Plan
1959	Khrushchev visits United States
1960	U-2 Incident
1961	Y. Gagarin becomes first man in space
	Berlin Wall constructed
1962	Cuban Missile Crisis
	A. Solzhenitsyn, *One Day in the Life of Ivan Denisovich*
1963	Nuclear Test Ban Treaty signed with the United States
1964	Khrushchev ousted from power
	L. Brezhnev named first secretary of CPSU
1965	M. Sholokhov awarded Nobel Prize for Literature
1966–1970	Eighth Five-Year Plan
1968	Nuclear Non-Proliferation Treaty

	Red Army crushes Czechoslovakia's Prague Spring
1969	Soviet and Chinese forces clash over border issues
1970	Solzhenitsyn awarded Nobel Prize for Literature
1971–1975	Ninth Five-Year Plan
1972	Strategic Arms Limitation Treaty (SALT) with the United States
1974	Solzhenitsyn expelled from Soviet Union
1975	Helsinki Accords
	Joint Apollo-Soyuz space mission
	A. Sakharov awarded Nobel Peace Prize
1976–1980	Tenth Five-Year Plan
1977	New Soviet constitution
1979	Invasion of Afghanistan
1980–1981	Solidarity in Poland
1980	Moscow hosts Olympic Games
1981–1985	Eleventh Five-Year Plan
1982	Brezhnev dies
	Y. Andropov named first secretary of CPSU
1983	U.S. President R. Reagan calls Soviet Union an "evil empire"
1984	Andropov dies
	K. Chernenko named first secretary of CPSU
1985	Chernenko dies
	M. Gorbachev named first secretary of CPSU
1986–1990	Twelfth Five-Year Plan
1986	Chernobyl nuclear power plant accident
1987	Intermediate Nuclear Forces Treaty (INF)
	J. Brodsky awarded Nobel Prize for Literature
1988	Russia celebrates one thousand years of Christianity

1989	Berlin Wall falls
1990	Germany reunified
1991	War in the Persian Gulf
	B. Yeltsin elected president of Russian Federation
	Strategic Arms Reduction Treaty (START I)
	Coup to overthrow Gorbachev fails
	Soviet Union ceases to exist
	Leningrad renamed St. Petersburg
1993	Constitutional crisis results in bloodshed
	New Russian constitution
1994–	Islamic rebellion in Chechnya
1995	Duma elections
1996	Yeltsin wins reelection
1999	V. Putin replaces Yeltsin
2000	Putin elected president of Russian Federation
	Nuclear submarine *Kursk* sinks
2003	Putin's United Russia Party wins Duma elections
2004	Putin wins reelection
	Beslan school hostage crisis
	Putin moves to reassert primacy of the "center" over regional and provincial institutions

Appendix C

Rulers

Emperors (tsars) of Russia—House of Romanov

Alexander II	1855–1881
Alexander III	1881–1894
Nicholas II	1894–1917

Provisional Government—Prime Ministers

Prince George E. Lvov	1917
Alexander F. Kerensky	1917

Soviet Era—Chairman of the Council of People's Commissars

Vladimir I. Lenin	1917–1924

Soviet Era—General and First Secretaries of the Central Committee of the Communist Party of the Soviet Union

Joseph V. Stalin	1922–1953
George M. Malenkov	1953
Nikita S. Khrushchev	1953–1964
Leonid I. Brezhnev	1964–1982
Yuri V. Andropov	1982–1984
Constantine V. Chernenko	1984–1985
Mikhail S. Gorbachev	1985–1991

Russian Federation—President

Boris N. Yeltsin	1991–1999
Vladimir V. Putin	1999–

Appendix D

Population Data

Population of the State

1870	86 million
1897	125 million
1913	166 million
1920	137 million
1939	171 million
1950	178 million
1960	212 million
1980	265 million
1991	290 million
2005	143 million

Nationalities as Percentage of Population

	1897	1926	1959	1979	1989	2002
Russians	47.11	52.9	53.8	52.4	50.8	79.8
Ukrainians	20.3	21.2	15.4	16.2	15.5	2.0
Belorussians	4.9	3.2	3.1	4.8	5.8	0.6
Poles	6.7	0.5	0.2	0.4	0.4	0.1
Uzbeks	—	2.7	2.8	4.8	5.8	0.1
Tatars	2.9	2.3	2.8	2.4	2.3	3.8
Kazaks	—	2.7	1.7	2.5	2.8	0.5
Azerbijanis	—	1.2	1.7	2.1	2.4	0.4

Ten Largest Cities (in millions)

1897		1990		2005	
St. Petersburg	1.3 million	Moscow	8.8 million	Moscow	10.4 million
Moscow	1.0	Leningrad (St. Petersburg)	5.0	St. Petersburg (Leningrad)	4.7
Warsaw	0.7	Kiev	2.6	Novosibirsk	1.4
Odessa	0.4	Tashkent	2.1	Nizhny Novgorod (Gorkii)	1.4
Lodz	0.3	Baku	1.8	Ekaterinburg (Sverdlovsk)	1.3
Riga	0.3	Kharkov	1.6	Samara (Kuibyshev)	1.2
Kiev	0.3	Minsk	1.6	Chelyabinsk	1.1
Kharkov	0.2	Gorkii	1.4	Omsk	1.1
Tiflis	0.2	Novosibirsk	1.4	Kazan	1.1
Tashkent	0.2	Sverdlovsk	1.3	Rostov-na-Don	1.0
Wilno	0.2				

Index

About the Editor and Contributors

BARBARA C. ALLEN is assistant professor of history at La Salle University. She received her PhD from Indiana University in 2001. She has published in *Jahrbücher für Geschichte Osteuropas* and *Revolutionary Russia*. Currently she is working on a political biography of Alexander Shliapnikov.

MARTIN J. BLACKWELL received his PhD from Indiana University in 2005. He is currently a visiting assistant professor of history at the University of Central Arkansas, and is preparing for publication a monograph on the return of Soviet power to Kiev during World War II.

RANDI B. COX is associate professor of history at Stephen F. Austin State University. She received her PhD from Indiana University in 1999. Her scholarly interests focus on the history of advertising and consumer culture in Soviet Russia. She recently published "NEP Without Nepmen! Soviet Advertising and the Transition to Socialism in the 1920s" in *Everyday Lives in Revolutionary Russia* (2006).

DAVID C. FISHER is assistant professor of history at the University of Texas at Brownsville. He received his PhD from Indiana University in 2003. His most recent publication is "Western Hegemony and Russian Ambivalence: The Tsarist Empire at the 1876 Centennial Exposition in Philadelphia" in *Comparativ*. His article, "Russia and the Crystal Palace in 1851," will be published in *Britain, the Empire, and the World at the Great Exhibition of 1851*.

KEVIN C. O'CONNOR is assistant professor of history at Gonzaga University. He received his PhD from Ohio University in 2000. He is the author of *The History of the Baltic States* (2003) and *Intellectuals and Apparatchiks: Russian*

Nationalism and the Gorbachev Revolution (2006). Recently he published *Culture and Customs of the Baltic States* (2006) for Greenwood Press.

DANA M. OHREN received her PhD from Indiana University in 2006. She is an assistant professor of history at Indiana University-Purdue University Indianapolis. Currently, Dr. Ohren is preparing a book about military conscription policies in late Imperial Russia.

THOMAS S. PEARSON is professor of history, and provost and vice president for academic affairs at Monmouth University. He received his PhD from the University of North Carolina in 1977. In addition to journal articles and book chapters focusing on the development of the *zemstvos* and local government, Dr. Pearson is the author of *Russian Officialdom in Crisis: Autocracy and Local Self-Government, 1861–1900* (1989, reissued 2004). He has also written about leadership issues in the late Soviet and post-Soviet periods.

JERRY PUBANTZ received his PhD from Duke University in 1973. He recently accepted the position of professor of history at the University of North Carolina at Greensboro. He is the co-author of numerous works including *The New United Nations: International Organization in the 21ˢᵗ Century* (2006) and the award-winning *To Create A New World? US Presidents and the United Nations* (1999). His articles have appeared in *Social Forces, Alternatives, Arabies Trends, Politics and Policy,* and the *International Journal of the Humanities.*

TAYLOR STULTS is an emeritus professor of history at Muskingum College. He received his PhD from the University of Missouri in 1970. He is the editor of *Fifty Major Documents of the 20ᵗʰ Century, 1950–2000* (2004) and is responsible for the most recent update of Melvin R. Wren's *The Course of Russian History* (1994). Dr. Stults has published articles in the *Russian Review* and contributed to several historical biographical dictionaries including *Statesmen Who Changed the World, Nobel Prize Winners: Peace and Economics,* and *Biographical Encyclopedia of Twentieth Century World Leaders.*

FRANK W. THACKERAY, a former Fulbright Scholar in Poland, received his PhD from Temple University in 1977. He is a professor of history at Indiana University Southeast and director of the history program. He is the author of *Antecedents of Revolution: Alexander I and the Polish Congress Kingdom* (1980), as well as several articles on Russian-Polish relations in the nineteenth century. With John E. Findling, he edited *Events That Changed the World* (1995–2001) and *Events That Changed America* (1996–2000). He also edited *Events That Changed Germany* (2004.) He currently co-edits *The Greenwood Histories of the Modern Nations* series.

CHARLES E. ZIEGLER is professor and chairman of the political science department at the University of Louisville. He received his PhD from the University of Illinois at Urbana-Champaign in 1979. He has published numerous works including *The History of Russia* (1999), *Foreign Policy and East Asia: Learning and Adaptation in the Gorbachev Era* (1993), and *Environmental Policy in the USSR* (1987). His articles have appeared in *Political Science Quarterly, Comparative Politics,* and *Asian Survey.* He is a former Senior Fulbright Scholar to Korea.